The Black Register

Critical South
The publication of this series was made possible with the
support of the International Consortium of Critical Theory
Programs and the Andrew W. Mellon Foundation.

Series editors: Natalia Brizuela and Leticia Sabsay

The Black Register

Tendayi Sithole

polity

First published in 2020 by Polity Press

Polity Press
65 Bridge Street
Cambridge CB2 1UR, UK

Polity Press
101 Station Landing
Suite 300
Medford, MA 02155, USA

ISBN-13: 978-1-5095-4206-2 (hardback)
ISBN-13: 978-1-5095-4207-9 (paperback)

A catalogue record for this book is available from the British Library.

Library of Congress Cataloging-in-Publication Data
Names: Sithole, Tendayi, author.
Title: The black register : essays on blackness and the politics of being / Tendayi Sithole.
Description: Cambridge, UK ; Medford, MA : Polity, 2020. | Series: Critical south | Includes
  bibliographical references and index. | Summary: "Drawing upon Africana existential
  phenomenology, black radical thought, and decoloniality, Sithole offers a new way of
  thinking about the contemporary relevance of seminal thinkers such as Wynter, Cesaire,
  Shakur, and Biko"-- Provided by publisher.
Identifiers: LCCN 2019033286 (print) | LCCN 2019033287 (ebook) | ISBN 9781509542062 |
  ISBN 9781509542079 (pb) | ISBN 9781509542086 (epub)
Subjects: LCSH: Blacks--Study and teaching. | Blacks--Race identity. | Anti-imperialist
  movements. | Radicalism.
Classification: LCC CB235 .S57 2020 (print) | LCC CB235 (ebook) | DDC 305.896/073--dc23
LC record available at https://lccn.loc.gov/2019033286
LC ebook record available at https://lccn.loc.gov/2019033287

Typeset in 10 on 12pt Sabon
by Fakenham Prepress Solutions, Fakenham, Norfolk NR21 8NL
Printed and bound in Great Britain by TJ International Limited

For further information on Polity, visit our website: politybooks.com

Contents

For my three mothers: Lebohang, Dikeledi, and Maduma

Acknowledgments

This book has been a long journey. At least I was not alone in this long walk. I was part of the chorus of the long song and many interlocutors to it, near and far, have kept it alive. I am thankful to them.

I would like to thank Victoria Collins-Buthelezi for her encouragement and friendship, which led to her soliciting this manuscript. Natalia Brizuela is also worth mentioning for her warm messages of encouragement and being an interlocutor. In addition, I wish to extend my appreciation to the editorial collective of Critical South in Polity Press, of which these two aforementioned comrade scholars are part. These include Judith Butler, Souleymane Bachir Diagne, Rosaura Martínez, Vladimir Safatle, Gisela Cantazaro, Françoise Verges, and Felwine Sarr. The invaluable support of John Thompson, the director of Polity Press, is humbling. Thanks to Evie Deavall, and my amazing editor at Polity Press, Susan Beer, who took me through this project with grace and loads of laughter.

The Africa Decolonial Research Network is always a home, and it is where this book was conceptualized right through to its completion. Thanks to my mentor, Sabelo "Mdala" Ndlovu-Gatsheni, for spearheading this collective. The Department of Political Sciences, University of South Africa, has been my home and it is where I found time to work on this book.

Jane and Lewis R. Gordon saw the work at its sketchy phase and inspired me to push on. I thank them for the journey we have travelled with it. They opened their home for my visits and their love is greatly appreciated as always. I also want to thank for intellectual support, as well as for warm friendship: Robin D.G. Kelly, Hortense J. Spillers, Ronald A.T. Judy, John and Jean Comaroff, James Manigault-Bryant, Linda Alcoff, Andrea Pitts, Charles Mills, Calvin Warren, Frank B. Wilderson III, Aaron Kamugisha, Paget Henry, Sarah Cervenak, J. Kameron Carter, Nathaniel Mackey, Dan Woods, Reiland Rabaka, Molefi K. Asante, Neil Roberts, and V.Y. Mudimbe. Tons of thanks go to Nelson Maldonado-Torres, Ramon Grosfoguel, Roberto D. Hernández, and Pablo Gonzalez, who are the uncompromising decolonial scholars who pushed me to sharpen my lenses. Laura Harris and Fred Moten gave me an awesome world of generosity, and I am deeply indebted as always.

The manuscript was gracefully engaged by Kenneth Taffira (may his soul rest in power), Cyprian Mpungose, Marzia Milazzo, Siphamandla Zondi, Luthando Ngema, Muntu Vilakazi, Lebohang Motsomotso, Boshadi Semenya, Zingisa Nkosinkulu, Marule Lentsoane, Maurice Vambe, Lunga Mkila, Mpho Maake, Kgomotso Masemola, Sam Raditlhalo, and Mante Mphahlele.

Thanks to Thabang Monoa, Sindisiwe and Salim Washington, Jessica Russel, Hlulani Mdingi, Tumi Mogorosi, Gabi Motuba, Katlego Pilane, Nombulelo Siwane, Aneesa Khan, Sipho Mantula, Edith Phaswana, Paul "Rude Boy Paul" Mnisi, Mosa Motha, Sibusiso Maseko, Julia Simango, Mwelela Cele, Lesley Hadfield, and Ontlotlile Seemela.

To my late uncle, Mohlalifi Jacob Lebele, who never lived to see this book, I would say *robala ka kgotso Letsitsi*. Many thanks to my brothers, Tshepo Lebele and Tshepiso Molepo, for your generosity. To my fallen comrade, Kasay Sentime, thanks for the critical reading of Chapters 1, 2, and 3, when this book was in its infant stages.

Tendayi Jr., Chanise, Sibusiso, Dyani wa Matekwe – you are the reason I breathe. I am glad we share the jazz spirit, and we sing Don Cherry chants together in corrupted notes of the avant-garde. My love for jazz is my love for you!

All my work is made possible by the prayers of Papa and Ma Sithole. All my love to you.

To those whose names I have forgotten to include here, *mea culpa*, and please know that I am always humbled by your support at different stages of this book. All the errors in the book are mine, mine alone.

Foreword

What precedes the black register?

Will it have been proper to associate what it is to record, or to bear again, with what it is to rule, or guide? To consider a problematic of visual alignment in (non)alignment with a problematic of aural atunement? The row, and its hard way, is part of an audiovisual seriality, a series of sensual problems and problems of sense, a spectrum of concerns for meaning, itself, that take a wavering, spectral, moaning line that won't and can't stop twisting, folding, creasing, and turning in return, finally, to feel. How is a movement of nonalignment braided with the movement of the nonaligned? The book that is now in your hands gives this as a South African question concerning Pan-African desire. Tendayi Sithole's *The Black Register* can't and won't quite keep it straight, in the canted *Wohnung* of black indigeneity, of what it is to have been *displaced in place*, to have been relegated to a homeland that *is not* home *at* home, to be exiled to a reservation, to live in and as what Heidegger calls "standing-reserve," which is genocidally to be taken as and for a resource, while also having been taken away from the general and generative beauty of being-resource in an unsettled field of sharing. The black register re-instantiates that sharing, while also recording that it has been taken. It is expropriative. It releases, rather than retakes, what has been taken. It moves in what it is to seek and practice anti-coloniality's embrace of displacement by way of the refusal of the colonial imposition of displacement, recognizing that

the brutality that attends this duality in and of displacement isn't
so much a European thing as it is that commitment to murderous
thingification out of which the very idea of Europe emerges.
The Black Register shows us how the black register works.
What is the relationship between displacement and registration in
Sithole's grammar? Black study is a field of open questioning and
Sithole is an accelerant of that fire, a proliferant of its recesses and
gatherings, and itinerant but unscheduled stoppages, and unending
terminations and broken persistences, which do not so much purify
as blur, in burning. The field is strewn with what Denise Ferreira
da Silva calls no-bodies, so that the non-opposition of decay and
bloom becomes our particular burden, a condition whose curative
immediacy we must devise a way to show and move. We are
constrained to practice this showing, to show this showing in our
practice of it. It is an empirical mysticism that abjures what the
beautiful ensemble we refer to is – that which Stuart Hall calls
the empiricist attitude. The black register overflows and undercuts
itself, is always more and less than itself, and this non-fullness and
non-simplicity is shown, registered, recorded, discorded, disordered,
and practiced in *The Black Register*.

On this broken edge, what's the relationship between analysis
and the all-at-once? Between world and subdivision? Maybe these
are François Laruelle's questions, which shade some of Bertrand
Russell's toward being turned inside out by Ed Roberson's. What if
mysticism, which is metaphysic's flesh and fugitive core, is Tendayi's
tendency to see the earth before the end of the world? For lack of
more precise terms, which the quest for greater precision always
exposes as a kind of devotion, let's call this being-empirical without
an attitude: no settled position, no emotional or epistemological
truculence, just this deep, shared, entropic sensing. Such seeing,
such registration, such re-gestation, must be under duress. There is
no redress of or for this ruthless restlessness. There's nothing but
the imperative to address it with(in its) absolute and unmediated
obliquity, tilted, off, side-eyed, glancing. Notice is bent, apposi-
tional. Blackness can't be registered but it does register because it
is registration. A way of measure that drives the will to account
straight, cold, geocidally crazy. What kind of account, and of what,
does the unaccountable give? Or does it give the account away? Or
is the account, in the unaccountable, foregiven?

Blackness does not give an account of itself in the black register
or in *The Black Register*. But this is not due to a puritanical

imperative against ethical experiment in the gap between description and portrayal. Somehow, predication is our funhouse. In the funnyhouse of the Negro we come up with nicknames for our prior and seductive resistance to their naming and we fall apart in the horror of how they try to tear us apart, to temper what remains off scale, which is their reaction to how *our* nickname ain't the same as *their* name even though they seem to sound the same. In other words, given that we can measure or record or account for neither what we are nor what they've done to us, what is the black register? An illicit, woven accounting of that which only has one name, the name of the one who kills the innumerable, the unnameable? Or, if what the black register is white, does its limit disappear in the disappearance of its object? Will the black register white's disappearance, in the lonely instant of the last analysis, as its own fade? Register's rich field of definition is like a field of proliferate recess. A test. But what are we testing for? There's the black register, the mechanical reproduction of subjectivity's residuum, and then there's the fact that blackness won't be registered. This is the line Sithole walks with the broken faithfulness of a man in black, the line between skin and livery indeterminate, Johnny Cash singing the body in question's questions, black skein, white masque, as Bongani Madondo might say.

What's the relationship between the black register and the real? What's the relation between the social and the psychic?

The "re" in register, the "re" in record, is of things, of *res*, of the real. What if the problem with Lucretius is that there is no nature of things? What if there's just the way *of* things, or maybe even a way *to* things, an approach, that is, in the end, in having no end, in its obliteration of ends, also a way *from* things, a veering away from things that is given, as it were initially, as a veering away *in* things, in black things, which makes them not quite understandable, or accountable, or to be registered? What if what precedes the black register is unprecedented? An approach not so much to things, even, but to the real, the realistic spot, the neighborhood, the holographic, holosensual field? But "re" is not only of things and their dispersion, emanation/coalescence, and sharing: it also bears the repeat, as if the peat of repeat is folded or pleated into things as their reverberation, the verberation or murmuration being already in the "re," already of the real, this buzz or hum or doubling or blurring of edge, the edgy edgelessness of things, their blue-black smokiness, like a garment – a

shawl or a warm woolen sweater, some kind of laborious weaving
wrapped with a tightness that works the difference between chemise
and skin – not so much worn but traversed and absorbed or imbibed,
as if it were Laphroaig. The record of the thing, the repetition of the
thing, is already in the thing which therefore constitutes the thing's
nothingness, its nonbeing in being more and less than itself. The
black register is where the dual delusion of the in/dividual – where
some infernal alignment will have occurred that posits separation
without difference rather than difference without separation – is
seen for what it is by we who refuse to see it and to be seen within
it. It has a grammatical effect. What if the sound pattern of English
took rhythm into account? What if rhythm messes with syntax in
a way that makes sentences not seem quite right? Is there a critical
writing that scans, sees, but as if from within what it sees, in a
way that defies normative scansion and the grammar it attends and
implies, a grammar/scansion that itself implies the hegemony of the
whole number? Sithole says a little prayer for us in a black musical
way, in a real, in an anarithmetical way, an Arethametical way, a
real, the real, arerererererethmetical way, an a-rhythmetical way,
a nonmetrical way, an acousmetrical way, a matrical way. His
sentences buzz like the bush of ghosts with words that are more and
less than themselves. The work is disintegratively anintegered. It's
Tutuolan in its atonal antotality, just as the black register welcomes
this constant gathering as that which won't quite come together in
having gone past. *The Black Register* is a bush of hosts.

What if one of the questions that the specificity of South Africa
requires you to ask is how the devolution from individual to
dividual, from disciplinary society to society of control, was already
given there in the intensity and particularity of a settler coloniality
that never had the brutal luxury of a myth of autochthony from
which a "demographic" problem could emerge? What if, here, the
demographic problem could never have been seen as anything other
than that which awaits the settler as he incorporates and excludes
"his" surroundings? There, in that place, in that social situation,
but also by way of the physics and sociology the unsettled allow
and demand and require, the Kantian/Newtonian metaphysical
and political laws of in/dividuality, or discipline/control or even
discipline → control break down. The black register sees and bears
and instantiates that breakdown, is what I want to say that Sithole
is saying. But how do you say that, in writing? What graphics don't

so much correspond to but bear that insight, as a matter of sound
and sounding? What entropy, what disorder, what revolt is borne in
every string of words? Again, this is a question concerning Sithole's
music. It is a question to be played on, and by, an African Pan.
Diaspora detached from practice in the enactment of identity is
the neoliberalization of Pan-Africanism, which was a neighborhood
thing or, more precisely, nothing but what we do in the realistic
spot, in its diffuse and irreducible nonlocality, out from abstractions of the nation-state in the nation-state's hold, underneath or
on the outskirts of the *polis*, in the place of dis/place/meant that
Clyde Woods and Katherine McKittrick and Abdoumaliq Simone
talk about with Sylvia Wynter and Amiri Baraka – the district, the
territory, the mill quarters, the demonic ground, the way of things
where in/dividuation breaks down. *The Black Register* feels that
and forms its own reverberations and Steven Biko is at the heart
of this, for Sithole, as Fanon's situated extension. Our Pan-African
desire is in and for a rent party, or a house party, for self-defense in
self-refusal. Not the real thing but the realistic spot because there is
neither a national structure nor a personal agent for our more and
less than political desire. The black register is theory's experimental
band practice, its anaTrinidadian panorama, and when we sit in
with Sithole and the ensemble he forms, and which forms him, in
prison's fetid, open air with Assata Shakur and George Jackson, in
massacre's continuance, we have to want to be ready because when
they play, they plays all that and then some. Reading Biko with
Mabogo P. More in the wake of Wynter reading Fanon, and Wynter
through the echo of Fanon and Aimé Cesaire in Biko, Sithole feels
and means all that, hearing, listening, looping, phonoseismographi-
cally feeding back, in measure, the immeasurable.

                                                            Fred Moten

Introduction: The Black Register

The animation of thought by those who have their humanity questioned presents an ontological scandal. It is here that the human question becomes central, and yet it is still raised as an ire by blacks who are dwelling in blackness. The stance adopted here is the one that undertakes serious reflections on foundational and constitutive problems that are marked by dehumanization.

In essence, thinking from blackness has always meant a set of critical attitudes whose stance means to occupy the position of those who are structured in opposition to dehumanization. This means that *to be* is to be at the receiving end of antiblackness – to be structured in relation to the world that militates against the existence of blacks – to have one's humanity called into question. It is, therefore, imperative to note that to be in such a position is to be rendered non-existent and not even have thought itself. Simply, it means that blackness must disappear in the face of existence. But this is bound to fail, as blacks continue to raise existential questions that scandalize the antiblack world.

The two important sites where blackness is located in terms of embodiment, and where the articulation of the modes of being becomes more clearly pronounced, are life and text. Life and text bring to the fore the embodiment of blackness, the cartography that maps out the ways in which blackness is coming into being, but that being is still put into question. The life and text of blackness are the important sites through which the ontologico-existential struggle enunciates itself and where fundamental questions emanate. The life and text are what blackness is in terms of assertion and not authorization, as blackness is militated against in the antiblack world. The place of blackness, being the subjectivity that is formulated in struggle – to live and to write in struggle – is the necessity to deploy discursive oppositions against the dehumanization that is called the black register.

The Category of the Black Register

The black register, hitherto described and not operationalized by any mode of definition, is here what might be referred to as the ways of thinking, knowing, and doing that are enunciated from existential struggle against antiblackness, and which dwell from the lived experience of being-black-in-an-antiblack-world which must be ended. It is here that blackness dictates its own terms of the existential struggle and sees the world from the perspective that refuses the universal disembodiment but dwells in the embodiment of blackness and as the site that generates existential questions. Indeed, these questions, which continue to haunt, and animate blackness are not new. They are – lock, stock, and barrel – what Wilderson (2010) terms "ensemble of questions," which are burdened by the long and dark history of black existential misery. The black register is, therefore, nothing novel and nothing magical. In short, it is not the conjuring of tricks. The hand of blackness has no magic wand, but the pen whose ink is the liquid (sweat, blood, and tears) that drips from the injured and suffering body. Clearly, the meaning and gesture of the black register is a witness account and expression of critique from the onto-epistemico site that has been rendered object and thus dehumanized. As the onto-epistemico intention, articulation, and actualization, the black register by operation is, in point of fact, a particular task of redefining the black condition otherwise. This otherwise is the radical insistence of breaking free from dogmatic claims but of continuing the longer tradition of black radical thought. The black register is not an attitude and expression whose sensibility is conforming to the orthodox line. The ways of thinking, knowing, and doing are always otherwise, and in their radically different orientation, they continue to forge ahead possibilities inside the belly of impossibilities; the latter which has been solidified by the longer history of disappointment with black liberation not being actualized. The fundamental question of black existence endures, and this is what authorizes the black register, the very thing that defines and concretizes it. For, if there was no antiblackness, there would be no black register.

By definition, nothing has been that of a brief duration when it comes to the black lived experience and what is worthwhile to record is that there is this thing called the black register, the mark of what is a *longue durée*. It illuminates the embodiment of the black lived experience and it is by no means declarative in the sense of prescribing a manifesto, but rather, it is the problematization of the problematic lived experience of the black. Gordon (2000a) makes it clear that blacks are not a problem, as they have been marked to be by an antiblack world, but rather, and as a matter of a condition they are in, and by facticity, blacks are *people with problems*. The existence of the black is problematic, and this is brought into being by the infrastructure of racism which is underwritten by the logic of antiblackness. That said, by modes of authorial inscriptions that blackness accorded and afforded itself, it can be said that the black register is thinking, knowing, and doing blackness as, according to Chandler (2014), a problem for thought. Added to this kind of an operation, it also means that blackness "experimentalizes being" (Carter and Cervenak 2016). That is why, by radical insistence, the black register can be called a "critical operation" and its modes of inscription authorize the grammar of blackness. This critical operation is, in actual fact, a mode of being in the world where the reality is the lived experience of being-black-in-an-antiblack-world.

What it is to be black, or what that means, is something apparent in the black register because it is the authorial inscription, and also, authorial intentionality that authorizes the modes of writing on the edge. This is a matter of life and death. The operative intention, its mode and constitution, is the reconfiguration and promulgation of conjunctions that pushes to the edge, and having to be black, and thinking, knowing, and doing from the abyss in order to erupt onto the surface of the world. This is no complicated negotiation but rather the assertion of possibility and (re)making things otherwise. The black register is there to disrupt, transform, and put to test what has been absolute and making declarations of what should be possible. The black register is an undertaking whose thematization embodies the interventions made here.

The black register is a (dis)position, an enunciation of radical statements and a place where blackness dwells. It is where thought is expressed – a stand that inscribes meaning, searching for this meaning, and making sense of this meaning – that is, the meaning of being black in the meaninglessness of an antiblack world which must be combated and re-configured otherwise. The semblance of justice is a façade and blackness is at the receiving end of injustice and the necessity, therefore, is to write meaning differently. This is where the black register as the ontological and epistemological imperative means thinking, knowing, and doing the work that is authorized by the standpoint against any form of injustice, subjection, and antiblackness writ large – say, dehumanization. As a form of assertion, the black register is oppositional. It is the refusal to be interpellated, appropriated, diluted, and tamed by the liberal consensus that structurally reads the question of subjection and antiblackness off the base. The liberal triptych of liberty, equality, and justice is, in an antiblack world, a register that renders blackness absent and mute. Therefore, the black register is blackness uttering for itself, and without being mediated. The black register is an "unknown tongue" as Carter and Cervenak (2016) state; thus, it matures into the irruption of what might be called the "communion of the whole" and it is here that unveiling serves as a revelation. It is the black register that Abdur-Rahman (2017, 684) brings to the fore; the "black grotesquerie" which reflects the "expressive practices" of formal disintegration and recombinant gathering – the assembly and anesthetization of remains – that opens pathways for as-yet-unrealized and as-yet-unimagined black futures. It is the black sayability in the face of unsayability. As such, the black register is the inscription of the denied, erased, distorted, muted, and censured grammar of blackness; the coerced expression that insists on saying things no matter what – the reorganization of the ordinariness of order – the unmasking and scandalizing of the status quo. To extend this idea, the black register is not only an opposition or critique, but the engendering of continuity, the elaboration of what has been done in black radical thought (the *longue durée* reformulation which can be said to be the bane of antiblackness). For the fact that blackness is denied, it nevertheless authorizes itself by refusing to be denied and it does this in its own way, without ingratiating itself, in order to be accepted. The black register is, in the face of this refusal, the critical combat against the official grammar and its sensibilities (order itself – say, antiblackness and its racist modes of authorization that denies any form of black subjectivity). Those who refuse are black and it is through the black register that they do not conceal; the refusal to be dispossessed and for them to possess life. The refusal that blacks face, and what it is on the brink of, is what Moten (2017) engages as a "radical refusal" – resisting forcefully and authorizing the modes of life that "persist in altered forms of diminished life" (Abdur-Rahman 2017, 683). It is the authorization of life and in authoring it through the means of coming into being by rewriting the script, where the black register "reconfigures the terms of contemporary black struggle by rendering the boundary between (black) living and (black) dying porous and negotiable" (Abdur-Rahman 2017, 683). The ability to think, and when it is something not worthy to be proven (when black radical thinkers combat antiblackness), cannot then, by any means, be surrendered. That is why the black register, blackness rewriting in its own name, is decisive and combative in its questions of charting multiple paths to liberation and the possibility of another world or even worlds.

The modes of coming into being are a clear evidence of having been expelled from living, thus coming back from the throes and the brink of death. The black register is, then, a radically transformative force, the insistence on life. By articulating another way of thinking, knowing, and doing, opening closed registers by way of inaugurating the possibilities of black grammar, is a way forward for the everyday life and its quest for liberation. A critical elaboration invents the presence of what has been reinstating itself, the re-making and re-imaging the world, the different ways of inhabiting the being of blackness in the world that is not supposed to be hospitable, but rightfully, the habitable world or worlds otherwise.

As the constitutive element of confronting antiblackness and rupturing possibility even in the mounted face of impossibility, the disorderly writing of the black register marks the bane whose insistent interruption is extending distinctive conjunctions in which the grammar of blackness records prescriptive and descriptive statements, which are never final but are deepened further and further. That is why the black register marks the writing that originates in the abyss. It is, at its operative functionality, the rewriting that does not revise what has been a canonical inscription, but the inscription of the grammar of blackness, the form of life that is denied writing itself into being.

It is not about giving a voice to blackness. It is, more properly, blackness rewriting the world. What is rewritten is what should be revealed as opposed to being hidden. What is of concern is what stands, according to Abdur-Rahman (2017, 698), "as black modes of being." Also, this is the rewriting of those who are made to exist and are thus making themselves come into being. The reconfiguration of order, the black register as the mark, is a "structure of opposition" as Chandler (1996, 78) names it, "is to overturn the hierarchy at a given moment." This, also, can be any given moment. For, it is a stand, an orientation whose attitudinal charge is to confront and combat antiblackness. The black register is a reconfiguration. It is blackness rewriting itself for-itself and from-itself – that is, in its own name and its own authorized grammar. The black register is generativity and articulation whose effort is the (re)-making of the world. Thus, its authorial intention is writing blackness into existence, to unveil what has been foreclosing blackness. "This movement above the veil experimentalizes a modality of black life that sees without being seen and can only register as being unseen, interrupting and augmenting this world's spatiotemporality with the assertion of an otherwise knowledge" (Carter and Cervenak 2016, 206). The black register unveils what has been a "veil entrapment" as Carter and Cervenak call it – that is, to see differently, to break from (en)closure to inaugurate and to necessitate rupture. The black register is, as a mode of reconfiguration, "building something in there, something down there" (Carter and Cervenak 2016, 213).

> Yet this aporic also functions in strategic political practice. In order to displace hegemonic institutions one can carry out the full displacement by crossing the threshold from open criticism to a declaration of authority. Without assuming power according to some existing institution within the status quo, any project of criticism is always open to a quite worldly and unkind intervention.
> (Chandler 1996, 87)

This has nothing to do with the absolute black authenticity which needs representation and narrative. Rather, what is at stake here is rupture that is evident in the practices of rewriting as unveiling. To rupture the given world and its closure, is what the black register is all about and its authorial inscription is "freedom's proper domain" (Abdur-Rahman 2017, 700). That is why there are radical demands. They embody what might be a radically different authorial statement. In the face of subjection, by any means necessary, liberation is demanded. The black register is the ethical operation of blackness liberating itself in its own name. It is a register that does not border on the generality and totality of the universal. Its specificity, hence it being called the black register, is bringing to the fore fundamental questions that must deal with the dehumanization of blackness. It is not a revision. It is a rewriting. Its imperative is authorizing the authorial modes of what might generally be called black writing or, more preferably, the black authorial inscription. It is breaking with the ranks. It raises fundamental questions. It is the eruption of what has been suppressed – a burst! That is why the black register is not an absolute inscription. It is, factually so, a beginning.

Epistemologically, it is to engage in different practices, which is to say that themes, genres, texts, discourses, critique, and so on are of who are struggling to become human, and they are different from those who are human, or who claim to be human by virtue of dehumanizing others. The notion of difference does not connote the preferred positionality; it is the one that is violently structured, the zone of non-being where blackness should be. This makes it important to point out ways in which thinking is done from this zone. Perhaps it is important to ask: What does it mean to have the black register and what kind of thought is produced from the dehumanized ontological domain of blackness being?

It is important to introduce the figure of the subject as that which is not black. If blackness has its humanity questioned, and it is still in the clutches of subjection and the structural relation of antiblackness, then it follows that the subject does not hold. What exists, then, is the black subject (the subject that is black or to be black as subject), the very instantiation of the subject proper. That is, the subject is the authorization of the human, and if there is no human, there is no subject. In the eyes of the antiblack racist, the black is nothing but the black, and the concept of the subject is to account for what the conception of difference that leads to violence, dehumanization, and death actually is. The black subject is not a subject of distinction or difference; it is, in the racist imagination, the *subject of not*: it is the subject which is not the subject, and this attests to the fact that there cannot be the subject where embodiment is relegated to the Fanonian zone of non-being.

The zone of non-being is in close proximity to the zone of being. This is the asymmetrical relation such that for there to be the zone of being there must be the zone of non-being. The zone of being is not a zone of its own; for it to exist it must feed itself parasitically from the zone of non-being. Privilege, which is the domain of life of whiteness, exists precisely because there is dispossession, which is the domain of blackness. The existence of civility is present on the basis of the form of barbarity it creates, something with which it compares itself. For there to be life there must be death. Not that life ends with death, but life exists side by side with death, and those who are in the domain of death are denied the forms of life. The Fanonian distinction of the zone of being and the zone of non-being is key to understanding the labor of thought at the limits of being. For there to be life in the just world, both the zone of being and the zone of non-being must be obliterated. Being structures how the world is made and these zones were created in order to displace blackness.

As it is written outside the register of the ontological, blackness inhabits the zone of non-being. Not only is this zone inhabited by beings – blacks are non-beings. The zone of non-being is not geographic to the point of being escapable; it is tied to black bodies whose transgression is nothing more than to appear in the world. To appear in the world, blackness is disciplined not to appear, and the zone of non-being serves the very purpose of eliminating blackness. If blackness imparts its modes of being, they become ossified, since the domain of being is not that of blackness. The zone of non-being structures blackness to be in the ontological void, the zone which is marked by death as opposed to life.

To live the life that is put into question is obviously to be in the domain of death. Having its humanity questioned and being structured by violence in the form of the banal and the everyday, blackness cannot claim any ontological status of being. It is the zone of non-being where blackness is declared dead at any time, which is to say, life under siege is the life which can arbitrarily be declared dead. It is the life that can be taken at will anywhere, anytime, and by any means. The suspension of ethics applies when it comes to blackness, for it is the life that is not life. The suspension of ethics means that there is no ethical necessity, as there is nothing ethical. The inescapable fact of the zone of non-being means that blackness is in the perpetual ontological state of capture. It cannot be a trap, but a permanent state of capture in which blackness does not choose whether to "play it right or safe"; the zone of non-being is a permanent state for blackness. Even those who claim to be in proximity to the zone of being find that this zone does not cater to blackness. There is no way that there can be a claim from blackness to be in the zone of being, as this is just an oxymoron.

The myth of upward mobility and liberal meritocracy as the way to get out of the zone of non-being and into the zone of being is a fallacy in that it does not deal with ending these two distinctions. The antiblack world does not see the human in blackness, but the black of black. What is important to state is the fact that the zone of being and the zone of non-being are racialized positions. There are no exceptions; blackness is marked at the level of corporeality, its appearance in the world, through being black, is a give-away by virtue of being hypervisible. In no way can blackness hide itself from being seen by the racist gaze, which sees not the human, but the black. The zone of non-being captures blackness in totality. The salient differences or discrepancies that are propagated by the class perspective, the perspective which has nothing to do with the bane of racialization, seems to suggest that there are blacks in the zone of being and that they are like whites. The fallacy in class analysis creates the impression that if blackness is in the domain of whiteness, then it is exempted from racism and dehumanization. The very fact of class distinction is the dismissal of binary positions such as the zone of being and the zone of non-being. According to this perspective, those zones are marked not by race but by class, and not race, but only class matters. The exaggeration can go to the extent of claiming that there is no such thing as these two zones, as all humans are the same, and what makes them different are circumstances – accidental and deliberate – that create class positions. The existence of class relations suggests relations, and these relations are those of whiteness. The obliteration of race would mean a classless society and the creation of the egalitarian world. Plausible as this may seem, the erasure of race leaves intact the racist infrastructure of antiblackness.

According to the class perspective, there is no race; put simply, race is just a social construct and therefore it does not exist. This inscription of the statement does pander to the sensibilities or bad faith of race denialists. In fact, it is correct to say, from the limits of being as the zoning of sub-ontological difference, that there is no race, but there is race that is dehumanized and there is race that humanizes itself from the very fact of dehumanization. There is no race as floating signifier, but there *is* race in its actuality, enactment, expression, classification, and labelling. Race signifies the extent of dehumanization that defines who is human and who is non-human, who lives and who dies, who is included and who is excluded, who is superior and who is inferior. Race will not be engaged in terms of calling for its complexity and its elusiveness. Race does not exist in so far as it is made to be elusive, the very deliberate act carried out to deny its existence.

What if race exists, not as a floating signifier, but as the burden of blackness? If race exists it needs to be named as such and it needs to be excavated in terms of its dehumanizing infrastructure. It is racism that creates those who are in the limits of being, not the alienated, exploited, and dominated, but – worse – those who are dehumanized in all facets of life and are rendered non-existent. To be outside the boundaries of being is to be racialized as that which does not exist. The very discursive labelling and other degrading effects are "add-ons" to dehumanization. Race exists only if it is referred to as actuality of race and racism – not racism as just a floating signifier, but race as dehumanization situated in the structure of the political life. Race has never been anything but antiblack racism. The kind of race and racism that is engaged upon here is antiblack racism because the world is antiblack and wants to exist by not seeing black bodies.

What is of importance here is the militancy of theory and its being the mode of subjectivity that, for Hardt (2011, 34), "opens up a new form of governance." This governance, it seems, is the creation of another form of life. What appears in this register is the neglect of the racialized injustices and of the ways in which the racist infra-structure hides behind governance, which still puts blackness behind precarious existence. The capacity of critique is important to Hardt, and its potency should unmask the hidden dimensions of meta-narratives, because nothing is a given. The limits of critique, says Hardt, are its limit in that it cannot transform and give alternatives to the existing power structures. The limit is at the level of political practice and propositions informed by theory. As such, theory in modernity and critique are nothing but the discourse domesticated by modernity itself. In brief, critique falls short in the call for the subjection of those who are racialized. They fall outside the domain of critique and theory as such.

If the task of theory is to mask the present, as Hardt suggests, and in the spirit of collectivism, "we," it is then important to ask: Whose present is it, whose past and whose future? And, in inventing this present, what if in the "we" the present is hellish or the past an invention being secondary primarily because time does not matter? What if the invention of the present is the reification of the very same hellish present? Of course, the call here is not for the invention of the future or the past. The call is for the end that must come first and invention will then, as a result, be taken upon. From Hardt, what emerges is the fact that theory in inventing for the present calls for the politics to renounce the form of governance, and in its militancy, theory gestures the modes of self-governance of the "we." It is not clear to whom reference is being made when Hardt (2011, 21–22) writes: "We should have the courage, then, together to make an exodus from the rule of authority, to throw off our habits of obedience, and to realize our capacities to govern ourselves."

It seems to Hardt that the present is the condition that needs to be contended with. As Hardt (2011, 12) insists, "theory is characterized by specific relation to the present." The invention of the present seems to be rupture that will ultimately be located in what Hardt refers to as the "terrain of struggle" – the site where power is negotiated and contested. This means transforming the selfhood of the "we" and its relational status to the world. In this terrain, the "we," according to Hardt (2011, 31–32), "struggle to destroy the modes of control and constitute not only a new life for themselves and others but also the world." Militancy of theory aims to create a new world and as a terrain of struggle it has a different form of relation to the world. It is the one in need of transformation and it needs a new prefiguration – it must produce different forms of lives. It is from this world that different outcomes manifest. The world of the "we" in the terrain of struggle negotiates and contests for power. This suggests that critique through militancy of theory is a political intervention informed by the desire to democratize. If the world can be democratic through transformation, the militancy of theory would have fulfilled its task. This does not naively suggest that this is a means to an end, but at least it is the manner in which the stakes for the struggle of the "we" are certainly safeguarded. As posited earlier on, the struggle of the "we" – modern subjects *qua* whiteness – is not similar to that of blackness positioned at the limits of being. The kind of world that militancy of theory produces and the one that the black register (where blackness is positioned as a radical critique) calls for are entirely different.

The call for transformation by the "we" means that the status quo remains the terrain of the struggle about negotiation and contestation. If to transform, then, is to maintain the status quo, for those outside this terrain of struggle and outside the militancy of theory, blackness in the ontologico-existential struggle means having different forms of politics outside the world as it is. Of course, this is not what militancy of theory is about, and the "we" as subjects of the political have sentiments and aspirations that are structured in modernity. Hardt's "we" has a different plight from that of blackness in the antiblack world. They are not plagued by injustice that still serves as the continuum of the past, which still haunts the present and those who are at the limits of being.

The utopic register for Hardt, then, is to destroy what he refers to as "our minority status" – and, while insisting on that, nothing is said about the racialized nature of the world. Indeed, for Hardt what should come to an end is not the world, and the stakes are not high for the life of the "we," for they yearn for democracy as the utopic destination. The militancy of theory, therefore, is confined to unmasking the structures of hierarchy and obedience and, once this is done, the ontologico-existential struggle for blackness is on the other side – the zone of non-being in which Hardt's "we" is not structurally positioned. Clearly, Hardt's world is not antiblack and its utopic destination and the constitution of the subject is the "we" who is the embodiment of the world. The nature of the antiblack world, which is organized through the infrastructure of antiblack racism and dehumanization, then, remains unexplored. This cannot be expected to be the task that Hardt has to carry out, and on that basis, militancy of theory is interpellated modernity and its Western episteme has no relevance to the ontologico-existential plight of blackness. By implication, then, the "we" cannot be said to apply to humanity writ large, since its world is dehumanizing to those whom it racializes. The universalistic posture of the "we," which suggests all humanity of the world, is by implication exclusionary, as blackness in this schema falls out. The totality of this narrative sees itself as not being obliged to account for the race question which calls for the unjust, violent, rapacious, hegemonic, and devastating conceptions of the world in the present. The world to come for the "we" and Hardt's militancy of theory has nothing to do with the end of the antiblack world.

The black register is the force of critique that comes from thinkers who are dehumanized, and who in turn question, define, and analyze so to frame the reality that they are in, and to unmask the forces that inform subjection. The world in which they are structured violates their existence, and they are committed to the project where they are lower in the pecking order of being, resurrecting from the existential abyss. Their project is that of critique in the form of the black register. In essence, the black register is the politics of life and confronting death – worlds that systematically and systemically produce dehumanization through subjection. The introductory intervention, then, is the theory that frames the parameters of thinking where to see, and to theorize is done from the black perspective, the perspective which is rendered superfluous, if it is considered a perspective at all. To distil the lived experience of blackness through understanding the blackened (non)-relation to the world that is antiblack is to come to terms with how the black register is animated.

Blackness objects to the distorted image that it has been given – to the point that it even refuses the kind of politics in which it is entrapped. This objection is fundamental in the sense that it is not the act of refusal, but of self-assertion, and in its own terms, which are not mediated according to the inscription of whiteness. It is to claim the ontological position in its own terms, without, however, wallowing in nostalgic performances, but viewing performance as the mode of critique that emphasizes the order of things as they are. It is to suture the fractures, to create a register from vast political ontological critiques, and to unmask subjection. It may, then, seem important to assume the position of resistance from those at the receiving end of violence.

These politics are more about structuring the demands of blackness in line with the sensibilities of the oppressor. The structural arrangements of power which effect violence that is directed at black bodies are such that they can command when blackness can be human and when not. Even if the gesture of recognition can be said to exist, by virtue of being the crafted narrative, the one done outside blackness, it will not help matters. It suggests that there is recognition, but it is nothing but a cosmetic gesture. The lived experience that witnesses the damnation of blackness is closely tied to the unmaking of the world and to fundamentally changing the place of blackness. This form of change does not need to come through blackness being acted upon; it must determine the forms of change it wants. If there is a myth to be dispelled it is that recognition matches the remedy for the crisis of blackness as a category of being in the world. For that world to come, it means that there should be ethical relations, but it does not mean having a form of teleology as a register of array in paradise; instead it means creating a path that makes it possible to imagine politics otherwise.

There is reason in black because there is, as Gordon (2010) registers, theory in black – that is, reason as the mode of articulating the lived experience of blackness in relation to the making of epistemic justice. The knowledge arrangement of the world is challenged, and the black register is the epistemological rupture that questions the making of the epistemic systems as the absolute truth through which the world demands that blackness not expand on its theorization. Blackness authorizes itself discursively by breaking the epistemological structures that police all forms of black thought. This articulation, as Gordon notes, is the expanding of thought, as blackness unmasks the falsity of white enclosure. If blackness is its own and regenerates its own grammar to install the structures of antagonism, then there is a possibility of thinking about the black register. What the black assembles is an attempt of meta-theory to locate being as the discursive center.

The black register does not claim any form of "Western equation," as Wynter (2006) puts it, and, as such, it does not claim any forms of superiority, as its task is to assert humanity and to see the obliteration of subjection which is being exposed in discursive practices that are founded on the politics of antagonism. Indeed, blackness is epistemologically eclipsed through Western epistemic violence – the provincialized form of reason – in its posture and expression as the universal, the only reason that is all encompassing and the most absolute truth, with its debates, differences and positions being nothing that is provincial. As Gordon (2011, 95) notes, knowledge has been colonized through "concomitant organization of knowledges into knowledge." If knowledge is colonized, there is one conception of reason, and this cannot be opposed. Reason, like the knowledge from which it derives, is also colonized, and blackness at the limits of being is on its exterior. The fact is that blackness resurrects from the domain of nothingness, which has been deemed as such by reason. It is in this resurrection that reason gets challenged. Moten (2018, 101) amplifies: "This means, in turn, arguing with the cunning self-consumption of reason that should in no way be accepted as standard." Reason, which can also be unreason/unreasonableness, is confronted by its accommodationist project, which insists that blackness must mimic reason in its Euro–North-American-centric posture without any form of opposition. It is necessary that there should be such opposition to what Gordon (2011, 98) terms "the effort to colonize reason." If reason is colonized, it will render stubborn social reality and the lived experience of those who are outside reason. Gordon is correct in referring to this mode of reason as unreasonable reason – the form of reason that poses as reason whereas it is not, in fact, reason.

It is the form of reason that is not reflective in any sense, and clearly, as it asserts itself as reason in the monolithic sense *strictu sensu*, it sees itself as justifiable. In short, unreasonableness does not admit its unreasonableness to itself; it is reason in bad faith.

Black reason is the creation of another world. At the level of metacritique, from black reason there is theory in black, and as Gordon (2010, 196) rightly states: "[T]heory in black, then, is already a phobogenic designation." The entry of blackness into the domain of reason and theory means the end of exclusionary sacredness of colonial domination. The entry of blackness into the antiblack world means phobogenesis – the stimulus of anxiety – as Gordon notes, the fear of reason being exposed as nothing but bad faith. This phobogenesis becomes exposed: "in an attempt to fool others, the trickster becomes the fool" (Gordon 2010, 201). Colonization of reason is trickery and it does not want to be seen for what it is. It masquerades as reason, which cannot be contested. Black reason, on the contrary, calls for the modes of critique and self-critique that unmask the fallacy of the complete nature of reason, including its canonical standing. This is, as Gordon asserts, to unmask the distortion of reality where unreason poses as reason.

The rule of a governing code has been that blackness is outside the domain of reason and there is no way that there can be a form of reason that will come from blackness. Therefore, the distinction between what is reason and what is not falls away simply because the definition of reason is *a priori* foreclosed. This is so because reason is the exclusive domain that expresses itself arbitrarily without any form of being unmasked for what it is. In this way, unreason that poses as reason, as Gordon forewarns, legitimates conditions where unreason solidifies itself as the regime of truth. Is this not what the antiblack world stands for, the world that justifies itself in being unjust to black bodies?

Black reason has been the politics of resistance and affirmation of life itself because this is something worth defending. In confronting the injustices unleashed upon itself, blackness has been at the limits of being, where reason reasons with unreason. Gordon calls for the articulation of the fundamental existential questions to heighten the necessity of black reason. In designating the concept of reason, Amini writes:

> [R]reason is the movable host of metaphors, metonymies, and anthropomorphisms: in short, the sum of human relations which

have been poetically and rhetorically tampered, transferred, and embellished, and which, after long usage, are seen to be fixed, canonical and binding.

(Amini 2010, 32)

What this unreasonableness is confronted with is the black register, which undertakes the modes of philosophizing and collapses systematization and solidity of reason – the Euro–North-American-centric linear narrative – which for Gordon (2010) is challenged by a series of fundamental questions about the social world. The black register comes into being through what Gordon refers to as the fusion of reason and culture, where illumination is primary by embracing contradictions. This mode of philosophizing lends credence to the philosophy of culture as "particularized loci for practices that in fact have universal potential" (Gordon 2010, 195). Even if the illumination would, for instance, reach that universalistic stance, it would not arrogate itself as a monolithic narrative – reason as reason in a solipsistic sense. "Thus, blackness is fundamental to the formation of European modernity as it is one that imagines itself legitimate and pure through the expurgation of blackness" (Gordon 2013, 729).

There is no cartography when it comes to blackness, and that is why it is the domain of nothingness, the utility of blackness being nothing as that which cannot be violated because its violation is something that cannot be accounted for: the technologies of subjection eliminate and deny complicity to all forms of reason that are generated from black bodies. Black bodies are damned blacks and they are not only inferior, but embody nothingness in the world that does not want them, the antiblack world. What is at stake in meditations in the form of the black register enunciated from different thinkers thinking black and who are in struggle has been and continues to be life itself.

Weheliye argues as follows:

For the relegation of black thought to the confines of particularity only affirms the status of the black subjects as beyond the grasp of the human. Given the hostility of slavery, colonialism, segregation, lynching, etc., humanity has always been a principal question within black life and thought in the West; at the moment in which blackness becomes apposite to humanity, "man's" conditions of possibility lose their ontological thrust, because their limitations are rendered abundantly clear.

(Weheliye 2008, 322)

According to Weheliye, black suffering is the signification of banality and the mundane of everyday life which refuses the state of exception. There is no state of exception in the zone of non-being, much as there are no "trace elements of calculability that deem some forms of humanity more exceptional than others" (Weheliye 2008, 323). What then becomes essential is blackness combating what is displacing, distorting, and dominating. It means that there must be a continued struggle for life, as this is the very basis of ontological attainment.

All is at stake, and nothing is not at stake for blackness. Having no ontological cartography in the realm of the ontological – considering the worse-off position of being clutched by subjection – dehumanization solidifies the domain or essence of life for blackness as neither there nor here except for survival and living side-by-side with death. What is left for blackness in the condition of survival is the fact of having to resist against depletion and non-existence. Gordon argues for metacritiques of reason, the forms of reason by those who are dehumanized are informed by the necessity of liberation to transform their existential reality and justification of this necessity of course. Metacritiques of reason are situated in the lived experience of blackness and they usher in discursive oppositions which Gordon signifies as politics.

> For politics to exist there must be discursive opposition. Such activity involves communicative possibilities that rely on the suspense of violence or repressive forces. In effect, that makes politics into a condition of appearance. To be political is to emerge, to appear, to exist.
>
> (Gordon 2011, 99)

It stands that the black register is politics, and blackness is indeed the political. For this to emerge and for the black register to stand, there must be speech, as subjection signifies the erasure of speech. According to Gordon, the erasure of speech has befallen blackness to create the condition of disappearance, and blackness is without a face. "As faceless, problem people are derailed from the dialectics of recognition, of self and other, with the consequence of neither self nor other" (Gordon 2011, 100). Gordon (2000a) also notes that black people are not problem people, but people with problems. These problems lie at the heart of the existential misery that blackness finds itself in, and they are the erasure of speech in so far as they do not allow any communicative practice. The enforcing of the communicative practice is a discursive opposition in so far as blackness forces itself, out of necessity, to speak. In the face of what seeks to eliminate them as a problem, this logic is problematic in that if the problem is black people, to eliminate them is the solution. Therefore, there is no ethical dilemma that arises in that the form of reason that prevails is solution seeking, and the solution is to eliminate the problem, which is the elimination of blackness.

What is at stake is the elimination of black life and the manner in which the historical scandal continues in the present. The antiblack world still exists; even though the celebratory discourse has proliferated to the point of institutionalization, this does not negate the fact that the limit of being is not the liminal position that is structured by the politics of temporality – it is the continued subjection where the definition of black life is still the domain of nothingness. What still remains at stake is subjection as the defining characteristic of blackness, and not its temporality, which is escapism that cannot be used as the basis; this means that there is no way the humanity of blackness can be brought into question. There is no use in exhausting the sublime site of blackness – the fundamental aspect of beauty which denotes that there is a transcendence of the pathologized; the unique aspect of blackness to be seized to create alternative life worlds. According to this thesis, there is something beautiful that can be illuminated within blackness. For blackness through the sublime has a lot to offer to humanity at large, and it is the center through which the sublime object of blackness, as Chipkin (2002) brings what Bascomb refers to as the "color of life," which shows the hidden troves that are embedded in the ruins of life. The grotesque is the sublime in so far as the political and cultural expressions of black life are "hidden within a treasure throve of potential" (Bascomb 2014: 149). The color of life as a discursive intervention is foregrounded in black modernism, which is a discourse that accentuates that there is black life, and to be at the limits of being is just a matter of temporality. This means that the limits of being can be transcended by blackness engaging the pathological through the sublime discursive intervention.

The black register is the regenerative force of the standpoint of blackness, for blackness to think for itself through the meditations of its own liberation. The black register means casting light on the darker side of modernity to expose what modernity hides. This does not mean that modernity is given light so as to redeem itself; instead, this light is meant to expose what modernity hides. In essence, the redemptive posture of modernity is exposed for its colonial systematization and the continued subjection that still afflicts those who are racialized. Since modernity is the economy of positive aspects and is posturing as redemptive, it is then exposed through the black register – the wretched engaging in the modes of philosophizing and theorizing – illuminating critique to unmask modernity and to expose it for what it is. In other words, what remains fundamental is the articulation from the epistemic site that was never even considered critique, coming in full force from the limits of being to give the perspective of the world. The black register pushes epistemic frontiers that center on the human question and the necessity of realizing liberation.

Where blackness enunciates itself, thinking from where it is, as Mignolo (2007) rightfully states, it takes a standpoint as a form of critique which then articulates the lived experience and modes of thinking that affirm the place of blackness in the world. It is to have perspective through which existence illuminates itself, where critique does not originate from the floating signifier where critique has no subjective point. "Blackness is the always already outside, but it also defines a space where things can happen" (Bascomb 2014, 150). Even though this might sound like some form of redemptive discourse that tames the stance of militancy of theory as per Hardt's articulation, blackness is still the site of critique and its existence has always been the oppositional politics for the very fact of being clutched in subjection. Mbembe (2002) reduces black critique to obsession with ghosts of colonialism and borders on the absurdity of "faked philosophies." It seems, therefore, that nothing warrants black critique from its own standpoint unless it is assimilated into race denialism by paradoxically asserting itself equal to the world. Not that this is the epistemological gesture that is available only where blackness has to be preoccupied with relationality to the world; blackness has to be the oppositional stance in relation to the world, so that its racialized logic can be destroyed. What is hegemonic is the delegitimizing of black critique through denialism, trivialization, dismissiveness, ridicule, and also phantom redefinitions, which are aimed at taming the bane of ontologico-existential questions that underwrite the black register. What is being waged against is the decadent position that black critique has reached an impasse and the world has changed from its racist infrastructure and has been more humane than ever before. It is clear from the view of Bascomb (2014) that black critique does not gesture the widely acknowledged legitimacy where blackness must justify itself to be convincing to the hegemonic structure and to be accepted. Giroux (2010) makes a distinction between the political (sovereignty, democracy, and public sphere) and politics (policy, juridical, administration, institutional arrangements) to understand the manner in which race operates in the realm of reason. According to Giroux, this distinction should be understood through ontological arrangements and the ways in which the question of justice features in the political realm. So, the political and politics as distinct entities are often collapsible into each other in the manner in which the state is confounded – that is, both the political and politics are melded in the ambit of the state. The state is engaged here in terms of relations of power, not its functions, distribution, or institutional arrangements. Rather, the state is the instrument of subjection, more so in relation to racialized bodies, which are perpetually criminalized, pathologized, and dehumanized. For the state to take this shape, it has to operate through the logic of race, which is, according to Gordon (2000a), the organizing principle of the antiblack world.

> The state determines who is human and who is property, who will be protected under the mantle of citizenship and who might be stripped of the rights it purports to guarantee, who will be a resident and who will remain alien, who will be declared friend and ally and who will be rendered a threat to national security, a plague to be exterminated, or an enemy combatant to be imprisoned and tortured.
>
> (Giroux 2010, 172)

If the state is accused of being unjust in what it determines in this above-mentioned paradigm of difference, the state will naturally refuse to account for the claims of justice made on it. It will refuse to admit that it is the state of subjection. In its modes of self-fashioning, the state will claim to uphold justice and distance itself from subjection. Badiou (2005, 100) notes: "The State, in its being, is indifferent to justice." The state has nothing to do with justice. For Badiou, justice is the politics that have to do with truth, and this has nothing to do with the functions of the state. Justice destabilizes the very order that the state is based in. The order that the state is based in is subjection, which gives the state its power.

To go beyond Badiou, what then if the state is the racist state? How indifferent is it then to justice? The question of injustice has been the one that has beleaguered blackness. It is the configuration of the racist state that injustice outlives itself, and yet at the same time, the racist state claims to uphold justice and that everything is held in the best interests of the citizens. Clearly, who are citizens in the racist state if not those against whom injustices are not directed? Citizens are not those who are racialized, since those who are racialized are stripped of their citizenship through the banal violation of the everyday. Even though the state continually violates, it will regard itself as promoting justice. So, those who do not feature in citizenship, even though they are documented as citizens, will be rendered by their race aliens in their own state. The state renders invisible those bodies whom it racializes. The state parades itself as not being racist, but instead acting on the basis of goodwill. If the world is antiblack, the state will be antiblack in that black bodies are unwanted by the state and also by the world.

The Category of the Unthought

The Black Register as thought from the outside of being, epistemic practices from the positionality of the unthought, puts blackness as a challenge to the world that denies the existence of blackness. The positionality of the unthought articulates "the world in which other people think their unthinkable thoughts" (Dabashi 2015, 7). These unthinkable thoughts do emerge not because they are obsessed with being different, but because the bodies that express those thoughts are marked as different and even non-existent in the realm of thought. Thinking unthinkable thoughts is the very basis of objecting to all modes of subjection. What follows are meditations in black, in which the register of blackness informs the basis through which subjection is confronted.

> The emergence and preservation of blackness, as the ontological totality, the revolutionary consciousness that black people hold and pass, is possible only by way of renunciation of actual being *and* the ongoing conferral of historical being – the gift of historicity as claimed, performed dispossession.
>
> (Moten 2013b, 238)

There is everything at stake for blackness. That is why there is a fugitiveness of refusal, objection. To think from the idea of conquest as having been and still being conquered calls for a different kind of thinking that has nothing to do with the call to abandon the idea of conquest. This is the fundamental reflective axis in that the call for the modes of being has to be understood from the life that is at stake. The strain that blackness lives in cannot be overemphasized, precisely because blackness has everything to lose in the antiblack world. This is the absurdity of intensification of the erasure of blackness from the realm of being. Those who are committed to the ethical questioning of the world do engage in the force of critique. Moten and Harney (2004) describe how the ethical questioning done by blackness is ridiculed as not being serious about change, not rigorous, not productive, and futile. This is banal in the sense that the standard is change, rigor, productivity, and success as defined by whiteness. This means that the domain of thought has to do with everything other than blackness. In essence, to have thought in the domain of blackness is a misnomer.

Indeed, the erasure of black thought shows that there is nothing that will ignite any means of accounting for the plight of blackness. The onus is then upon blackness to ignite itself, and to raise the human question in its scandalous form. It is to make a concerted effort to ward off any means of pacification or propagation of thought outside the domain of blackness. As a kind of discursive opposition to the thought that claims to be inclusive while it is exclusive, blackness comes with "property unknown"; Moten and Harney still emphasize the idea of conquest as the site in which black bodies remain located, and they call for ways in which to think seriously about the relocation of everything that has been erased. This property unknown, for Moten and Harney, connotes the epistemic break from the Western-centric consensus, and as blackness is the fugitive embodiment, "a thought of outside" then emerges as the terrain of thought; this is not the self-imposed marginality that comes as a choice of doing politics from the outside. To be in this space of no-space is not a matter of choice. It is the realm that is not accidental, but the deliberate perpetual continuity. Moten and Harney (2004) formulate what they call "the Undercommons," which is "the non-place that must be thought outside the sensed inside" precisely because it is the forceful epistemic critique of sociality and the demand of the world to be just.

What is then fundamental is the articulation of that which is rendered non-existent and subjectivity from the limits of being; it is that which liberates itself from the clutches of subjection. It is the subjectivity, as Mignolo (1999, 38) writes, of "an undoing and a redoing." What is being undone is *the inscription of the subject* – blackness as nothingness and redoing does not mean that blackness is becoming something – rather, a redoing is the assemblage of subjectivity to unmask the racist inscription of blackness as that which is nothing, and if it is to be killed, it cannot be accounted for, as there is no life to think of.

Nothing is expected from blackness, and if there is anything to expect, it still remains nothing. The doubting or the questioning of the humanity of blackness means that blackness is positioned in the zone of non-being, the world being better without blackness. And, having nothing to offer to the world and not being part of that world, there cannot be any black thought. It is the hegemonic of the Euro–North-American episteme and its technologies of subjection that see fit to be the perceptivity and the sole embodiment of thought. According to this frame, there is no black perspective to be thought of; hence the installed framework is that colonization of thought renders blackness devoid of thought and places it in the zone of non-being. If, then, there is thought that stands against this hegemonic claim, the thought that comes from those rendered nothing, the thought that comes in a form of discursive oppositions in order to affirm life itself, blackness is no longer defined; it defines itself, and yet at the same time, it admits that there is still colonization of thought be subjected to discursive oppositions, since subjection still remains. It allows blackness to reflect its ontological standing, which many times mask the injustices that are unleashed upon black bodies on the basis of their racialization.

What is important is not to claim easy victories that introduce celebratory discourses that propagate non-racialism, post-racialism, and transcendence while subjection continues. The idea of conquest is a starting point that shows that the world cannot go unquestioned and what is erased keeps on resurfacing not at the level of embodied appearance, but through enforced speech. This means to admit that there is subjection and that blackness is still dehumanized, and yet to make sure that there is will to live. This will to admit is important, and in no way suggests fatalism, nihilism, lack of agency. Rather, it creates discursive oppositions by means of "emergence of colonized epistemic practices" (Gordon 2013, 730), which admits to the condition of the colonized and having the will to end that ontologico-existential predicament on its own terms.

For the fact that blackness is at the receiving end of modernity and structured in its darker side, it makes itself the subject of statement, which does not necessarily mean that this will reorder the world. To articulate the lived experience of blackness calls for the specific ways of thinking that call the world as it is into question, for it is the world that exteriorizes blackness. The positionality of the unthought is the thought that nevertheless continues to think while it is rendered non-existent. Not that it must be legitimated – it is a double critique, as Mignolo (1999) states. The statement of the subject is the enunciation through which the question is approached – the lived experience of being at the receiving end of subjection. What, then, is proffered are meditations in black which have to do with the quest for liberation; this comes from blackness defining itself through discursive oppositions and ontologico-existential struggles. The position where blackness is articulating thought, as a form of discursive opposition, means that blackness is its own, since it is itself which is at stake. Therefore, there are no coalition politics, since the direction of subjection is targeting only racialized bodies. The form of thought that comes out of this space stands outside moral discourses that react to the suffering of the human.

The structure of dehumanization is based on a radical making and unmaking, both of which explain the life in the nervous system of antiblackness. The structure of dehumanization needs production that creates and destructs, privileges and dispossesses, tears and sutures, enriches and impoverishes, that lets live and lets die. Thus, the realm of life and its articulation could not be an all-inclusive project where the human is placed in the world. Blackness still remains dehumanized; it is signified on the domain of the excess of otherness. To see difference in everything that is outside itself, whiteness in creating blackness presents brutality as not anything grotesque, but sublime. So, whiteness is the domain of the human and blackness is the opposite, the very basis of being excommunicated from the realm of life.

The structure of dehumanization produces blackness as the haunted figure and has nothing to do with the myth of sameness, recognition, agency, and cosmopolitanism. To be haunted is to think outside of being and take the question of dehumanization seriously. Thus, the conception of the paradigm of difference is the basis on which to consider the human question. Difference is not the opposite of sameness in this instance, but serves to reify the fact that the difference of blackness is something that amounts to non-existence.

The position of the unthought is important precisely because it is necessary for there to be a black register. This, then, amounts to blackness having the capacity to position itself and to ask fundamental questions outside the hegemonic epistemic terrain that denies blackness its own humanity. This is because the structural position of being black in the antiblack world is to be a slave. The problems of blackness mean being ontologically located in the world; however, this locatedness is not that of the human being, but something exterior to humanity. To be here means life and death are collapsed into one thing in blackness as it does not matter whether blacks are alive or dead. What is safeguarded in the antiblack world is whiteness at the expense of blackness.

In pursuit of thought, blackness has to undertake risk and to recognize that there has never been a radical break, as subjection masks itself further to make sociality continue to think outside itself, the installation of alienation, as of the present not mattering and the future being something that actually does. It is in this trajectory that blackness is prevented from even accessing the past, naming its injustices, and the cruelty that it must account for. Subjection is, as Hartman and Wilderson (2003, 192) posit, "the same predicament, the same precondition." Blackness remains the same: there is no temporality or complexity; the structural position of blackness is what it suffers in a distinct form of being dehumanized. Moten (2003) articulates the question of resistance in blackness, and it is important to highlight the fact that it is coupled with assertion. The psychic structure of dehumanization is so intense that it persuades blackness to remain where it is under the watchful gaze of whiteness. If it makes a claim, in its own name and own register, blackness is accused of being a threat and of destabilizing the world.

In fact, the positionality of the unthought takes seriously the fact that the old is still new and the new is the old. The spectrality of the past is still the continued domain of the present. The kind that is pursued here is not a utopic register, but the sedimentation of the past, present, and future. The positionality of the unthought is the repositioning of the black body (Hartman and Wilderson 2003). This necessitates the modes of subjectivity that have everything to do with the human question. For blackness to reposition itself is to confront the mimicry that curtails any form of imagination that thought should come as that which is in its name. To reposition

oneself is to think with the other so to create the community of
life, the life which has been expelled and is now recomposing
itself. This is the re-imagination of life itself. This heightening of
imagination without any limitation – the possibility of reaching
that which is always fathomed as outside – the positionality of
the unthought means blackness becomes its own and heightens its
political imagination in the face of whatever form of skepticism.
Possibility lies within reach and this will mean imagining new
forms of life. Blackness does not engage in the gestures of wanting
to be accommodated and to position itself within the epistemic
structure of antiblackness: "Instead, it demands a radical racialization of any analysis of positionality" (Hartman and Wilderson
2003, 184). To take seriously the positionality of blackness is to
think seriously about the racial positioning of blackness and the
ontological structure that comes with it. This, then, explains why
black subjectivity is derived from the lived experience of being black
in the antiblack world.

The becoming – the reconfiguration of the subject – from
blackness means becoming the political agent (Hartman and
Wilderson 2003). It therefore means that there is no way that the
question of the political can be misplaced. The position of the
unthought is what Hartman and Wilderson call the "position of the
slave" whose problem is that of "crafting the narrative." To craft
the narrative means that blackness seeks to make a claim, naming
the injustices that afflict it for what they are. This crafting of the
narrative, as the position of the unthought, means that blackness
states its non-relationality to the forms of subjectivities that claim
to be universal, while they exteriorize blackness in the guise of
relationality. The blackened relation to the antiblack world is
nothing but non-relationality, since there is ontological elimination
of blackness. The crafting of narrative by blackness is not in relation
to the master's articulation of the narrative. The black relation is
non-relation in the sense that there is no narrative, but its crafting.
This problem means that the master has the narrative and crafting
it is second nature – that is, there is no effort claiming subjectivity
from the master, since this is a given. The slave, in contrast, is still
concerned with the problem of crafting the narrative as it is outside
the grammar of being human and its ontological constitution. This
should be understood in terms of the contrasting positionality
of being oppressed and being free. The slave is oppressed, while
the master is free. The freedom of the master manifests from the

freedom of the slave. Therefore, the narrative of the master does not need to be crafted, because the narrative is there to solidify the existence of the master, who has no constraints on his freedom. The slave is the embodiment of blackness, and what Hartman and Wilderson (2003, 190) emphasize is that "masters and slaves, even today, are never allies." The struggles of the oppressed and those who are not are not the same, and not only that, the asymmetrical ontological stand calls for different forms of political causes. The master oppresses the slave, and the latter is not regarded as the fully constitutive being.

So long as the asymmetrical relations continue to exist, there is no common cause to pursue, as whiteness depends on blackness to be free and to craft its own narrative. The narrative of the master does not have the aspirations of blackness, and it is clear that the myth of being allies is just that. It is a myth in that whiteness exists through its modalities of violence to maintain its position as master. To call for structural antagonism is to call for the positionality of the unthought and this category which takes seriously the modalities of violence that dehumanize blackness. In emphasis, blackness is denied humanity, so is its subjectivity. There is no form of thought that will be regarded as thought if it comes out of blackness, and the position of blackness is insurgency at the level of subjectivity in that it registers itself amidst all form of denial of its humanity. Blackness cannot be articulated outside subjection, and what appears foundational is the warning by Hartman and Wilderson (2003, 185) not to wallow in "celebratory narratives of the oppressed."

The past, the present, and the future are intrinsically linked, and for blackness there cannot be a break of the three. Blackness cannot be nostalgic about any sense of ontological purity, neither can it be proud that the present is better than nothing, and the future will be "the best of the best." There is nothing that never was of blackness, nothing was left untouched. Everything with regard to blackness is bastardized. The present and its future are already bastardized by the past, as it is in the past that black dehumanization was kick-started, and this condition still exists. To be black is to disappear, and this means that bastardization does not stop here, but delegitimizes whatever blackness articulates as something that is inferior, illegitimate, and constituting lack. This means that there is no going back to the romanticist past or even retrieving something of essence from the past. It is simply a matter of working things out from the present existential condition. Even the future that is said to be virtuous or something that holds a form of certainty is not so. What is at stake is not the life of blackness, since there is no life to speak of, but rather, blackness itself. Whether by historical accident or unavoidability of the human condition, to be black means to lead existence in the hellish condition of being outside the boundaries of being.

To subject the future to critique is not unusual, more so if the future is paraded as something that humanity should invest in, even at the expense of the present. Black life has been resistant and persistently constitutive in its past and the present. As the life to be liquidated, its militant resistance has been in the domain of survival. So, if the future is about to be created, it should not be based on the notion that things will be better while the present is not attended to. The future is presented as progress, and it is meant to be a better condition than the present. It means that the past that informs the present, as violation of black bodies continues, is something to be ignored. It presupposes that for there to be a better future, race must be abandoned because it is the pathology of the past and the burden of the present, which means that there will be no future. According to this reasoning, denial of race, there was racism in the past, and since the present has no racism (though it still continues in a structurally violent way), the future is what should be focused on. In other words, the future is the horizon of possibility and not of uncertainty. The future as the marker is identified as the era that has nothing to do with uncertainty in that it is the new moment. This is problematic in two senses. One, no one knows what the future holds, and if that is the case, it means that the future is the era of uncertainty. Two, if racism is traced from the past and often relegated to the past as having nothing to do with the present, it is fallacious to suggest that the future will be burdened by race. To mark the past, present, and future of race as separable is problematic, given that the living conditions of today are those of the past.

The future cannot be a destiny. The present has to be attended to. The making of the present means that the demand for fundamental change cannot just be cosmetic and the future cannot be considered as something distant, having nothing to do with the existential conditions that signify pathology of blackness. The future cannot be left to its own devices; it must be influenced or directed by the present. The future cannot be the distant time to be arrived at, to be postponed so that it remains a mere illusion. What should be radicalized is the present. If we are to talk of a meaningful future, the present must be meaningful. There is no way that the brutal past will be remedied by the future; the present has to come before as the remedy of the past. Moreover, when one is in the past, the present is the future. So, it is important not to defer the end of dehumanization to the future. Dehumanization should end now.

The Itinerary

What is offered in this book is a *capita selecta* of thinkers who called for the end of dehumanization now. In the first chapter, Sylvia Wynter confronts the figure of the Imperial Man, while Aimé Césaire, in the second chapter, unmasks the human subject in the colonial condition. Both Wynter and Césaire engage in the serious critique of the colonial condition by calling for the world of the human *qua* human. Successively, the book charts the terrain of the criminalization of black bodies that have to live in the shadow of death. The third chapter reads Steve Biko, who lived under a white supremacist regime and died in detention, as the outlawed subject. Biko's condition bears similarity with the incarcerated existence of Assata Shakur and George Jackson, who are featured in the fourth chapter as the authors of prison slave narratives. The basis of this is to show how blackness has been the domain of critical thought and this is related to a philosophical tribute in the fifth chapter of Mabogo P. More, who makes an original critique of antiblackness and calls for a just world. The sixth chapter shows that bare life is not an adequate conceptual structure for understanding the ontological scandal of Marikana. Finally, the concluding chapter takes the concept of the subject seriously and resituates it within the ontological domain of blackness.

In all these chapters nothing is conclusive, except to say that *The Black Register* is a continued search for the human subject that reconfigures the world that is outside subjection. Therefore, it is the end of subjection that all chapters are about. It is fundamental to raise existential questions that do not conform to the status quo of human rights whereas there are still those who are dehumanized. Wynter, Césaire, Biko, Shakur, Jackson, and More offer their own meditative registers and are in conversation with each other. What ties them together is their own plight and commitment to creating another world – another world is possible!

1

Sylvia Wynter:
Contra Imperial Man

The modern colonial world cannot be divorced from the processes that brought the human into being. This also includes the reversal of such processes through the logic of dehumanization. The manner in which humanity assumes its place in the modern colonial world signifies the excess of difference and this is not natural or a given phenomenon by the creation of the human and the non-human. To account for the human or to install such an ontological category in the modern colonial world is to encounter that which is not human. This creation comes out of the fabrication of being that the human is *itself*, *for-itself*, and *in-itself*. For it is the logic that sees the human as a given and not linked to the processes of social formation. Indeed, this has instilled the fallacy that the individual is prior to sociality and the human is a transcendental subject who can also be said to be separate from the embodiment of being and its relationality to the world. This is the subject positionality of the Imperial Man – the figure of the human who is both last and foremost human against all others who are different and who are solely non-human.

The modern colonial world produces the human through difference precisely because its logic of racism is the one that dehumanizes what it differentiates. It is the infrastructure of racism that enforces the classification, demarcation, location, hierarchization, and zoning of the human. This, of course, is done in the pure logic of difference. To facilitate dehumanization and give it some moral relief, justification of difference is nothing but the mask of dehumanization itself. In the greater scheme of things, Sylvia Wynter is the important figure to engage the human question in the manner in which the making of the modern colonial world is revealed and such a world unfolds in its mutations while affirming its position in maintaining the ontological distinction of superiority and inferiority. Wynter confronts the modern colonial world by unmasking its legitimation of ontological distinction and showing its installation of *Man* – the figure of the human who is human against the rest of those different from it and the ways in which the figure of Man is that of Imperial Man. Just because there is a different ontological standing that claims superiority, Wynter assumes the solidity of her marginalized, violated, exploited, alienated, and dehumanized blackness as a site of subjectivity. The signature of being in the ontologico-existential struggle – Wynter's "yours in struggle" – is to show her contra positionality to the Imperial Man and the supposition that her political commitment is that of continuity and not temporality.

Wynter's work is not only a declaration of intent; it is a call for the unmaking of the colonial world. As such, it is the work of the political and its subjectivity that is informed by confrontation of dehumanization and a move to the creation of the human. There is, so to say, no human in the modern colonial world, but the Imperial Man with his phallic power and those whom he dehumanizes. For Wynter, the epistemic shift of studying the human condition from the existential point of damnation and being in contradiction with the Imperial Man is to assume a clear stance of the rebel. Not only does she differ for the sake of differing, she also demystifies that superiority of the Imperial Man. This is fundamental, since the figure of the human is not that which is created by the Imperial Man, but the human – *After Man* – the creation of the human in the world comes into being through ontologico-existential struggle. What does it mean to then think the human differently from the dehumanized position and to be contrary to the Imperial Man? This does not pertain only to thinking the human differently, but to be in confrontation and not in the terms that the hegemonic Imperial Man dictates in his epistemic strictures. What Wynter's meditations keep on harking back to is the figure of the human contra Imperial Man which leads to the unmaking of the modern colonial world.

The Imperial Man

The Imperial Man is an individual, the subject of self-definition and self-justification. He does not claim or emphasize this standpoint because he is the embodiment of the world. If everything in human history is to be narrated, it should be done through the triumph and pageantry of the Imperial Man. Weheliye (2008, 323) also adds that the Imperial Man is the one "who could define himself as the universal human." This is the imposition of the disembodied embodiment, the very configuration of blackness as that which is defiled, making it nothing that exists. In this case, human history is thus mono-narrative and overly totalizing as it cannot be something outside the Imperial Man. Wynter (1995) highlights the historical event of 1492, which marks the conquest of the Americas as the kick-starting of the Imperial Man's overrepresentation in the making of the modern colonial world and the continuity of its aftermath. Wynter has been at the receiving end of events resulting from 1492, as the other in the colonial-centric historico-existential experience. It is this era that attests to the logic of voyages of discovery having led to the inauguration of the unmaking of the world. It is in this configuration that the modern colonial world is in favor of the Imperial Man, which in turn is the very opposite when it comes to those who are located at the existential abyss.

In point of fact, the racialized, colonized, criminalized, exploited, subjected, and more acutely, blackened subject, is the sole creation of the Imperial Man. This then allows such a subject to be the target of and vulnerable to dispossession, oppression, and dehumanization. This subject is, in the eyes of the Imperial Man, the negative of the human. Wynter, by standing in opposition to the Imperial Man, clearly shows how standing on the side of liberatory politics that are destined to bring about the end of the Imperial Man is an indomitable task that requires politics of commitment. This form of politics is met with fierce resistance by virtue of its contradictory positionality against the Imperial Man. Wynter destabilizes the foundations of the modern colonial world and pathos and logos which privilege the Imperial Man. Maldonado-Torres (2007, 190) writes: "Instability is often met with force of edicts, rules, regressive propositions, reforms, imprisonment, or even bullets." Wynter assumes the positionality of being near to death, for she is the blackened subject who stands contra Imperial Man.

The contra positionality – the politics of liberatory opposition-ality and affirmation so to say – articulates the pain and agony of being black, even while that pain is denied. It is to act against the very co-optation and to refuse to be consumed by the Imperial Man. To be consumed is to be rendered complicit and to have nothing to do with liberatory politics. Wynter stands in the contra positionality which Maldonado-Torres refers to as the "grammar of dissent." This grammar does not bow to the subjection of the Imperial Man in his structures of modernity and its attended eclipse of political imagination. What informs Wynter's instability is not chaos for its own sake, but rather the terrain of the practice of liberatory politics of the very form of the livelihood of the blackened subject.

The subject formation of the Imperial Man is the self as complete. It is the self as a conqueror which, as Maldonado-Torres (2007, 245) notes, provides "a solid foundation of the self." The expansionist logic is what informs the Imperial Man; the beginning of history and its aftermath are those of the Imperial Man. Nothing has been there before the Imperial Man, and if there are lands that happened to be expropriated, they are regarded as empty lands without people; not only that there were no people – there have never been any people before and even after the conquest. More crudely, their ontological superfluity and invisibility mean that everything begins and ends with the Imperial Man. The Imperial Man, as Ferreira da Silva (2015, 91) amplifies, "rules as the transcendental-empirical king." To be such is to be an oversized figure which is ontologically created by projects that reify dehumanization since the operating logic is to exercise lordship as a form of dehumanization.

This then leaves the way for the Imperial Man to question the humanity of the colonized where the Imperial Man claims superi-ority while inferiorizing others. The ego-politics of the Imperial Man inaugurates, as Wynter (1989, 640) argues, "the Self of Man and its instituted mode of subjectivity/subject, conceptualized as a selected being and purely natural organism." The Imperial Man is not defined, he defines himself and he has the absolute right to define others to the point of defiling them. The Imperial Man's power of definition also determines who lives and who dies. The life of the black is wholly dependent on the will of the Imperial Man.

> This *man*, who depends as everyone else does on the social world for his being, sees himself as independent of it precisely because he expects it as conditioned by him and for him ... His model becomes,

in a word, himself, which issues the realm of a contradictory
solipsism – the self as world by virtue of a denial of *others* without
whom the self could not have been posited in the first place. It is
this inhabitation that constitutes an obstacle to the emergence of the
human.

(Gordon 2006, 248 [emphasis original])

The Imperial Man is against sociality, and even the holistic constitution of humanity. For the Imperial Man, there are no humans
outside himself. That is why fixity of difference is the key ontological
marker. It is important to consider difference in terms of those who
are here and those who are out there. To be here means to be in the
realm of life and to be out there is to be in the shadow of death. It
is to be violated in such an extreme form that to be out there is to
be a non-entity. The Imperial Man does not see the conciliation of
the here and out there since difference is vital. As such, to maintain
ontological purity, which is merely a narcissistic attachment, is to
claim that those who are out there will contaminate the ontological
purity of those who are here. That is why, as Gordon notes, the
imposition of the genuine world poses a threat to the Imperial Man.
This imposition is necessary to end those who are here and those
who are out there.

To affirm his existence, the Imperial Man imposes himself as God
over those he seeks to dominate or already dominates. The role of
claiming to be God comes through the excess of self-definition. The
Imperial Man knows very well that he is not God, but he makes
an institutionalized, naturalized, and normalized subjection – the
demand to want to be regarded as superior by those whom he
oppresses. If the Imperial Man claims to be God, tacitly or not, the
logic of difference will be reinforced to see Man *qua* Man as one
ontological dimension and the Imperial Man commanding lordship
over the rest of organisms and species. Indeed, the projection of God
by the Imperial Man is simply a distortion of himself.

The one under the sight and control of Imperial Man is forced to live
in conditions where her and his worth augments in direct relation to
her and his self-evisceration, that is, to the devaluation of her or his
own body, identity, and culture. Since Imperial Man structurally and
semiotically functions as God, the holy call to imitate God becomes
an explicit act of violation.

(Maldonado-Torres 2008, 114)

The Imperial Man, as Wynters insists, is not God, let alone his representative. It is in Wynter's work that the challenging of the orthodox occurs in how the politics of representation are used and always skewed in favor of the Imperial Man. In the same way, to say the least, this orthodoxy is "a *theocentric* view of the relation between God and man" (Wynter 1991, 255 [emphasis original]). It is this view which is embedded in hierarchization and also the claim of having proximity to God, if not being God. Indeed, the justification of the Imperial Man of being closer to God or being God is the fact that the Imperial Man justifies his existence as unquestionable. In simple terms, the Imperial Man is closer to God or is God himself by virtue of being the Imperial Man – the being above all beings – reason, standards, and morality being some of the currencies that border on the omnipotence. This then leaves the infrastructure of violence to be the figure of the arbitrary; the Imperial Man has unlimited excess of lordship over those whom he marks as inferior, if not non-human. It is Cartesian logic to be a transcendental subject while those who are inferiorized and dehumanized cannot be transcendental, let alone subjects of the human. It is only the Imperial Man who is the human, and who assumes the ontological category of *Man* as Wynter shows. The ontological cancellation of those the Imperial Man inferiorizes and dehumanizes is nothing but the eschatological escalation (in fallacious terms, of course) to create its other. The Imperial Man produces certain forms of humanity which are hierarchized into superiority and inferiority. These form the existential composition of the world – the modern colonial world – where in the logic of difference the Imperial Man determines the fate of humanity as being superior or inferior. The condemnation of other humans to inferiority means that they have no existence and it cannot be justified. Therefore, their existence, being insistently a hellish one, inaugurates subjection as the exercise form of human relations.

It is, from Wynter's standpoint, that the Imperial Man is confronted directly and his claims to invention being nothing that make him come closer to creation. To claim what rightfully belongs to God to himself, the Imperial Man creates the impression of being the master of the world and all the species and things on earth should be subjected to his lordship. Placing the Imperial Man in a different positionality allows for Wynter's contradiction. This means that there is no pre-existing or given – that is, it *is there* by virtue of *being there* as if there are no existential formations. This claim is falsified by Wynter, who shows that the Imperial Man is the product of invention and this is tidily closed to forms of existence that take prevalence in the modern colonial world. The production of the racist infrastructure which condemns those who are racialized is systematic, systemic, and continuous subjection. Wynter's opposition rests on black subjectivity which is informed by the clear task of unmasking the deceit of the Imperial Man. To think from Wynter's standpoint is to be in direct opposition to the Imperial Man precisely because the very idea of his supremacy is falsified and the call is for such a figure to come to an end.

The lordship of the Imperial Man as the master means the right to own everything without any limit. To be in the world is to be in the absolute possession of the will and excess of the Imperial Man. The destiny of the black subject, as the other, is decided without any regard to the black subject, who is regarded as nothing. For there to be the possibility of the colonizing of minds, bodies, and souls of the black subjects, the Imperial Man states clearly that they have no relationality with themselves. They are made to see themselves through the eyes of the Imperial Man. The Imperial Man is a sovereign subject, as Agamben (2005) notes, and has free reign over others who are regarded to be outside humanity and exterior to God. The fact that they are dehumanized finds justification through the moral denigration exacerbated by the Imperial Man and to engage in what Wynter (1991, 257) refers to as the "theocratic and arbitrary model of divine creation" – the creation of the other through theological justification.

It is with will and excess that the Imperial Man is legitimate, as Wynter puts it, to the discoverer, conqueror, expropriator, and even the claim to be God. The notion of being a hyper-figure of man of God, which means being in constant opposition to those who are steeped in sin, means that the only way to create existential harmony is for them to repent. The leitmotif of the Imperial Man is to partake in some form of God's function to rule over the "lower order of reality" (Wynter 2003, 287). The ego-politics of being God is justified through reason, which is something said to be external to blacks. The absence of reason means that blacks are not human beings. The Imperial Man, having reason, assumes a propensity of what Wynter calls the higher degree of spiritual perfection. Therefore, this mark of paradigm of difference postulates the "new iconography of irrationality, to its new postulate of 'significant ill'" (Wynter 2003, 304). The paradigm of difference is accelerated through a plethora of significations. This gives way to the single field of power to unleash subjection as a form of life to those who are considered different (Sharma 2015).

The manner in which subjection operates in this theological construction of difference, the Imperial Man, the man of God, signifies that the black subject is fallen flesh. To be signified as fallen flesh is to be permanently fixed in the abyss. It is to be outside the spirit and to be in permanent sin simply because the Imperial Man renders blacks to be sinful by nature, as Wynter shows. By implication, the fallen flesh is the signification of evil. The embodiment of sin does not require those who are niggerized to commit a sin, since they are sinful by virtue of being black.

The paradox, as Wynter (1984) points out, is the fact that the redemption of the fallen flesh is to be baptized via Christianity. But still, the very signification of being the deviant other by virtue of being black remains, with no possibility of becoming fully human. To be the fallen flesh is to be beyond redemption, yet this is the very negation of baptism, which counts for nothing. Therefore, there is no chance for the invention of blackness as human, as the Imperial Man denies every form of ontological possibility. Consequently, the black is the black as the Imperial Man imposes, to be seen as far from God and not only that, as still godless. Wynter (1984, 36) writes: "At this level of Otherness the 'negro' was not even considered, since he was not imagined even to have languages worth studying, nor to partake in culture, so total was his mode of Nigger Chaos."

It is Wynter who clearly shows that such a figure is rendered as deviant. It is the figure which cannot govern itself and its modes of everyday life. As such, to be relegated to the existential abyss is nothing but the moral virtue of the Imperial Man to come and change the black subject. The Imperial Man is "genetically *redeemed*, whose other, is necessarily the genetically *damned*" (Wynter 1991, 273 [emphasis original]). It is on this basis that Wynter affirms that this is the way in which epistemological orders have been built.

> Modernity, then, introduces ego-politics into the world of theo-politics, an early modernity bears witness to the gradual marginalization of the theo-politics by ego-politics of knowledge, in which a new God is born: modern Man.
>
> (Maldonado-Torres 2014, 652)

Fanon (1990, 32) opposes the fallacy of the Imperial Man to call for God's way as "the ways of the white man, of the master, of the oppressor." For if the Imperial Man is God, he constantly forces this gesture to come into being, to imprint on the psyche of those over whom he lords through practices of domination, exploitation, pillage, and dehumanization. The Imperial Man strikes fear and he wants to be absolute, if not the omnipotent pious. The fall of man is, as Wynter shows, the figure that is enslaved, expropriated, and legitimately to be eliminated. This happens without any moral dilemma because the bad faith of the theological with its guise of redemption permits the Imperial Man to be the figure of excess who can dehumanize at will without any form of accountability. The spread of the gospel and evangelization of the Imperial Man is not meant to redeem, but to dominate. The expansionist logic of the Imperial Man is that of colonizing racialized bodies and also the psychic damage that is the attendant part of subjection.

The Imperial Man is the fraternity of what Maldonado-Torres (2008) calls the community of masters – the patriarchal infrastructure of the modern colonial world – the world of domination and dehumanization. Indeed, the emergence of the Imperial Man led to the credence and justification of civilization and the birth of the Imperial Man as the lord of the modern colonial world under the fraternity of the community of masters. The imperial formations of the world, according to the ethos of the community of masters, propagate the supremacy of their being at the expense and inferiorization of others. As Maldonado-Torres (2008, 13) infers, it "defends the condition in which mastery is to be achieved concretely at all costs and in which this can only be answered by actually eliminating the slaves." The community of masters signifies the patriarchal infrastructure since its modes of subjectivity equate to signification of violence. The operating logic is, of course, that those who are differentiated should be dehumanized and made submissive, passive, and even complicit in their own oppression. It is the community of masters that the Imperial Man is accountable to; that is to say, the collective of individuals as Imperial Men constitutes the formation of the community of masters. It is Imperial Reason that serves as the glue that keeps them together, since its main motif is the dehumanization of blacks.

The Imperial Man is the individual – a being in the full sense of being – the master of his Other, the world and the rest that is in it. The idea of race, as the organizing principle (Gordon 2000b), gives the community of masters legitimacy in bad faith that their responsibility is to question the humanity of the racialized black subjects. The Imperial Man has no moral obligation to humanity at large, but only to the fraternity of his own – the community of masters. The motif and aspiration of the community of masters border on the elimination of the other. There is nothing that calls for communal life with regard to the community of masters as they value "ethics of power needed to maintain alive a pathos of domination and self-control" (Maldonado-Torres 2008, 53). As self-acclaimed transcendental subjects, the community of masters see it as their duty to be the individual – Imperial Man as self *qua* self – in the Wynterian sense, the individual as human and others as not human.

The logic of the community of masters, as Maldonado-Torres contends, is only war, violence, and death. This takes place in the realm of excess and in relation to those who are racialized. The racialized subjects are nothing that can count for being in the human fraternity because they are the fallen man. The fallen man is lorded upon, and war, violence, and death serve as justificatory practices. As Maldonado-Torres (2008, 24) laments, these practices "are not foreign elements in Western culture but logical results of dominant paradigms of thinking." They determine the very episteme of the community of masters and the manner in which that is translated to the modes of existence. The modern colonial world is made to be the place that makes *homo polemos* a necessity and naturalized to be the state of permanent war against racialized bodies. The Trinitarian slogan of liberty, equality, and justice, as Maldonado-Torres points out, becomes suspended when the racialized subject comes into being. Even though this slogan is universal and inclusive in gesture, it does not extend to those who are in disfavor with the community of masters.

It is important to note that the Imperial Man sees himself as a complete subject and also the one with high moral currency. That is why belonging to the collective fraternity of the community of masters affords him a high sense of legitimacy; even if such a figure is accused of being immoral, that accusation will not stand, for everything he does is virtuous and all actions are done in the best interests of civilization. What the community of masters continues to serve, as their sole purpose, are the interests of the modern colonial world through what Maldonado-Torres (2008) calls "imperial guardianship." In serving this role:

They create new subjects that must be relocated to the productive
and exploitable, dispossessed to be modern, disciplined to be
independent, converted to be human, stripped of old cultural
bearings to be citizens, coerced to be free.

(Stoler and McGranahan 2007, 8)

It seems as if, from the extent of brutality visited upon the racialized
body of blackness from the process that Stoler and McGranahan
underline, there is no clear articulation of ontological devastation.
This, of course, is the master morality code of the Imperial Man
claiming to be doing good to those whom they dehumanize.
That is, the Imperial Man knows what is best for the racialized,
dehumanized black subject. It seems as if those who are subjected
to imperial guardianship do not have any form of agency, and
that they have been saved from themselves. Even if they validate
the constant fluidity of the imperial formations and their degree of
differentiality, this does not negate the stasis of war, violence, and
murder which continue to haunt them.

Suspension of morals takes place through Imperial Reason, which
is dictated by what Maldonado-Torres (2008) refers to as master
morality. The community of masters imposes a certain notion of
master morality – that is, a certain kind of morality which is not
morality. Maldonado-Torres identifies two practices which master
morality rests upon, both being responsible for the very formation
and constitution of the community of masters. These practices are
conversion and persuasion. It is these two concepts that form the
dominating logic and if they do not work, war, violence, and death
are deployed as disciplinary tools to put racialized bodies in their
place. Maldonado-Torres (2008, 43) writes: "Master immorality
is exclusive at best and homicidal at worst." This pertains to the
manner in which morality is used to mask the dehumanization of
other human beings who are perceived as different. It is for this
reason that morality is suspended when subjection is applied to
blacks and there is no sense of moral contradiction or conscience.
There is no conscience to speak of precisely because morals are
suspended. Master morality is the logos and pathos of dehumanization. Even in its mode – discursive and ideological – it has no
moral content whatsoever except to mask the underlying logic
of domination. Propagating morals while suspending them is the
very foundation of dehumanization. The acts of violence, war, and
murder are propagated "as altruistic acts made in the service of

God" (Maldonado-Torres 2008, 117). Therefore, it is important to point out that there is no such thing as master morality without the community of masters.

The condition of existence – being in the world – is founded on master morality and the will to live or die is the absolute possession that is outside the self faced with the condition of existence. The existence of the black subject is reduced to damnation as the Imperial Man and his collective formation of community of masters have the will and power to lord over the life and death of their other. That is to say, the other lives not out of his own will, but that of the Imperial Man. The life of the other does not matter and its depletion is made not to have any moral currency because there is no moral attachment that is due to the other. Letting the other live or die is a superfluous condition because there is no excess without *exteriori* – everything goes when it comes to the other by virtue of not being human.

To confront the Imperial Man *qua* community of masters, whom Wynter labels as Man – the very antithesis of the human – is to show the essence of the contradictory positionality. That is, Wynter's standpoint means that she defies the Imperial Reason of the Imperial Man and also the community of masters. What is the foundational logic of the community of masters if not dehumanization par excellence? It is from the perspective of blackness that Wynter inaugurates the moment where blacks must speak for themselves and in their name. It is important, therefore, to place the Imperial Man as the figure whose time has come to an end. The commitment should be that of seeing the resurrection of another conception of the human – the one outside the invention and distortion of the Imperial Man. This is the human who exists and who has no baggage of being violated.

Niggerization

The stereotypical images that are inscripted on the black body are used, as Wynter shows, to detach life from black bodies and to fixate them to people with nothing and to make dispossession legitimate. The Imperial Man dehumanizes blacks through discursive formations and the weight of language to "*induce* the specific mode of perception needed by a culture-specific order, and to thereby orient prescribed behaviors needed by that order" (Wynter 1995, 20). It is to legitimate signification of blackness as what Wynter (1995, 21) refers to as "the absolute lack of the optimal criterion of being as well as of rationality," and for them to be also relegated to the realm of absolute negation. In this formation, blacks become an extreme form of otherness where to be black is to be a nigger. Blackness in a niggerized form, Wynter (1994, 49) contends, is signified to "incarnate the most atavistic non-evolved Lack of the human." That forming part of language is to have the power to name, and doing so in a manner that is dehumanizing. It is through language that blackness is obliterated from the face of the earth.

The modern colonial world is the hallmark feature of imperial statecraft. The imperial formation as the attendant feature of state-craft is the norm rather than the exception. This then eliminates any form of imagination outside the Imperial Reason. Inevitably, the imperial formation is self-justified and does not warrant any form of opposition. The imperial formation then assumes the pseudo mantle of the universal. As Stoler and McGranahan (2007, 13) clearly state, imperial formations are "derived from an acknowledged and often an unexamined European prototype."

Gordon (2000b, 375) writes: "For the racially formed, the sites are often the body and the metaphysics of group association. For both, there is an epistemology of closure and dialectics of disappearance and extinction." Niggerization essentially means, as Sexton (2006, 251) insists, "dwelling at the absence of the human presence." To be niggerized is to be non-valued, that which has no change or even transcendence. To be niggerized is to be *as it were* and that which *will never become*. This ontological fixity means the atavistic signification is a given. This is made in the logic of the Color Line, which Du Bois ([1903] 1997) stated prophetically would be the problem of the twentieth century. In addition, this problem goes beyond that time, since the aftermath of subjection continues and race is the organizing principle of the modern colonial world (Gordon 2000a). The modern colonial world, which includes the imperial project, is the anti-ethical par excellence. To be clutched in subjection, the racialized and the colonized body is made to be "not so much as a prison but an inescapable sign of murder" (Maldonado-Torres 2008, 114). The modern colonial world in the configuration of the empire is commanded under the lordship of the community of masters.

For Wynter, the Color Line is the one that affirms the paradigm of difference, which is the logic of the modern colonial world. It is in this existential fault line that the Color Line, as Wynter (2003, 315) suggests, is "drawn institutionally and discursively between whites/nonwhites." It is not out of choice to be niggerized, but the making of the Color Line which gives a niggerized body "a thematic structure" and Farley (1997, 474) argues that it is "a social practice rather than a natural object." It is the imposed signification which marks the legitimization of dehumanization. The radicalization of difference is structured by the imposition to "live in the *poesis* or *autopoesis* of 'Man'" (Wynter 2006, 20). In a call against niggerization, Wynter argues for a new definition of the human. This means that the responsibility to redefine lies solely with the niggerized. It is they who must redefine the human and repose the fundamental question of the human in their own epistemic and existential register. Indeed, it is clear from Wynter that this is the collective effort which is also seen as responsibility to one another. This is evident in the mode of "we" and not "I." Being contra niggerization is not an individual effort, but a collective one in that niggerization is not about the individual but the collectivity of blackness. Maldonado-Torres has this to say:

> Racialized subjects are constituted in different ways than those that form selves, others, and peoples. Death is not so much an individualizing factor as a constituting factor of reality. It is the encounter with daily forms of death, not the They, which afflicts them. The encounter with death always comes late, as it were, since death is already beside them.
>
> (Maldonado-Torres 2007, 251)

What is being revealed here is that to be niggerized is to be expelled from humanity and to be structured is to be at the receiving end of death. It would, therefore, be insignificant to signify those who are niggerized as if they were fully ontological while their humanity is questioned. They exist in social death as Patterson (1982) notes and as Wilderson (2003b) amplifies, they are constitutively dead. For the forms of selves, other, and peoples that Maldonado-Torres referred to earlier only make reference to those who have ontological density. To be niggerized is to be put to death. It is to be dead while alive.

The profound consequences of having Humanness defined against Black beings means that the project of colonization and the ongoing works of coloniality have produced for Black people a perverse relationship to the category of the Human in which our existence

as human beings remains constantly in question and mostly outside
the category of *a life*, removes an existence marked by social death.
(Walcott 2014, 93 [emphasis original])

If the human question continues to be outside blackness, its genres
are used against blackness. What is solidified is the condition of
unfreedom that gridlocks blackness into damnation and not life.
This is an inescapable position of social death without any form
of ontological possibility and transcendence. Wynter is on point
to argue that the mode of overrepresentation of the Imperial Man
is to erase blackness where the central mechanism is the work of
socializing blackness into niggerization. The conquest of the black
by the Imperial Man is the latter's overrepresentation as the figure
"which overrepresents itself as if it were the human itself *and to be
the sole determiner of who is human or not*" (Wynter 2003, 260
[emphasis added]). It is, therefore, poignant for Wynter to state
that niggerization can be understood as a form of excess elaborated through representing blacks as nothing but those clutched in
"their extreme nigger form" (Wynter 2003, 307). It is to ensure
that blackness becomes nothing, even to the extent of them seeing
themselves as nothing. Thus, to be a nigger is not to be oneself,
but to be the creation of the Imperial Man. It is Fanon (1970)
who puts it succinctly that blackness is the creation of whiteness.
Gordon (2000b) rightfully points to the irony that the very institutions that created blackness are the ones that detest blackness and
blackness is nothing but the collection of blacks. To see the black
is to see nothing but blacks, and no human beings. It is this very
idea that gives a clear understanding of niggerization. But then,
Wynter also proposes in the Fanonian spirit that the wearing of
masks is the mode of overrepresentation of the Imperial Man.
Even if there are prospects of asserting existence, the presence of
the mask means that there is no face, but a mask. To be signified
as a nigger is to be faceless, that which contains layers and layers
of masks.

Since the positionality of Wynter is contra the Imperial Man, it
clearly appears that signification of the nigger is only dehumanization, and Wynter's standpoint is against such dehumanization.
Instead of being faceless and having layers and layers of masks,
Wynter (1995, 50) calls for the installation of "a new contesting
image of the human." Having this image does not mean being
human, but human in the making.

With this population group's systematic stigmatization, social inferiorization, and dynamically produced material deprivation thereby
serving both to 'verify' the overrepresentation of Man as if it were
the human, and to legitimize the subordination of the world and
well-being of the latter to those of the former.

(Wynter 2003, 267)

Wynter (1984) mobilizes the concept of "the Lack-State" to point
out the number of ways in which being niggerized is to be something
that amounts to nothing. The Imperial Man signifies those niggerized
as "black and lacking significant subjectivity" (Maldonado-Torres
2014, 639). To encounter those niggerized is to come close to those
who have no religion, souls, or even humility. Wynter remarks that
Fanon's attempt to escape the hellish circle of subjection has been
met with failure. For there to be the Imperial Man, there must be
a nigger – the exterior construction in the ontological abyss – the
nigger has no sense of the self because he is not one's self. The sense
of the self is relegated to the absentia. Even if there can be so-called
empirical proof that there is the sense of the self in blackness, the
signification of the nigger collapses all the ontological essence. To
be niggerized is to be crushed by the racist infrastructure. It is to be
brought into a reality that is violent and interpellating.

The organization of the modern colonial world means niggerization as Fanon's depersonalization. Wynter makes a constant effort
to expose the systems of meaning by means of imposed signification
that give legitimacy to niggerization. The nigger is the construction
of the Imperial Man's racist fantasy which is actualized into reality
in a dehumanizing way. For the Imperial Man to say "you are a
nigger," the black ceases to exist and, as Fanon (1970) points out,
to be niggerized is to be assigned the ontological status of being a
subject of failure. Being the subject of failure is solidified so as to
make the modern colonial world to be unjust. It is in Wynter (2001)
that the burden of failure is exposed as deliberately constructed
at the level of genetics – that is, blackness being negative while
whiteness is the opposite. It therefore shows that niggerization is a
form of desire by whiteness to claim narcissistic identification. For
whites not to fail, blacks must fail. This asymmetric dependability
is the logic that holds the modern colonial world together. Also,
it is important to point out that the genetic inscription is a fallacy
if it is to be linked with blackness and failure. For Wynter (2001,
42), the Imperial Man depends on "normative definition in 'white'

terms." The Imperial Man then creates the deviant other. Yet, there seems to be no deviance other than to be the fallacy of justification that blackness and its pathologifical attachments are nothing but failure which is genetically inherent. For the mere fact that there is this failure, niggerization legitimates dehumanization. It is to be in stasis without any form of possibility. Therefore, the nigger is left to his own devices of self-destruction and pathologification. The nigger is nothing since there is no human being in that the Imperial Man signifies who is human or not.

Whatever they own does not belong to them, and as such, they are enslaved objects who have no claim to anything. Plundering, expropriating, looting, and dispossessing is the logic of violence whose target is that which is nothing. Therefore, there cannot be any moral upheaval, as what is violated is not in the grammar of morality – the violation of the niggerized is legitimated and therefore justified. Niggerization means there are no human beings in blacks and they are "irrational beings, and not as human beings; they are below mankind, but above monkeys" (Maldonado-Torres 2014, 640). The infrastructure of racism is dehumanization of other human beings who are relegated to the ontological status of the nigger.

Wynter's subjectivity is interjection. It stands in the opposing direction of the Imperial Man who commands the making of blackness. This interjection is contrary to obedience and complicity in one's own death and that of others. It is the interjection that one's defense against death is also the defense of others. For death does not target the individual but the niggerized. Wynter's interjection is the positionality of being "at the nearness of death, and at the company of death" (Maldonado-Torres 2007, 257). To rid this pathological attachment, there must be the assertion of the will to live. This does not come at the will of the Imperial Man, but the force of will of those who are niggerized. It is then justified that they assume the positionality of being contrary to the Imperial Man by rebellion.

The Rebel

Wynter says no to the Imperial Man as the rebel *à la* Camus, and when she thinks of herself, she says yes. That is to say, Wynter refuses by saying no when her freedom is trampled upon and she says yes when she pursues the realization of that freedom. To say no is not only to litigate, but to liquidate the power of the Imperial Man and to depose him from being a master. Being exploited, alienated, enslaved, and dehumanized is what the rebel says no to. Wynter (1984, 28) forcefully writes: "In decolonization, there is therefore the need of a complete calling in question of the colonial situation." It is to be the rebel, not by choice but the circumstance of being colonized that there must be this moment of radical questioning. If the rebel says no, it is to say "this has been going too long," "so far but no farther," "you are going too far" or again, "There are certain limits beyond which you shall not go" (Camus 1956, 19). The rebel tells the Imperial Man straight to his face: No! This affirmation of the self is how Wynter as the rebel and her act of refusal signifies the contra positionality to the Imperial Man. The rebel redefines the human question by waging the existential struggle rooted in the politics of being. It is to say, as Wynter (2003, 331) forcefully concludes: "The buck stops with us."

For Wynter, the Imperial Man will not be allowed to enjoy any form of excess from her and the rest of the humanity that is oppressed and with whom she is thinking, as she is part of them by claiming to be theirs in struggle. Wynter is in struggle with the rest of the racialized bodies and this is not accidental, but the force of circumstance dictates that there should be this struggle. Wynter is the rebel because she does not subject herself to any obeying code and she asserts herself through refusal. As Camus (1956, 19) writes: "Rebellion cannot exist without the feeling that somewhere, in some way, you are justified." But it needs to be clearly noted that this is not ego-politics where the rebel thinks of the self as a transcendental subject. To be at the exterior of being is to be in the positionality where assertion is needed and to weed out oppression and other existential pathologies.

As the rebel, Wynter is concerned with the refiguring of the human. By inserting herself in the existential struggle to become human differently, and from the vantage point of not being the figure of the sublime but that of the grotesque, Wynter assumes and advocates the positionality of the rebel. As the rebel, Wynter stands for the figurative truth, the one unwanted by the modern colonial world. It is to turn the hegemonic existential arrangement upside down and to break whatever is sealed. It is in this positionality that humanity matters. The relentless pursuit of liberation makes Wynter launch strong propositions and refutations of subjection that still afflict the racialized body, condemning it to the existential abyss. This then creates the *damné*, those who are "all" – the all of blackness in the clutches of subjection – not the individual as the rebel has, according to Camus (1956, 22), "a feeling of identification with other individuals." For the rebel to claim the affinity of the category of "all" (the *damné* so to say), the destiny is to "[undermine] the conception of the individual" (Camus 1956, 20). For Camus to declare: "I rebel – therefore we *exist*" [emphasis original] is to confront the Cartesian cogito and to render it meaningless in the world where the life of the *damné* is at stake. For Wynter, of course, the right to exist is not a given, it must be fought for through combat breathing.

To rebel in order *to be* means that knowledge and awakening of consciousness is the formation of subjectivity that enables the discursive practices that come from blacks in order to realize liberation. The rebel is resurrected from the *damné* not as the figure of exception, or that which is superior to *all*, but part of the all. The politics of authorship, as is clear in Wynter's case, make existential demands of liberation and for there to be the new human beyond the Imperial Man. The existential demands of the rebel require no concessions, but they shutter the order which has been imposed by the discursive strictures and closures of the Imperial Man.

In the battlefield of the episteme and of consciousness, something that lies ahead is the political commitment of the rebel. The locus of enunciation and subject formation of Wynter is foregrounded in the epistemic break. It is "an instituting act of this new mode of revolt" (Wynter 1989, 639). The call for an epistemic break is not only discursive; it is the ontological necessity that enables the resurrection of the new human. Acting upon oneself and for the care of all who struggle for humanity is to challenge the very foundation of subjection. By articulating the position of being black in the antiblack world means that Wynter has a certain understanding of being human and the existential question is framed. Eudell and Allen (2001, 3) acutely point out that "the kinds of questions she poses are usually not the ones compelling to the hegemonic Western academic establishment." The will to live and relentless pursuit of the just world is worth not compromising as there is a lot at stake. The rebel is the figure of the political with the discursive formation of thinking anew outside the confines of the Western epistemic strictures and its disciplinary solipsism and rigidity that hide behind objective knowledge. In the main, the rebel of this nature is foregrounded in the existential lived experience of the damned.

The modes of writings by Wynter are those of the rebel in the full sense of the word. They mobilize all forms of weaponry resources and the poeticism evokes images of the relentless pursuit of victory – the rebel with the cause and its realization. The urgency of creating the new poetics are outside the edifices of the Imperial Man and necessitate the pursuit of liberatory politics. If being the rebel is to want only total liberation, subjectivity should be the stretched imagination and use the conceptual arsenal to impose the meaning of being human in the world. Thus, being a rebel is not a matter of choice, but of necessity.

Fanon writes:

> This is sufficient explanation of the style of those native intellectuals who decide to give expression to this phase of consciousness which is in process of being liberated. It is a harsh style, full of images, for the image is the drawbridge which allows unconscious energies to be scattered on the surrounding meadows. It is a vigorous style, alive with rhythms, struck through and through with bustling life; it is full of colour, too, bronzed, sun-baked, and violent. This style, which in its time astonished the people of the West, has nothing racial about it, in spite of frequent statements to the contrary; it expresses above all a hand-to-hand struggle and it reveals the need that man [sic] has to liberate himself from a part of his being which already contained the seeds of decay. Whether the fight is painful, quick and inevitable, muscular action must substitute itself for concepts.
>
> (Fanon 1990, 177)

The conception of style is not aesthetic validity, but Fanonian combative breath (Agathangelou 2011). The images that it evokes, which are clear in Wynter's oeuvre, signal the damnation that the black subjects are subjected to, and the symbolic codes of the Imperial Man which serve as strictures that do not permit access to the lived reality of the world. To be in the damned position, the black subject is made to be obedient through the penal code and its forms of torture and dehumanization. But then, as it is commonly obvious, every form of subjection is met with resistance. Fanon's native intellectual, who is Wynter as the rebel, mobilizes concepts which translate into muscular action and the form of consciousness solidifies the bonds of solidarity among the damned. This comes through the rebel being, as Fanon (1990, 179) acutely notes, "an awakener of the people; hence comes a fighting literature, and a national literature." For what is at stake is made to be visible – that is, as Fanon would counsel, everything wholly depends on them and it is they who are at stake. The vigorous style is the one that Wynter assumes as the rebel to absolutely rupture the strictures that the Imperial Man has solidified as unintelligible and which the colonized subjects will have no access to. But the rebel contra Imperial Man, Wynter, breaks this hellish circle and reconfigures the whole apparatus of subjection and calls for *After Man*.

The installation by Wynter is that for the rebel, there has to be a pursuit of a just cause. To be contra Imperial Man, this is significant through the poetics of decolonization that Wynter undertakes. These poetics are solid and consistently politically committed to see the new world. For this world to come, the rebel must continue with the just cause and refuse to be a pawn of the Imperial Man and his subjection. Wynter heeds Fanon's warning by not throwing herself into Western culture and making it her own. As she is the rebel, she assumes the role of what Fanon signifies as the native intellectual. It is to be in the zone of occult instability, as Fanon says, and to be grounded in the existential conditions of the *damné*.

Wynter's textual practice is the one which gives the *damné* the full account of their existential conditions and which also makes them confront subjection. It is in Wynter's subjectivity that Fanon's combative breathing is evident – the rebel's indomitable will to fight for the politics of life in the clutches of subjection – its strictures signifying nothing but suffocation. "Combat breathing names the mobilization of the target subject's life energies merely in order to continue to live, to breathe and to survive the exercise of state violence *and the violence of the Imperial Man and his fraternity of the community of masters in the service of empire*" (Perera and Pugliese 2011, 1, emphasis mine). Combat breathing as the will to live, as Perera and Pugliese insist, is fraught, traumatic, and can be fatal. As Agathangelou (2011) notes, combative breathing is the existential struggle of the *damné* against the infrastructure of subjection. Maldonado-Torres (2006b, 203) states that the "damné live in hell from which there is no escape." This signifies the continued presence of social death, as Patterson (1982) notes, and the structuring of ontology of racialized bodies. Wynter as the rebel *qua* combat breathing "practice[s] a 'default' from this order to wrestle for life" (Agathangelou 2011, 211). The rebel identifies with life and in this instance, it is life to come since the politics of antagonism are waged in the colonial zone with its imposition of hellish existence fraught with the brutality of genocidal impulses of the Imperial Man. Fanon's combat breathing is to be underlined in relation to the rebel being contestatious, as Agathangelou notes, to signify politics as politics of ontology. To be in the state of combative breathing is to be haunted and for the rebel to fight for existence is to inaugurate the possibility of the new forms of life. It is to be in the nexus of decolonization – the contra positionality of Wynter – what Fanon clearly puts as the meeting of forces which are diametrically opposed, their encounter being marred by violence. The co-existence of the rebel and subjection is the space where combative breathing occurs.

If it is accepted that combat breathing is the politics of ontology in as much as Wynter's positionality of the rebel shows, then it is plausible to punctuate the fact that the rebel is in pursuit of the will to life and the politics of ontology cannot be conflated with a death wish. Wynter disrupts the Western discursive formation as the rebel who is concerned with bringing back life (Agathangelou 2010). The *damné* are not in conflictual relations of violence, but they are structurally positioned in its antagonistic relation which justifies the logic of absolute elimination.

> Rather, it is a force grid, where positions of *contingent* violence are segregated from positions of gratuitous violence. Positions of contingent violence are segregated from positions of ontological incapacity; there are those (flesh and matter that are never subjects) who have no immunity from genocide, captivity and fungibility (i.e. gratuitous violence) in world politics.
>
> (Agathangelou 2010, 699)

Wynter's contra positionality means that she is against what Agathangelou calls ontological suffocation. Wynter must, Agathangelou insists, engage in "theft of air" for the existential struggle to be waged as "combat breathing enables alternative worlds and worldviews" (Agathangelou 2011, 219). There is no option for Wynter but to engage in the politics of commitment and to be the rebel that confronts the Imperial Man. As the rebel, Wynter refuses to be in service of the Imperial Man whose gravitas of discursive formation "requires those being slaughtered to *pretend to be part of the living*" (Agathangelou 2010, 722 [emphasis original]). This refusal is the demand to breath, since subjection is ontological suffocation par excellence. For those who breathe because they cannot breathe as life is suffocated out of their bodies, it is in the Wynterian sense that combat breathing is a necessity. That is why the theft of air should not be just temporality, but the very being of the black. It is to insist on life and not to survive. That is, the freedom to breathe can be made by those who demand to breathe for they are the ones who are suffocating. To insist on living in this sense is not just to live, but to wage the existential struggle – the will to live as insisting to live and not as a given. Evoking the colonial disciplinary tool that the rebel is always wielding is tantamount to neglecting one fundamental aspect, namely that *the rebel is always at risk*. Being at risk is not a choice that the rebel makes; it is a given that for the *damné* to exist is at the will of the Imperial Man and to be at the mercy of this will is to be at risk.

What matters for the rebel is the principle of saying no. Also, the rebel does not seek to live in bad faith by being complicit with subjection, nor to have any allegiance to the Imperial Man. Also important to note is that there is no impulsion to avenge, but to insistently assert the existential condition that is just and to be in absolute defense of life; to demand the fundamental change of life, as it is the call of the rebel. As Camus correctly puts it, to confront injustice is to call for the reign of justice. "The rebel, on principle persistently refuses to be humiliated without asking that others should be" (Camus 1956, 24).

To rebel, in this sense, is to enunciate subjectivity from the positionality of the all "to promote epistemic and cultural decolonization" (Maldonado-Torres 2006b, 205). The rebel, in the Wynterian sense, keeps the human question largely intact for there to be decolonization. The rebel assumes the epistemic foundation that is necessary to chart the terrain for complete liberation. Wynter sits well in this discursive terrain and with her solid political commitment as the rebel, she makes no claims to the unusual truth, but bears witness to the testimony of the *damné* in the modern colonial world. The *damné* are in the existential position where they produce knowledge not for its sake, but as testament to the modes of their lives of social death. It is from being concerned with the question of dehumanization that Camus (1956, 21) writes: "Knowledge is born and conscience is awakened." This is clear in Wynter's oeuvre, and not only that, both knowledge and conscience are subjected to the subjectivity of the *damné*. This means that the knowledge they produce is informed by the existential rebellion which is decolonial in intent.

Decolonial *Scientia*

From the vantage point of the Imperial Man, epistemic privilege which is entrenched in the Western episteme with its colonial virus solidifies the notion of truth. In this instance, truth only means that which comes from the Imperial Man. The meta-narrative is the absolute – what starts and ends with the Imperial Man. The epistemic privilege and Western episteme are closed systems. Consequently, the epistemic shift of Wynter, as Mignolo (2015, 107) notes, is where "her intellectual disobedience" emerges and her dissenting world views are emphasized. Note, too, that Mignolo draws attention to the fact that it is not the human and humanity, but rather the significations that make the ontological effect. This ontological effect, as Mignolo clearly points out, is central to Wynter's work in that its epistemological framework accounts for the *damné*. Gordon (2000b, 376) emphasizes "suspending certain questions in favour of others." From this vantage point, what is essential in situating a human study in the modern colonial world is to create spaces for ontological upsurge where affirmation of life takes the principal stance. If not, Gordon (2000b, 376–377) warns that "they will become that which is acted upon without emergence, without defiance, resistance, and agency." What is called for, essentially, is the opposite and to move from the vantage point of bad faith, which is inhuman.

This imposes the limits of the Imperial Man as nothing but a scandal, and his episteme as nothing but the regime of epistemic totality with its mirage of totality (Mignolo 2015). For Wynter, as Mignolo (2011) insists, what is fundamental is responding and de-linking from the imperial *scientia* and by (re-)installing decolonial *scientia*. Imperial *scientia*, the exclusive episteme of the Imperial Man under the guise of the universal, invests in epistemic closures in order to totalize subjectivity and the very being of the colonized, racialized, and black subjects – the *damné*. That is why, as Mignolo argues intensely, decolonial *scientia* is of relevance to those who suffer the colonial wound, and these are the *damné* who are interested in generating the politics of life and not the descriptions of Imperial Man masked as life. The very descriptions that the Imperial Man imposes are closures and they propagate the truth that is far from the truth itself. Mignolo (2015, 108) opines: "The epistemologies of les damnés do not seek to arrive at a perfect or true depiction of the Human, for there is no Human 'out there' beyond the Western imperial conception of Man/Human from the Renaissance on."

In so far as epistemic questions and interventions are concerned in the modern colonial world, there is no such thing as having the floating signifier of the universal as the validity of truth, if it is an imposition that refuses any form of refutation. By placing strong emphasis on the *damné's* socio-historical formation, subjectivity, existential condition, and the organization of the modern colonial world, among many other things, decolonial *scientia* opposes the Imperial Man *qua* the community of masters from putting the *damné* in existential hell and using epistemic infrastructure to militate against their existence. It is also to place strong emphasis on the fixity of the hierarchization of the colonial existence as a given in which the idea of race is solidity. Decolonial *scientia* is the exposé of the Imperial Man, and it does not claim to be truth of the universal, but of the *damné* which the Imperial Man denies due to his subjection that reinforces fallacy as truth. It is clear, when Wynter engages in decolonial *scientia*, that she does not call for the corrective discourse, but the unmaking of the imperial *scientia* and this does not assent to any form of essentialism, strategic or otherwise.

Wynter is relegated to the margins, as she is not interpellated in the Western episteme. Decolonial *scientia* is "the difference of thinking with sources that have been to some extent marginalized by the West" (Maldonado-Torres 2007, 241). This marginal positionality is not natural but deliberate, as she challenges the very foundations of the Western episteme. Wynter does this by insisting on decolonial *scientia*, the elaboration of a new science of the human infused with the liberatory intent and realization. For Gordon (2006), it is the study of the human subject and also the contribution of its constitutive being. The ontologico-epistemic project that foregrounds the necessity of studying the socio-historical forces that re-institutionalized, naturalized, and normalized in the modern colonial world is what decolonial *scientia* aims at. It is, in Wynter's sense, to unsettle the architectonics of subjection and their elaboratory frameworks and the infrastructure of the modern colonial world. This constitution is that of the liberated world which all humanity deserves, but the very thing denied by the antiblack world. The Imperial Man and the community of masters as the custodians of the modern colonial world, as Sharma (2015, 179) asserts, "produced new social formations, and it is *within* these formations that struggles for decolonization have taken place and continue and need to take place."

Wynter's discursive practices authorize those who have been objects of knowledge and who "remain as recipients of still new orders of injustice, dehumanization, and suffering" (Maldonado-Torres 2006b, 203). They are made, in ontological terms, to have nothing to hold on to (Hudson 2013). To authorize, as Wynter charts, is decolonial *scientia*, which calls for the end of monologue and opening up of epistemic ruptures, which is the clear gesture of being human. More precisely, Fanon's sociogeny and Wynter's leap of the sociogenic principle *qua* decolonial *scientia* emphasizes the will to live. In this way, Wynter is able to pose fundamental questions about the human, and not in the abstract sense, but the human in the dehumanized existential position. It is the sociogenic principle that enables the methodological formulation and stance that signatures Wynter's work.

The embodied experience of the human is what requires thinking from the bodily experience, since it is at the level of the body ontological that erasure takes place. The body as the very site of specificity is ontologically absent. This absence is not through metaphysical death, but social death. Wynter is not choosing to be ontologically absent – to be the *exteriori* – she is there because she is racialized, and to be in such a positionality is *to be there* out of choice. In short, to be a *damné* is to be made to be there. Just like Fanon, Wynter (2001, 31) calls for a "new conception of the human," and one foregrounded on "the importance of *experience*, or the necessity of experience." The existential experience of blackness is structured by the antiblack reality and it is important for blackness to articulate itself from the position of being the anomie of the antiblack world. What is it like to be black? This question is pursued by Wynter to engage Fanon's sociogeny to account for the lived experience of blackness in the antiblack world.

Fanon's conception of socialization of the black being and that as something limited categorically by culture, as Wynter suggests, is also linked to the manner in which disciplines have reified the conception of the human and continue to do so. This entrenches the difference in how the human question is dealt with. Even human identity, human behaviors and socialization are shaped by the discipline as an extension of the colonial process that is embedded in dehumanization. What comes to be identified with blackness is being at the receiving end of dehumanization. The discipline is fraught with the high element of epistemic violence that dismantles the very idea of the black being, as there are no blacks in the discipline. Wynter presents the existential question *à la* Fanon: what does it mean to be human? Not only must the response be external, but it must be what blacks should create themselves by moving being human and also the leap after Imperial Man. Wynter continues through Fanon's meditation and coins what she refers to as the sociogenic principle, which intimates the sense that the black has been made not to be itself, and that which contradicts the imposed version of the Imperial Man. It is the Imperial Man who wholly claims to be the self of the self, and the self in itself. In other words, Wynter, like Fanon, calls for the self in its own making by resisting subjection, depleting it completely and allowing the emergence of the human. Wynter (2001, 37) makes it clear that the sociogenic principle is a "counter-manifestation with respect to human identity."

The Imperial Man is exposed through the sociogenic principle as a peddler of lies and deceit in terms of defining who is human or not. For the mere fact that this is the sole determinant of the Imperial Man, Wynter exposes the form of epistemological and ontological violence that comes with this fixing of the contradictory array archetypes of stereotypes. This comes into being through what Wynter (2001, 48) refers to as "coercive semantic technologies," which are merely a "programmed and artificial sense of the self." To excavate the fundamental implications of being black by applying the sociogenic principle, Wynter explicates how cultural constructions of blackness as the deviant other find expression. She foregrounds the manner in which the definition of blackness as that which is non-human is entrenched. The sociogenic principle, Wynter argues, is not a natural scientific object of knowledge. She calls for the existing absolutes, which are then turned into targets of criticism. It is to call for them as mere narratives relevant to a particular existential context and not the universal as the meta-narratives. Wynter fiercely argues against the infrastructure of normativity which is normatively defining the present as being the existing finality.

For Wynter, the discursive practices of decolonial *scientia* show that there is no eclipse of imagination since there is a lot at stake and to account for – that is, Wynter is in relentless pursuit of liberation at all costs. It is in the imagination that there should be a leap to actualization, which questions the known and thus results in the upsurge of the unknown. This might, at times, be the marker of impossibility and not seeing the actualization coming into being. Wynter, having a passionate attachment with the *damné*, makes their existential condition be the very thematic area of her oeuvre. This is fundamental, as Pillay (2004, 95) warns, to "a lack of sharing the 'imagination' of the masses." If this imagination is about liberation, then it is important, as mentioned before, that the rebel's positionality of the "all" serve as the tie that binds. Maldonado-Torres (2007) affirms that since decoloniality is the leitmotif of this *scientia*, what is fundamental is to evade death, and not only one's own death, but that of others as well. These ties are a construction of Pillay's notion of "a collective will" where the awakening of the masses and the consciousness make way for pathways to coming into new humanity and liberation. For Mignolo (2015), decolonial *scientia* is well intentioned in *good* and its virtue is to create the humane world. If decolonial *scientia* is anything to go by, it then means the whole reconfiguration of the ontologico-existential condition and the inauguration of liberation for the better humanity to come.

Practices of Freedom and the Politics of Being – *After Man*

Asking the question, "What about the Human?" is to pose a different question about freedom. This means that Wynter "advocates the radical reconstruction and decolonization of what it means to be human" (Weheliye 2014, 12).

> It is to suggest that freedom is grounded on a set of human practices that challenge what we are at the specific historical moment. Thus, there is no radical thinking about freedom without the human, not as a figure of essence on fixed human nature, but rather as an assemblage figure of concrete historical practices with lived experiences that are deposits and sediments in time.
>
> (Bogues 2012, 46)

Pillay requests ways of thinking that call for the dissolving of Man and also its decentering, to strip Man bare from the naturalness of being Man as subject. For Pillay (2004, 101), the challenge is "to displace Eurocentrism from the pedestal it occupies and from where it made pronouncements on culture, politics, economy, and society, that enabled the writing of a different Man." Wynter's meditations are more different utopic registers and decolonial pathways – that is, *After Man*.

Fundamentally, what is key in Wynter's intervention is the charting of new imaginations of freedom. Not being prescriptive but diagnostic, Wynter takes seriously into account the complexity of the modern colonial world and the manner in which the shift of markers of difference elude the ways in which practices of freedom take place. The way in which the human is rethought by Wynter is to take seriously propositional knowledge and the manner in which the new humanity should come into being. Freedom is not a *telos* precisely because it does not suggest the end but the means of something. It is then predicated on the idea that it must be practiced, by means of praxis to say the least. Its fulfillment, realization, attainment, and reach have a desired effect for the human condition. But that cannot be enough, solely because subjection is so interweaved in dehumanization. What then appears to be the precise intervention is not freedom *per se*, but its practices, which are linked with the politics of being. Of course, this is the ontologico-existential domain of the *damné*.

For there to be freedom, there need to be practices that are fashioned meaningful praxis. This is not to suggest the end, but the ways in which the political is imagined and not its *telos* as *a priori*. The horizon should go beyond the *telos* and to foreground the lived experience of subjection as something that requires the constant critique and unmasking in all its tropes of captivity, deprivation, and crushing objecthood. The idea of building a better future should not just be the monotype and reductionist tendency of removing subjection without having the contradictions of freedom itself, by putting its meaning into constant radical questioning. The practices of freedom will call for the utopian suspension and to take seriously the present which demands freedom now. Therefore, the practices of freedom do not deal with freedom as a distant horizon, since it needs to be seized in the practices of the present. That is, the aspirations of freedom are not worthy to be postponed as they are part of the lived reality of the *damné*. The contemporary challenges are much more demanding and they become complex in such a way that they demand constant vigilance, as freedom can fall into populist uses and abuses. The practices of freedom as the politics of being do not contain a conclusion.

Furthermore, Wynter (2003) asserts that it is the *damné* who engage in the practices of freedom that comprise different facets as they are excluded and invisibilized. For Wynter, the practices of freedom will have to put forth the conception of the human, and thereby define such a figure from the positionality of the *damné*. It is continued resistance and also the moment of radical questioning. Even if freedom is said to be installed by removing the old order of subjection (and that freedom is really the defining order), this does not mean the absence of freedom. That is why it is important to have the moment of radical questioning that does not take the human question for granted, with the pitfall that humanity is a given to all. The politics of being, as Wynter (2003) argues, are "waged over what are to be the descriptive statements of the human, about whose master code of symbolic life and death each human order organizes itself." The practices of freedom at the moment of radical questioning confront "the legitimation of the ruling gentry's hegemony" (Wynter 2003, 319). It is this hegemony that constricts, undermines, frustrates, manipulates, and even denies freedom as it propagates the notion that the *damné* are naturalized not to be free, as they cannot exercise control, self-constraint, self-regulation, and reason; thus imperial guardianship is for their better good. Since the *damné* are made to be located and represented outside the law of nature by the Imperial Man as subjects, Wynter (2003, 320) stresses that they are "weeded out by the 'iron laws' of nature." It then means that the subjection of the *damné* and their nullifying of freedom are necessary.

It is clear that Wynter is not a making a plea for freedom. The plea for freedom is merely a mute scream, the scream which falls on deaf ears, so to speak. There is nothing realizable by making a plea for freedom as it should be seized by those who want it. It is their freedom that is curtailed, and they must fight for it. Of course, the means of resistance, insurgency, and oppositional politics are some sites of practices of freedom as politics of being; it therefore seems self-justified for the Imperial Man to thwart these existential gestures with the outcry that they create disorder. In the maintenance of order, the Imperial Man is then justified in exercising violence against the *damné*. Wynter's conception of "undeservingness" is essential here as applied to the category of the *damné*, which inscribes the idea that they do not deserve to be free. If they dare to claim freedom on their own terms to end subjection, this is seen as a provocation and the violation of the modern colonial world, which is under guardianship of the Imperial Man and the community of masters. It is through the ruling hegemony and its naked violence that the purpose is to crush any dissent of the *damné* and to make them passive if not complicit in their own subjection. As Wynter (2003, 328) asserts, the *damné* are prohibited "from realizing themselves as fully human within the terms of our present ethnoclass genre of the human." Mbembe (2001, 29) concurs with Wynter: "The original meaning of freedom, therefore, has to do with letting human beings be the human beings they are meant to be." To let them be means that it must be of their own accord and not by the will of the Imperial Man. The will of the Imperial Man is scandalized by bad faith and he has no desire to loosen his grip on the squeezed life of the *damné,* as the implication of letting be will be the end of the Imperial Man.

The practices of freedom mean, as Mbembe (2001, 29) correctly notes, that "freedom is not a state of being or quality one possesses once and for all, but a mode of activity, a praxis." What remains clear is that practices of freedom are a continued struggle and the *damné* must continue to fight for the will to live and to live as human. For there to be *After Man*, the Imperial Man must cease to exist and the beginning of life should be that of the humanity to come. Practices of freedom, as Radhakrishnan (2008, 118) asserts, mean that Wynter "stands for values that are revolutionary, trans-formative, and in dire avant-garde transgressions of the norm. This would take the form of a macropolitical ideological confrontation with the status quo." Indeed, it is now clear that the Imperial Man is the one who does not enable. The practices of freedom as the politics of life pose a challenge to the status quo. The Imperial Man cannot be expected to play the role of an enabler when his interests are at stake. Therefore, in a benevolent form, the Imperial Man enables while he disenables. Freedom matters to the Imperial Man as something that cannot be conceded, let alone shared. Freedom should always be out of sight and out of the reach of the *damné*. To reify the paradigm of difference, the Imperial Man's stance is insist-ently that no freedom should prevail for the *damné*.

Perhaps the most challenging thing is that the practices of freedom are forever haunted by subjection, since they are not only sanctioned, but outlawed. That is why they are met with systematic, systemic, and continued violence as they symbolize threat, whereas, paradoxically, the threat is the very violence directed at the *damné*. In order to set afoot the new human and the humane world, there is no choice but to continue to engage in practices of freedom, since this is the virtue of the politics of being. This is the sole duty of the *damné* and nobody else's. They are, as Radhakrishnan (2008, 95) asserts, "creating the very subjectivity that they want to be, rather than representing a nature that is already there." Wynter's meditations on practices of freedom and politics of being politicize the *damné*, and their political demands are based solely on freedom. Their political unconscious, which has been interpellated in the colonial unconscious as the infrastructure of subjection, produces the politics of being as the existential struggle launched only to obliterate subjection. This obliteration is absolute in the sense that it means *After Man* – not the end of the event, but the end of the infrastructure of subjection – the end of the Imperial Man, the community of masters and the modern colonial world. To leap to the ontologico-existential condition of *After Man,* Wynter's politicization blows open "the blockage that disconnects the historicity of temporality from the temporal historicity" (Radhakrishnan 2008, 133). But then, the idea of temporality is entrapped in that it does not take into account the *longue dureé* of subjection, including the life of its aftermath, which continues to reproduce subjection in subtle and yet dehumanizing ways. The history of the present and the postcolonial things to come, as Radhakrishnan posits, should not be understood solely as the problematic of binaries. The binaries continue to haunt the lived presence of the *damné*, and yet they continue to serve the makeup of the colonial infrastructure for it to remain intact. It is important to submit here that binaries are not a problem *per se*, but the manner in which they signify the human is indeed a problem. This signification continues to be binary – the human and the non-human. Obliterating the binaries without having to radically question subjection and its aftermath will prove futile. The human who is said not to be human at all (the *damné*) cannot place the emphasis on temporality and historicity, due to being exterior to time and space. The *damné* are deemed, on one hand, to be outside time as they are old, primitive, savage, and nothing modern. On the other, they are said not to own land, and whatever form of colonial dispossession that emptied them of space is deemed not to be a violation, as they are people with nothing.

To make realizable the world of the human and the reinstallation of the human as the subject, there should not be mimicry of the Imperial Man. The insistence should be on building that world of *After Man*; the world of the humanity to come. This means that the practices of the human and the politics of being are "causing a permanent alteration or rupture" (Gagne 2007, 253). It means that they will not be what they used to be and neither will they turn out to be what they are expected to be. The permanent alteration or rupture is the radical mutation of bringing the world outside the epistemic strictures of subjection. The world is not that of Man, but the world of the human. Consequently, the configuration of the practices of freedom by the *damné* means that they are preoccupied with freedom and seeing the absolute obliteration of subjection. For this to happen, it is key to engage in the politics of radical questioning by exposing the scandal of the human.

2

Aimé Césaire and the Scandal of the Human

If the human is the figure of life, it means that the existence of the human is a given. The human is part of the world and the world is where the human exists. To exist, in this instance, essentially means that the human is the embodiment of life itself. In other words, the existence of the human not only depends on the will to live, but also the preservation of life in the world which offers the ontological and existential possibilities of the right to life. The end of the human is the end of life – that is, death. There is no human in death because life has ended and even the figure of the political cannot be understood in the absence of the human. If then the human is the figure of life – a given existence – the human is the one who lives in the world. But then, what about the non-human? It seems, for obvious reasons, that the human is not the non-human and in the realm of existence both are irreconcilable. There cannot be the non-human in existence but rather, the non-human is synonymous with non-existence. The non-human is akin to that which inhabits nothing and cannot exist or be killed. It is to be outside the world, to have no location and life is superfluous.

For the non-human nothing is a given because there is nothing that counts for life. To be exact, the non-human is not the ontological figure that results from the processes of invention, but rather, ontological destruction. This form of destruction does not stem from the natural order of things, but the dehumanizing practices that serve the absolute purpose of creating the human.

These practices do not emerge in a vacuum and their source is the non-human. In short, it is the human who creates the non-human as the latter is not the source of self-creation. For there to be the non-human there must be dehumanization by the human who is in charge of the very antithesis of life, the end result of dehumanization being to warrant death with impunity. The ontologico-existential positionality of the non-human is to be a colonized subject, the result of colonial subjection – that is, dehumanization par excellence. Colonial subjection, the human eliminationist logic and the racist infrastructure of keeping the ontologico-existential status of the human and non-human intact. It is important to demarcate the human question by understanding the human subject (the human) as the complete subject and the colonized subject (the non-human) as the subject of lack. This distinction is fundamental in accounting for the ontologico-existential question of the human.

If the colonized subject assumes subjectivity and the modes of affirming its existence in the narratives are incarcerated by colonial subjection, it means that these narratives will be informed by the desire to be liberated. This mode of affirming is not giving an account to the lived experience of being a colonized subject, but to critique dehumanization that is inaugurated by colonial subjection and the desire to be liberated that is aimed at reconstituting the non-human as a subject. The narratives that stem from subjectivity of the colonized subject take the question of the subject and its relation to the world – existence writ large – seriously. The colonized subject who is expelled from the fraternity of the human is the one who is in the abyss of dehumanization. While this being the superfluous figure of the non-human, the mode of questioning brings the upsurge of the politics of insurrection and affirmation of existence.

What is at stake for the figure of the non-human? Even if the answer suggests that it is life itself, there is a lot at stake. In order to account for this question it is essential to turn to Césaire. Not that Césaire will give prescriptive answers, but will give a form of diagnosis to the question that faces humanity in the colonial contact, which is nothing but a scandal. It is from the positionality of being a colonized subject that the human question is brought to bear. In the mode of radical questioning, it is then relevant to ask the fundamental question that Césaire asked in relation to colonialism, what it is, more *fundamentally*. It is clear that colonization is the technology of subjection that animated the politics of constantly putting the humanity of the colonized subjects into question. For Césaire to pose this question, it does not connote its variant – what is colonialism? – this is the very mode of questioning that does not account to the systematic, systemic, and continuous nature of colonial mutation. Césaire's effort to add the word "fundamentally" to this question means going beyond the established meaning of colonialism. The question is constituted differently because it is asked by the colonized subject in the clutches of dehumanization. It is to understand colonization as an event of the past. This fundamental questioning exposes the devastation, dispossession, anguish, brutality, and death of the colonized subject as a result of colonization.

Essentially, Césaire offers an important perspective of a colonized subject. In other words, the non-human thinks about the question of the human through the ontologico-existential positionality of being dehumanized. This, therefore, means that the affirmative sense of the human and the non-human will depart from different genealogies and trajectories and would chart their modes of questioning in different decolonial horizons. Césaire departs from the genealogy of being a colonized subject. Its trajectory is the advocacy of life in the face of dehumanization. Its decolonial horizons are the creation of another world outside *faux* humanism, which is nothing but dehumanization. In Césaire, a decolonial struggle is conducted in the spirit of taking the new human outside the colonial infrastructure. This will be elaborated on by showing how Césaire confronted the idea of Europe, his deployment of a decolonial critique and the ways in which Negritude is charted in the terrain of decolonized ethico-political. The fundamental point of emphasis is that Césaire signifies the politics of life – the resurrection of the human from dehumanization through the creation of a decolonized world. It is in this world that the new being will emerge through the politics of insurrection from the ontologico-existential positionality of dehumanization.

Europe and its Other

The idea of Europe is the construction and expression of difference. Its myth of origins "reinforce the formation of adversarial world-view" (Delantry 1995, 16), and it is based on nothing by the superior–inferior complex, where Europe is at the apex of civilization and is the bastion of humanity. "Furthermore, Europe is the point from which all the other figures must be viewed" (Pagden 2002, 51). The construction and the expression of difference and exclusion aim to keep the human in purity, while persistently creating the non-human through dehumanizing practices. This occurs through the idea of Europe as a civilization and its finding its exteriority through conquest and enslavement under the rhetorical guise of civilization. Civilization is a positive outlook. It is a linear progression of the betterment of humanity. A charge with a good cause to humanity and its manner of progression suggest the common good and it being applicable to the whole of humanity. The specific aspect of civilization is prefaced here by Césaire, who illuminates the European contact with what it dehumanizes. The testimony below serves as amplification thus:

> I am talking about societies drained of their essence, cultures trampled underfoot, institutions undermined, land confiscated, religions smashed, magnificent artistic creations destroyed, extraordinary possibilities wiped out.
>
> (Césaire 1972, 43)

It is from this testimonial account that dehumanization is made visible. These ontologico-existential maladies did not occur in a passing historical phase; they are continued practices of dehumanization. It is in this configuration that the human is synonymous with Europe and its other is the non-human. It is then the self-arrogance and the excessive form of narcissism that the idea of Europe equates with civilizing others. "Césaire writes at a point when the disenchantment with Europe accelerates" (Maldonado-Torres 2006a, 124). It is from Césaire that Europe is exposed as being indefensible and as having nothing to offer humanity. The idea of Europe as "a system of 'civilizational' values" masks its very form of barbarity. Delantry (1995, 31) writes: "To imagine Europe involves the privileging of a particular discourse over others." Not only that, it also means the elimination of others. The elaboration of the idea of Europe is sustained through systematic and continued dehumanization. European civilization is a myth that claims to have a deep connection with humanity, whereas it is, in fact, the opposite of its propagation.

Nowhere is civilization claiming to be particularistic in its departure and arrival – it is all encompassing – the site of humanity *in toto* and yet its self-justification for generality is masked under the auspices of universalism. The positive outlook of civilization is nothing but the masking of lies and deception. Civilization is lauded as the making of European modernity. Its spread is propagated as necessary for those who are in need because the idea of Europe seems to suggest that it knows what is good for its *exteriori*. Césaire (1972, 42) unveils the propaganda of civilization thus: "They talk to me about progress, about 'achievement', disease cured, improved standards of living." This is indeed the propaganda of the idea of Europe and its civilization. It postures itself as the civilization that has something to offer to humanity. It is within this propagation that there is excessive accentuating of what is good for the human – that is, to be civilized is to rid oneself of barbarism. To be civilized is to be human and thus all humans must be civilized according to the standardization of the idea of Europe.

If civilization brings life to the fore, the life in excess of the positive, it has to take the human into account. Indeed, it does. But, this conception of the human happens at the exclusion of other humans on the basis of their racialization and having their humanity questioned. To civilize them in rhetoric simultaneously means dehumanizing them. The masking of the gravity of ontologico-existential violence faced by the colonized subject who is clutched by the genocidal impulses of European civilization with its logic of elimination brings Césaire to the conclusion that this is a civilization of death. It is the destruction of the human and makes the bodily presence of the colonized subject to be a flesh – the superfluous ontological entity. If there is anything that the civilization of death warrants, it is the dehumanization of those whom it considers non-human and who, by implication, are the aberration of civilization. Therefore, the idea of Europe means that civilization is a pursuit at the expense of the humanity of those whom it marks as different and non-human. For Césaire (1972, 47), the cries of Europe are "'kill, kill" and "let's see some blood." This comes at the cost of death – that is, to be dehumanized in such a way that that there is no possibility of coming to life. Césaire unmasks the rhetoric of civilization thus:

A civilization that proves incapable of solving the problems it creates is a decadent civilization.

A civilization that chooses to close its eyes to its most crucial problems is a stricken civilization.

> A civilization that uses its principles for trickery and deceit is a
> dying civilization.
>
> (Césaire 1972, 31)

The indictment of Europe by Césaire assumes the subjectivity of a
slave to a judge. To judge Europe as a civilization that is decadent,
stricken, and dying suggests that there is nothing to gain from
Europe. Césaire (1972, 32) boldly insists that: "What is serious
is that 'Europe' is morally, spiritually indefensible." The lies and
deceit of European civilization are subjected to exposé because
"[t]he dossier is indeed overwhelming" (Césaire 1972, 65). They
are foundational and constitutive to the idea of Europe. Césaire
confronts the civilization that justifies colonization and for him this
is a sick civilization and, as such, it is morally diseased. By relying
on trickery and deceit it lurches from one form of denialism to
another, while masking dehumanization practices. For this civilization to affirm its existence, it must continue to dehumanize. Its
idea is the maintenance of the superiority complex. As Ndlovu-
Gatsheni (2012, 423) succinctly notes: "[T]he conquerors assumed
a superiority complex and assigned inferiority to the colonized."
This ontologico-existential positionality legitimated all sorts of
dehumanizing practices. That then sustains what Pagden (2002)
argues to be its desire to demonstrate and explain its superiority
over others. The idea of Europe, in its self-image and narcissistic
desire, becomes "the house of liberty and true government" (Pagden
2002, 37). It positions itself as a model to which all whom it inferiorizes must gravitate – that is, the other in the idea of Europe must
be civilized, become like Europe, but not become European.

Césaire postulates that there is no such thing as civilization in the
colonial zone. There cannot be civilization while there is dehumanization. Colonial subjection does not compel any moral currency
because it is justification in itself, and it goes without any limit
because what it confronts is nothing but the non-human. That is
to say, there is no ethical requirement for that which is non-human
and, for such a figure to be brought into being, civilization needs to
take place in the absence of this figure. It is not human; it should
be acted upon by being civilized, even without its concern. What
underwrites civilization is violence, destruction, and death – that
is, dehumanization, and yet the discourse of civilization continues
to claim the pedestal of being the higher good for those whom it
dehumanizes. The rhetoric of civilization seems to suggest that the

human is at the center. If that is the case, it has been clearly shown that it is not the colonized subject, since this subject needs to be civilized.

> Europe itself appears as an evil demon of sorts in Césaire's text. Now, its evil character not only shows in deceit, but also in the propagation of violence and death as well as in the naturalization of institutions, ideas, and practices that perpetuate social death and colonial violence. Instead of a process of methodic doubt, the *condemned* went through a process of method suffering for their alleged lack of humanity.
>
> (Maldonado-Torres 2006a, 130 [emphasis original])

It is impossible for a civilization of death to be a civilization of humanity. It would need another name and, if civilization is anything to go by, then there is no such thing that will suit its propagation of the positive outlook. Not being in generality of course, those who are at its departure (the human subjects) should not see it in the same light as those who are at its arrival (the colonized subjects). The latter bear the trauma of being dehumanized and having nothing to hold onto, as their humanity is systematically, systemically, and continuously being called into question.

The conception of the human, if that is the phenomenon of the European man, means that there must be the dehumanized. This is the ontological figure that is outside the politics of life and is confined to death. To be relegated to such an ontological status is to be made something that is not essential. Not to be essential is not to be a subject of history. It is to be its aberration, hence the insistent erasure from history. Foucault suggests that history imposes its laws on the analysis of production and analogue structure to connect these organic structures. Foucault (1989, 237) insists that these organic structures, which reside in the order of things, "opened the way to successive identities and differences." Indeed, the context in which history is engaged by Foucault is not at all the history that deals with the human in the colonized context. The successive identities and differences that Foucault refers to are within the idea of Europe. As such, as Santos (2007, 2) asserts: "[B]eyond it, there is only non-existence, invisibility, non-dialectical absence." The idea of Europe creates the exclusionary world and those who are in the colonial zones "inhabit the world of superfluous invisibility" (Maldonado-Torres 2006a, 125). The history that Foucault

is making reference to faces the ontological scandal when the
non-human and dehumanization are introduced. For this history
to be engaged upon there should be the history of consciousness. It
is the history that does not deal with those who are ontologically
located in the paradigm of regulation and emancipation, but rather,
the paradigm that is outside universality. The colonized subjects
qua non-human are located in the paradigm of violence and appropriation. It is this latter paradigm that is littered with the scandal
of dehumanization. That is why its history is distinctive and yet it
assumes the history of consciousness.

The history of consciousness is informed by what Marriott (2012)
characterizes as the political act of questioning. What is brought
into question of course is the actual colonial imaginary of dehumanization. These questions mean the reconfiguration of history, and to
be located in the subjectivity of history of consciousness essentially
means colonized subjects writing their own historical narratives.
This is the historical narrative that gives an account of the dehumanization, and also the invention of the historical problem from
the colonized subject that re-imagines the ontologico-existential
questions outside the idea of Europe. For Marriott, the history of
consciousness frees the colonized subject and it allows the breaking
of the path of the human and the creation of other historical codes
which call for epistemic shifts. The affirmation of the history of
consciousness is not only the epistemic critique of colonialism, but
it is "contesting colonialism in a more general description of its
language of time" (Marriott 2012, 53). Marriott continues:

> The leap beyond history, and first of all, that very separation
> between history and invention, is not simply to counter the ways
> in which history has been used to justify supremacists' claims and
> effects, but to escape the normal teleological form of writing, and
> so refigure life as event. Everything that imprisons the capacity for
> infinite realization, everything that presents the past as criterion, as
> is the case with "historical" judgment, is felt to be incommensurable
> with that leap, not akin to the ceaseless work of invention.
>
> (Marriott 2012, 46)

The history of consciousness is not that of incarcerated subjectivity
which is steeped in the empiricism of the human. The history of
consciousness means the unsettling of the meta-narratives of history
that write off the colonized subject. The idea of Europe with its

human subject sees history in its epoch breaks that are steeped in teleology. The colonized subject is not an historical empirical subject or the obsessively postcolonial temporal subject. Therefore, the ontological and existential standpoint of the colonized subject – the non-human and that of history is irreconcilable – the writing of history is without the consciousness of the colonized subject. The history of consciousness in Césaire is foregrounded in political commitment. This commitment means thinking and writing the colonized subject to emerge as a human subject in history among many other histories. It is to make the colonized subject understand that thinking and writing the history of consciousness is to face the ontologico-existential struggle of being colonized.

Where there is violence and appropriation, Santos (2007) argues, there is a specific social territory – the colonial zone – the place-lessness of the non-human. The form of law that governs the colonial zone is the law of things – that is, the law that legitimates dehumanization and its destructive practices. It is the law that explicitly denotes that the colonized subjects are illegal by virtue of being things. Their existence is aberration from the law. This clearly means that the colonized subjects fall outside the paradigm of human rights because they are things. They have no rights and, essentially, there are no human rights for non-humans.

The idea of Europe justifies colonial subjection but in the form of a guise by distancing itself from dehumanization. The mask of civilization is used to claim the moral high order. For Césaire (1972, 40), "colonization: badgehead in a campaign to civilize barbarism, from which there may emerge at any moment the negation of civilization, pure and simple." The ontological status that is granted by Europe to those whom it dehumanizes is that of the non-human. It automatically implies that dehumanization does not produce a human, but the dehumanized – the colonized subject. What does it mean to be a colonized subject under the idea of Europe and its logic of dehumanization? The idea of Europe is the actualized colonial fantasy. It is what Césaire refers to as "barbarous faith" – the paradigm of war (Maldonado-Torres 2008) that is infused with genocidal impulses of dehumanization. It is, as Césaire (1972, 76) charges, "[v]iolence, excess, waste, mercantilism, bluff, conformism, vulgarity, disorder."

> More radically still, what is it that ails "modern civilization" inasmuch as it is European? Not that it suffers from a particular fault or from a particular form of blindness. Rather, why does it suffer

from ignorance of its history, from a failure to assume its responsibility, that is, the memory of its history *as* history of responsibility?
(Derrida 1995, 4)

Being the decadent civilization that it is, Europe will not engage in
the history of responsibility because there is nothing to account for
in its *exteriori*. Its history of dehumanization is self-justified in the
sense that the human is that which deserves responsibility while
the case is the opposite for the non-human. The acts of dehumanization cannot be seen as a particular form of blindness as Derrida
suggests, nor can they be seen as suffering from ignorance. It should
be clear that Césaire's indictment of Europe does not stem from the
misconception that it was ignorant, absent-minded or as Irele (1992,
201) argues, "lost in a similar attitude of nonchalance" – it was, in
more fundamental ways, "an act of calculated aggression." Irele
even insists that these acts were not metaphorical but they were of
literal significance. The idea of Europe and its civilization "wrought
such devastation as to have turned the stomach of decent humanity
everywhere" (Irele 1992, 202). The refusal to see the ontologico-
existential destruction of the European other is located in its
civilizing machine which is always righteous, even in the face of is
heinous acts. If Europe is confronted with the facts of its brutality
against its other, it will still insist on its self-justificatory practices
because the other is not human and nothing can be accounted for.
Derrida (1995, 70) writes: "I am responsible to anyone (that is to
say to any other) only by failing in my responsibilities to all the
others; to the ethical and political generality." It is important to
highlight that the other that Derrida is referring to belongs to the
domain of the human. That is, the ontologico-existential entity
which has relations with the world. Therefore, there is no such thing
as the history of responsibility, and the one that Derrida suggests,
if there is any, applies to Europe only and not its colonial subjects.
This then negates Derrida's conception of European complicity
being a fault, ignorance, and failure. The implications of this trio
suggest that the European deeds of dehumanization occur because
of some historic error, which then is still a form of atonement only
if historical responsibility is taken into account. Césaire (1972,
45) truthfully notes that "Europe is responsible before the human
community for the highest heap of corpses in history." The responsibility that Europe has, is to itself, and has nothing to do with the
colonial subject. The manner in which responsibility is constructed

is something that cannot be negotiated in the domain of those who are regarded as non-human.

Whether Europe acknowledges its history of responsibility or not, this does not alter the existential precariousness that befalls the colonized subject. Dehumanization practices that are the embodiment of civilization thrive on the ontological destruction informed by genocidal impulses. The European deeds of dehumanizing the colonized subject come into being even through the propagation of morality. But for the mere fact that the dehumanized are not human beings, there is no moral caveat that haunts Europe in that its dehumanization is justified on the basis of acting against that which is not human. For this is the case; there is no history of responsibility that pertains to the colonized subjects. The issue at stake is that there is only a history of responsibility in so far as it extends to the treaties between human subjects. To have humans engaged in the ontological contraventions is to call the aftermath and the latter to account for its historicity. In other words, the deeds of violations of humans (which are not dehumanization of course) call for the rectification of historical wrongs. Even if humans fail to reach an agreement or fail to rectify their historical wrongs, those who are affected will still remain human. What is essential to put forth is the fact that there was no act of dehumanization; the ontological equation was that of human *qua* human. In the idea of Europe, humans are bound by the ethical responsibility to each other as they make civilization *a priori*. For humans to be subjects of civilization is to propagate the notion of the ethical life. The essence of the life world of the human subject in the idea of Europe is the ontological triad of liberty, justice, and equality. Of course, this is the ontological privilege that can be enjoyed by human subjects to the exclusion of the colonial subjects, who are deceived into believing that these ontological privileges are extended to them, while they are actually not. The colonial subjects are those who fall on the outside and the ontological scope of history is filled with distortion, erasures, and inferiorization of the colonial subjects. The latter do not feature in the historical catalogues as subjects of history, but as its objects. In the colonial imaginary of the idea of Europe, there is nothing that was done to non-humans because they do not exist, and no history of responsibility can be extended to them. Therefore, there is no historical accounting for that which is not human. They are not human and, as such, their existential precariousness is the fault that they brought upon themselves. For, if they had been properly civilized or had not been trapped in their backward and barbaric ways, as this colonial imaginary purports, they would not be in any form of existential mystery.

The indictment of Europe from the colonial subjects is different from that of the European subjects; the latter engage the idea of Europe from the positionality of being human *qua* human. What remains an ontologico-existential scandal is the fact that the colonized subjects confront the idea of Europe outside the grammar of the human. Not only is Césaire offering a damning critique of the idea of Europe and its decadent civilization, he also charts a way through which the colonized subjects can be the judges of Europe. In amplification to Césaire, Heller (1992, 15) writes: "All great promises of the eighteenth century – the progress of knowledge, technology, and freedom – now appear as so many sources of dangers and decay and manifestations of decadence." There is no-one who anchors the idea of Europe in the ethical sense, more so from the colonized subjects, like Césaire. The terrain chartered by European civilization is what Heller (1992, 17) calls "the victorious power of accumulation," which occurred at the expense of humanity as it is informed by the destruction of humanity. This is the route of ontologico-existential destruction, which means, for Europe to live, its civilization must destroy. This means there is nothing redeemable and the idea of Europe is a self-created mythology – the decadent civilization as Césaire argues – a civilization of death. In the eulogy form, Heller (1992, 22) writes: "Europe, the mighty, the leader of the world, no longer exists; Europe, the source of inspiration for all higher cultures, has been exhausted. May her soul rest in peace."

It should be noted that Heller's locus of enunciation is the critique of Europe from within, and from the positionality of the human subject. The damning of Europe as being decadent is nothing but the expression of disillusionment and disappointment. This is far from Césaire's criticism, which is different in the sense that Europe is engaged from its underside and from the positionality of the colonized subject – the non-human. Thus, it is also important to note that for Césaire, Europe had nothing to offer; it was not, as Heller argues, a source of inspiration for humanity at large. To be specific, there is nothing inspirational about Europe from the receiving end of the colonized subjects. The colonial subjection that has plagued Césaire's ontologico-existential milieu triggered him to engage in the ontological critique and to confront Europe as nothing but a scandal. Therefore, Europe is not dead,

as Heller eulogizes; on the contrary, it still exists and its dehumanizing practices are still accelerated. Indeed, Césaire is not asking
Europe to redeem itself. There is no moral appeal in his critique
since this will fail to recognize the masked dehumanization
practices that are still systematically and continuously applied in
mutating forms.

Humanism as the False

From the idea of Europe, humanism is a totalizing phenomenon in
that the posture of Europe is that of giving a sense of humanism to
humanity at large. Europe cannot offer anything to humanity while
claiming the ethical stature of humanism. If Europe is the epitome
of humanism, its reach is within itself. Humanism does not extend
to those to whom Europe puts their humanity into question, or to
say the least, those who it considers to be its other. The colonized
subjects, even the gestures of humanism, are extended them; this
is nothing but assimilation. They are given a false sense of being
human because they are still dehumanized. From Césaire, it has
been demonstrated how his stance towards Europe has been that of
indictment. If there is nothing indefensible with regard to Europe,
then its assertion of humanism those whom it dehumanizes, clearly
suggests that there cannot be humanism in the colonial condition.
This condition is nothing but dehumanization.

The idea of Europe and its propagation of humanism borders
on narcissistic self-presentation and it is a spell to hook those
who are less sceptical of it, but it is in Césaire's poeticism that the
scandal of Europe is coming out into the open. As the metropole
that creates colonies and creates itself as a bastion of civilization, it
is the very idea of Europe and its scandal of dehumanization that
Césaire is turning his back on. The question of the human subject
in humanism does not raise the ontologico-existential scandal. For,
humanism is there to give to humanity and to affirm the politics of
life. These are the politics that are propagated in the absence of the
colonized subject since there is no existence to speak of so far as
the colonized subject is concerned. The systematic, systemic, and
continual erasure of the colonized subject in the face of humanity
deprives humanism of the grammar to articulate this socio-politico-
historical account. Ndlovu-Gatsheni (2013, 263) charges us thus:
"Western humanism informed by coloniality is in crisis." But due

to the imperial arrogance of Cartesian subjectivity and its perversity of bounded reason even in the face of unreasonableness, humanism will still be forcibly propagated as if it is inclusive to the fraternity of humanity at large. Even if there is undeniable truth from the side of the colonized subjects that humanism is irrelevant to them still, humanism will even be blind to the complicity of the colonial subjection and dehumanization.

It is important to register that the conception of the human *à la* the idea of Europe is the Cartesian subject. The human as crafted in the idea of Europe as the one who is in relation to the world. For this world to be inhabitable in the ethico-political sense, humanism is the spirit of ontologico-existential relation. In short, the world should be civilized and, for it to be such, humanism needs to be foundational. Mouffe (1993, 12) argues that humanism "does not imply the rejection of modernity but only the crisis of a particular project within modernity, the Enlightenment project of self-foundation." Clearly, humanism critique within modernity itself has nothing to offer nor can it be expected to be of any service to humanity at large. When Mouffe mentions the achievement of equality and freedom for all, there are those who are written outside this register – the colonized subjects. This is humanism that has nothing to offer to humanity because it is constitutive and foundational to the idea of Europe, let alone the fact that there is no mention of the colonial question by Mouffe – that is, the colonized subject is absent from this theorization of humanism. To extend such humanism to all humanity while it is exclusionary in practice and intent, is to be oblivious to the fact that humanism means the idea of Europe. The antidote that Mouffe offers as radical democracy also has nothing to do with the colonial question.

Mouffe brings to the fore the figure of the political that is at stake and that faces the possibility of elimination. The concern that Mouffe highlights with the elimination of the political is the gains of the democratic revolution. This existential struggle that Mouffe seeks to wage is not the ontological burden that plagues the colonized subject. For the latter, what is at stake is elimination of life itself, the very thing that humanism does not cater for. It is, therefore, important to ask: What is at stake for the colonial subject in Césaire's thought? Indeed, for Mouffe, what is fundamental is the democratic revolution, and it is a clear testimony that there is nothing ontological and existential at stake. And, if this is itself, something that is at stake, that becomes evident to Césaire.

For Mouffe (1993, 3), the political is "a dimension that is inherent in every human society and that determines our very ontological conditions." The ontologico-existential condition of the colonized subject faces dehumanization. The concept of the political is the ontologico-existential positionality of the human subject and not the colonized subject. There are no gains of democratic revolution to speak of in terms of the colonized subject. Therefore, the political in Mouffe's formulation is the human subject. And it must be stressed that Mouffe's subjectivity is that of the idea of Europe as the universal construction. In other words, humanity is viewed in a totalizing form from the vantage point of Europe. The political becomes a nameless subject in its form of totality. If Césaire's subjectivity is brought in confrontation with Mouffe's conception of the political, what emerges is the need to account for the ontologico-existential conception of the political. This accounting would mean naming the political – that is, Mouffe being specific that she is only referring to the human subject. To be sure, the human is a given to Mouffe and yet the struggle of Césaire is not the return of the political because there has never been such in the dungeon of dehumanization. For the struggle that is necessary for Césaire, what is fundamental is not to defend any gains because there have been none in so far as the colonized subjects are concerned. The struggle for the colonized subject is to become human. What is at stake is life itself, and death is a concern. In short, the democratic revolution, its gains included, is not worth fighting for if there is no life at all.

Césaire's criticism of European civilization is indicative of the fact that there is no humanism, but only *faux* humanism. What is hidden is colonial violence that is coupled with sadistic acts of dehumanization. It is this humanism that masks the desire of domination and its actualization. It is the idealism which is always a distant horizon to those whom are removed from the ontological status of the human. *Faux* humanism is, as Césaire (1972, 31) notes, "the crowing of barbarism that sums up all daily barbarisms." To really show that this is a scandal, those who propagate this *faux* humanism "pride themselves on abuses eliminated" (Césaire 1972, 43), and in their cause, they propagate transcendence, while not attending to the real ontologico-existential concerns that have to do with complicities of colonial subjection and its dehumanization practices. In the claim of seeing nothing but the human, this eliminationist perceptive justifies the dehumanization of the colonized subjects. Césaire writes:

They talk to me about local tyrants brought to reason; but I note that in general the old tyrants get on very well with the new ones, and that there has been established between them, to the detriment of the people, a circuit of mutual services and complicity.

(Césaire 1972, 43)

Césaire turned his back on Europe and he writes:

As I leave Europe
The irritation of its own cries
the silent currents of despair
as I leave Europe
timid in its recovery and boast
I wish for that egoism which is beautiful
Which runs risks
And my ploughing reminds me of a ship's relentless prow.

(Césaire 1970, 63)

In leaving Europe, there is no way that a damning testimony cannot be made. Having to witness dehumanization through *faux* humanism Césaire brought to bear its deceit and lies, which are embedded in Europe's propagation of civilization. Césaire (1970, 64) writes: "My memory is surrounded by blood. My memory has its belts of corpses." Having witnessed the barbarity of Europe to the colonized subjects, it is right for Césaire to give a poetic testimony, a damning account and unmasking the egotistic boast of European humanism and its narcissistic irritations. To leave Europe is to embark on the re-affirmation of the human – that is, the ontological figure that will be created, but not through *faux* humanism because the latter does not have the colonized subject in mind. Fanon's exposé to *faux* humanism is telling:

Let us waste no time in sterile litanies and nauseating mimicry. Leave the Europe where they are never done talking about Man, yet they murder man everywhere they find them, at the corner of every one of their streets, in all the corners of the globe. For centuries they have stifled almost the whole humanity in the name of a so-called spiritual experience.

(Fanon 1990, 251)

Faux humanism is opposed by Césaire in that it is not a gift to humanity as it claims to be. If, then, Europe does not grant anything to humanity, it takes away from humanity by leaving them empty of their ontological content. There is nothing but an empty gesture in the politics of the gift. The colonized subjects are dispossessed and there is no gift in dispossession. "Europe pretends to 'give' generously to the colonized but that which it gives is inessential" (Maldonado-Torres 2006a, 133). It is inessential in so far as it is nothing. To give nothing is not giving at all. Not only is this deprivation, it is also dispossession – that is, on top of being dehumanized, this is not an event, but a continued lived reality. Dispossession *qua* dehumanization is what lies in this *faux* humanism. In other words, *faux* humanism does not give humanity; it takes everything from humanity. *Faux* humanism is what Maldonado-Torres (2006a, 133) refers to as "the European imperial gift … which takes away from the colonized the very possibility of giving: that which the colonized could give has been taken 'away from them'."

The colonized subject who is locked in the status of being non-human cannot be made human by the human subject. The colonized subjects do not need humanism as advanced by the European human subject. The latter propagates humanism in the name of all humanity, while knowing that its non-human other is nothing human and will not even be allowed to become part of the human fraternity. There is nothing to reach, but only a distant horizon for the colonial subject, leaving the latter in an existential abyss and not having any sense of locatedness. What *faux* humanism offers as a gift to the colonized subject is assimilation. The colonized subjects will be given a false sense of being human, while they are dehumanized. For assimilation to succeed, the colonized subject must believe in the lies and deceit of *faux* humanism, which are packaged in the idea of Europe. For those who gravitate to this *faux* humanism, what happens to them is to be left in the neurotic economy of obsession and desire to be human, or thinking that they are human while they are not. They will claim to be human while they constantly witness their daily dehumanization, which they will stoically suppress through bad faith.

To be assimilated is to feel the devastating weight of dehumanization. It is, to a large extent, to feel the essence of being human violated and vanquished, yet ignoring this scandal of dehumanization. To be assimilated is as good as being elevated to nothing, but still being a non-human.

What racial history produces, or threatens to do, is an organization of power that, ceasing entirely to be a humanism, has become

violence itself: a system of control that can be all-encompassing
because it cannot be compassed in turn by *subjects*.

(Marriott 2012, 52 [emphasis original])

The assimilationist trait of *faux* humanism is evident in Césaire's
critique and this proves to be decadence par excellence. "If assimilation exploits the logic of a promise by perpetually maintaining it
as *no more than such*, then colonialism must obviously produce a
subject who is dirempted, who is as much frustration as hopefulness"
(Marriott 2012, 68 [emphasis original]). To the colonized subject to
be invited to humanity still means the absence of invitation as the
possibility of becoming human is not realized. With its masked
gestures, assimilation is informed by the absolute inhalation of the
colonized subjects. As Scharfman (2010) notes, assimilation takes
the colonized subject away from itself.

Scharfman argues that Césaire is a humanist who is informed
by the utopian vision of liberation. For Garraway (2010, 83),
"Césaire's Negritude is predicated on an attitude of continuous
solidarity, openness, and engagement with all others as its condition
of possibility." This was expressed, as Rabaka (2010) notes, as a
site of subjectivity that is informed by nothing but liberatory subjectivity. This is the Negritude that does not take the human as a given,
but that which is involved in ontologico-existential emergence and
continued invention. This is not Negritude that is concerned with
reaching the mythical past, but the assertion of humanity yet to
be found. It is the Negritude that is foundational to the human
question and its version of humanism is not foregrounded in the
idea of Europe. It is, so to speak, decolonial humanism. Césairean
Negritude poetically articulated thus:

> my negritude is not a stone,
> nor deafness flung out against the clamour of the day
> my negritude is not a white speck of dead water
> on the dead eye of the earth
> my negritude is neither tower nor cathedral
>
> it plunges into the red flesh of the soil
> it plunges into the blazing flesh of the sky
> my negritude riddles with holes
> the dense affliction of its worthy patience.

(Césaire 1970, 75)

Césaire charts the terrain the ontologico-existential position that Negritude affirms – that is, the spirit of decolonial humanism. Rabaka (2010) argues that this positionality is not that of universality, but specificity, which is focused on becoming human from the standpoint of the colonized subject and its subjectivity to be such. It is also indicative of the manner in which the colonized subjects claim their humanity in the world. But it is important to register the fact that this claim and assertion to humanity is made in the belly of the civilization of death. However, this does not mean that decolonial humanism is a state of utopian arrival where the colonized subject is the human *qua* human. There is no ontologico-existential standardization that is pursued while plagued by the idea of Europe with its claim of the human as the totality of being. Rather, the struggle of decolonial humanism is not a derivative of *faux* humanism with its logos of civilization of death, but a coming into being of a new subject which clearly emanates from Césaire's politics of life and also its affirmation. The affirmation of the politics of life would not have existed if there was not dehumanization taking place. The politics of life in Césaire's outreach of decolonial humanism point out at the ontologico-existential horizon that the idea of Europe and its *faux* humanism insistently resist just because for it to live, it finds its justification in dehumanization.

This is the Negritude that is distant from the romanticist poeticism, assimilation, ethno-philosophy, history by nostalgic comparison, and derivative discourses.

> Negritude, therefore, from Césaire's point of view, is wide-ranging and grounded in black radical politics and a distinct Pan-African perspective: a purposeful perspective aimed not only on 'returning' to, and reclaiming Africa but, perhaps more importantly, consciously creating an authentic 'Africa' or 'black' self in the present.
>
> (Rabaka 2015, 179–180)

To be exact, it is the Negritude that is concerned with the predicament of being dehumanized in the world. Diagne (2011, 188) writes: "The affirmation of the self was a natural reaction to colonial domination." Negritude as the affirmation of the self signifies the refusal to be dehumanized. This is the continual struggle where life is affirmed and it is a constant exposé of the lies and deceit of civilization concocted by the idea of Europe. The idea of Europe is the one that negates life that is only preserved for those who are imperial subjects. The affirmation of life in Césaire is Negritude. According to Jones (2010, 176) "Césaire's existential affirmation even extends to the living cosmos." The totality of life is what Negritude is, and the resistance of colonial domination is the confrontation of the very thing that denies life. To bring the question of dehumanization to the fore in Negritude is to stretch Césaire further and to the ontologico-existential location of the colonized subject in the matrix of dehumanization. "Césaire's epistemological orientation was also pragmatic; he distributed a priori approaches to knowledge and truth, whether idealist or materialist" (Wilder 2015, 21). It rightly points to the source of colonial subjection as the maker of Patterson's (1982) conception of "social death" since the latter points acutely to the matrix of dehumanization. It is clear that in Negritude as decolonial humanism, colonial subjection is not an event that needed the anti-colonial struggle for there to be antagonism. This is only reasonable or actualized after the end of the modern colonial world. To emphasize, the world as it is has to come to an end in that it creates those who are human and non-human through the logic and organizing principle of race. It is this logic that justifies dehumanization.

Decolonial humanism is not a response to colonial subjection, it is its diagnosis, dissection, and also its call to come to a total end by the struggle waged by colonial subjects, not some juridical decolonization where the colonialized subjects still remain caught in dehumanization. Also important to mention is to maintain that colonial subjection is taken seriously in its afterlife, it has hidden and operates in a mutated form. The fact that colonial subjection and its dehumanization practices are institutionalized, naturalized, and normalized, are the very things that Césairean Negritude is concerned about. As Rabaka (2010, 120) attests, Césaire's Negritude is "simultaneously seminal, radical, evocative, and obtrusive." Garraway (2010) correctly notes that Negritude has been reduced to mean nativism, racial essentialism, ideological mystification, unradical, unrevolutionary, and ineffectual. Garraway also notes that Césaire's Negritude has more revolutionary emphasis, but that did not spare Césaire from Fanon's criticism. Fanon's (1970) fundamental criticism was that Negritude steeped itself and believed in the racist constructions that the colonizer created. Despite this, it is clear from Césaire's Negritude and Rabaka's (2010) obser-vation that it is committed to bring the human into being and to end dehumanization. Indeed, Césaire's Negritude with the leap of decolonial humanism is the condition of the possibility of subjectivity that destroys the edifice of the colonial subjection (Garraway 2010).

What Marriott (2012) brings to light is the danger of celebratory utopian imagination which is steeped in teleological writing – the narratives which advocate the end of juridical colonialism as the end of the history – the danger of ignoring the aftermath of colonial subjection and its devastating effects of dehumanization. Marriott continues to warn that this celebratory utopian imagination can continue to create the myths of myths and this can lead to the incarceration of meaning. It can be added that the meaning of humanism will be the rhetoric of *faux* humanism and the form of subjectivity will be the one that informs the subjectivity of the colonized subject. To be steeped in writing the human subject in the teleological form of the end of history is the perpetuation of dehumanization in that there will be denial of the continued existence of colonial subjection. Césaire's decolonial humanism and its horizon is against *faux* humanism with its rhetorical dispositive. What remains clear from decolonial humanism is the making of history among many other histories – that is, the very basis of history of consciousness. The combating of dehumanization is what Césaire's decolonial humanism is all about. To be human is not to have humanism as conferred by the dictates of the idea of Europe. To be human in the way of its own accord, means that decolonial humanism takes a different trajectory that even calls the modern colonial world into question. It is a decolonial humanism that creates the world where humanity is shared. It is the invention that seeks to destroy colonial imagination – a real leap – the birth of the new human being.

The Return

Césaire's decolonial critique is foregrounded in the positionality of the colonized subject's will to become another human being. Césaire inserts the conception of the human to come, and this form of becoming is outside the confines of the modern colonial world, which must come to an ultimate end for the new humanity to be born. If Césaire's Negritude is anything to go by, then, "the return" is another decolonial move which has to do with the recovery of the subject, but by means of the subject returning to itself. Rabaka (2010) rightly argues that Césaire's conception of return cannot be reduced to reclaiming the mythical past, but the recreation of the authentic self. In other words, to return does not mean the nostalgic exercise of romanticizing the past and wanting to go back to its myth of purity and essence. As has just been mentioned, the return is not a retrieval of something from the past. Césaire writes:

> For us, the problem is not to make a utopian and sterile attempt to repeat the past, but go beyond it. It is not a dead society that we want to revive. We leave that to those who go in for exoticism. Nor is the present colonial society that we wish to prolong, the most putrid carrion that ever rotted under the sun. It is a new society that we must create *and that is the society of the human.*
>
> (Césaire 1972, 52 [emphasis added])

Césaire's conception of the return is, as Marriott (2012, 65) accurately notes, "metaphorics of becoming and transfiguration, to be an invention worthy of the name." In becoming human, colonial subjects will not become a copy of the human subject in the sense of the idea of Europe; they will become the new human in the absence of the modern colonial world. This will be the invention of the human subject outside colonial subjection and its dehumanizing practices.

Césaire's subjectivity is an "insurrectionary activity," which essentially means that through the conception of the return, the colonized subjects engage in a political activity that is aimed at bringing fundamental change. That is why, for Irele (2011), Césaire's "critical commentary" on colonialism has always being radically incisive. The notion of return, therefore, marks the contours of sustained critique of the colonial condition. Concretely, the return implies "the struggle that awaits to recuperate an alienated identity, and a prioritizing of personal awareness as the condition of possibility for political action" (Scharfman 2010, 114). This insurrectionary move from being non-human to being human plays an "important role in the task of rethinking the nature and the dynamics of our self-formation process" (Henry 2000, 275). This form of return is the self-extrication of the colonial subject from the incarceration of dehumanization. It is the confrontation of dehumanization where subjectivity is charted on the terrain of creating the human.

For the return to be actualized, dehumanization practices of colonial subjection need to be exposed. Henry (2000, 278) argues for "throw[ing] off these masks and reclaim[ing] our humanity." The effort to rise to the level of the human subject or to be elevated to such is counterproductive in that dehumanization is not dealt with. For the colonial subject to become human there must be an end to dehumanization. The return, as it were, is to return to the politics of life where the colonized subject does not pathologize itself, but stands *for-itself*, *by-itself*, and *in-itself*. This means that the return is returning to historicity and in a continued dialectical form. That is, the form of dialectic that does not have a thesis as its *telos*. It is the continued ontologico-existential struggle. Therefore, this return is grounded in the concrete lived experience of life worlds where the past is part of the present cemented in the colonial wound (Rabaka 2010). The return is not the return of the human to be recovered from the past. The return is the effort of creating another human outside the matrix of dehumanization.

What is important is for the colonial subject to rediscover itself and this involves "a more complex articulation of time and repetition" (Marriott 2012, 64). The return is not the return to the mythical past and its purist essences, but a return to invent a new human amid the ontologico-existential incarceration which places the colonial subject in the dungeon of morbid historical fixity. It is also through the return to the self that the meaning of the colonial subject would then mean to be human. This then brings to light the fundamental fact that there is no past to return to because the past is fraught with elisions and absences. The past is that which, simultaneously, *was* and that which *never was*.

The advocacy of the return by Césaire means to offer, as Maldonado-Torres (2006a, 119) acutely notes, "new grammars to do critique" and chart the terrain for decolonial futures. It is in these new grammars that the insurrection of the non-human comes into being because the colonized, as a non-human, engaged in the return to the self. These politics of insurrection point to the ways in which the ethical, the political, and the intellectual confront colonial subjection. Césaire's conception of the return calls for the epistemic project and ontologico-existential practices that require "alternative thinking of alternatives" (Maldonado-Torres 2006a, 123). This would mean that, not only the colonial subjects question the alternatives that are offered by the idea of Europe, but the constant critical reflection of their own alternatives. This is profound in what Maldonado-Torres refers to as the "decolonial turn."

The decolonial turn (different from the linguistic or the pragmatic turn) refers to the decisive recognition and propagation of decolonization as an ethical, political, and epistemic project in the twentieth century *and twenty-first century*. This project reflects changes in historical consciousness, agency, and knowledge, and it also involves a method or series of methods that facilitate the task of decolonization at the material and epistemic levels.

(Maldonado-Torres 2006a, 114 [emphasis added])

The emphasis of the return in Césaire means the colonized subject is the political in the making; that which is informed by the will to live. The ontologico-existential form of the colonized subject in the state of insurrection would mean the will not to exist as a colonized subject, but as a human. If there is something that ever was, the colonized subject was a human being. But it is clear in Césaire that this is not the positionality to return to, as it has nothing to offer. The return of being human does not suggest that the colonized subject was a subject before colonial subjection. Already, the colonized subject is in the ontologico-existential ruin of dehumanization. The return that is emphasized is the return to the self-in-decolonial consciousness. The necessity of this return suggests two things. First, the return to the self is a redefinition of being human while being committed to waging the ontologico-existential struggle against all forms of dehumanization. This struggle is waged within a new form of subjectivity – the self-in-decolonial consciousness – that is, the intentional commitment of breaking the superior–inferior complex of colonial subjection. This redefinition also means not seeing oneself as the extension or the mirror of the idea of Europe. The self returns to the self as human *qua* human. Second, the return to the self means adopting what Maldonado-Torres (2008) refers to as the decolonial attitude informed by the phenomenology of love. It is clear in Césaire that the love for humanity is what informs the return to the self. Phenomenology of love transcends the lies and deceits that lie at the heart of the idea of Europe. This is the love that projects ethical relationality of the humanity that is about to be born. Fanon (1990, 254) counsels thus: "But if we want humanity to advance a step further, if we want to bring it up to a different level than that which Europe has shown it, then we must invent and we must make discoveries." Fanon is clearly instructive in calling for the creation of another human in a different world – a decolonized world – a world of liberated humanity.

Uprooting the colonial subjection from the dehumanization and to engage in the continued search for humanity, Césaire's conception of the return is rooted in the politics of life. The politics of life are the politics of creation. What is created enables the infusion of the ontologico-existential conception of the non-human into being a human being. The existence of the colonized subject having being a questioned humanity, and not only is the radical desire, as Bogues (2006) notes, and to bring an end into this questioning of humanity – that is, to absolutely eliminate dehumanization, is the necessary task of Césaire's conception of the return. That is why Césaire's return is the confrontation of dehumanization and the elaboration of the politics of life which set the radical desire afoot. The task is much bigger for Césaire to account for the non-human, the very ontological position he is in against the human subjects who "realize themselves as boundary maintaining systems" (Wynter 1984, 44). They make the colonized subject to be *a thing* that is studied outside itself and rendering it as not its own self.

In no way will the colonized subject be exempted from the preoccupation of the politics of life, since it is life itself which is at stake. It is these boundary maintaining systems that ontologically re-inscribe the asymmetry of the human and the non-human; the orders of the fallacious and mythical propagated as the truthful absolute and what Wynter refers to as the regime of normative definition and its negative stigmatization. To return to being a human being means the assertion of life and this is nothing that can be bastardized as anything poetic because in Césaire's poetic there is a radical desire, which is the politics of life. This radical desire is not to be like the human subject in the Cartesian sense, because the human subject is foregrounded in the will to power, where the colonized subject's radical desire is the will to live. For there to be such subjectivity on the colonized subject, there must be a return to the self in the ontologico-existential formation of the human being in the decolonized world. If the colonized subject ceases to be non-human, which is the domain of non-existence, the radical desire propels the colonized subject to break ties with the idea of Europe. Césaire's resignation from the French Communist Party in 1956 serves as testimony to this. To be sure, it was clear from Césaire that the French Communist Party did not care about the plight of the colonized subject, and there was no colonial question in the Party. Césaire ([1956] 2010) illustrates clearly how the positionality of the colonized subject is different to that of the worker, to whom the notion of the struggle in the French Communist Party is centered around. By privileging the worker, the colonial question is erased and the Party is accused by Césaire of its inveterate assimilation, unconscious chauvinism, fairly simplistic faith and all this "dogmatizes in the name of the party" (Césaire [1956] 2010, 149).

It is this resignation where Césaire engaged in attitudinal defiance, and embarked on a return to the self. For Césaire has fallen victim to colonial paternalism of the French Communist Party as an assimilated colonized subject. Césaire was nothing else but a black face of the colonial infrastructure – the French Communist Party – the space where there was no colonial question but assimilation as *a priori*. Césaire did not exist as a full subject in the Party; he remained non-human in the impasse of colonial paternalism. It is important to interrogate Césaire's claim in the resignation letter when he writes:

> I believe I have said enough to make it clear that it is neither Marxism nor communism that I am renouncing, and that it is the usage some have made of Marxism and communism that I condemn. That what I want is that Marxism and communism be placed in the service of black peoples, and not black peoples in the service of Marxism and communism.
>
> (Césaire [1956] 2010, 149–150)

Césaire is, in a paradoxical way, mistaken in terms of the colonized subject in relation to Marxism and communism. It is not the issue of the colonized subject being served and being in the service of Marxism and communism. These two ideological forces removed the ontologico-existential concern of the colonized subject, and privileged the position of the worker. This makes clear the fact that there will never be another variant of Marxism and communism, since the French Communist Party bestows its duties upon the colonized subjects and then imposes its own distorted ideological version. The French Communist Party, Césaire ([1956] 2010, 150) rightfully asserts, "still bears the marks of the colonialism that is fighting." This is reason enough to break away from such a political formation since it still reproduces the dehumanization of the colonized subjects. In order to return, Césaire writes:

> Suffice it to say that, for our part, we no longer want to remain content with being present while others do politics, while they get

nowhere, while they make deals, while they perform makeshift repairs on their consciences and engage in casuistry.

(Césaire [1956] 2010, 151)

Césaire clearly highlights the ontologico-existential of the colonized subjects being acted upon. This has clearly been indicative under the semantic blasé of comradeship, class struggle, solidarity, and unity of workers against imperialism and so on. Nothing will be mentioned about the colonial question by the French Communist Party and all other Westernized leftist movements, since the colonial question creates a scandal. In the subjectivity of the French Communist Party there is no colonial subject but the worker – that is, the human subject who suffers from alienation and exploitation, not the colonial subject who suffers from what Wilderson (2003b) refers to as fungibility, accumulation, and death – the very things that testify to the worthless life of the colonized subjects, their very thingification in Césaire's terms, which is nothing but dehumanization par excellence. The colonized subject cannot be accounted for, and if the colonial question was to be the fulcrum of the French Communist Party, the latter would have ceased to exist. For, it is the party of the worker who is human *qua* human, and not the colonized subject who is the non-human *qua* thingification. The worker is the embodiment of violence that dehumanizes the colonized subject. The mere fact that there was no colonial question in the French Communist Party means that the party was complicit in the dehumanization of the colonized subject. There was no concern in the party to dismantle colonial subjection since that would mean putting the worker at a disadvantage. The logic being that, for the worker to live, the colonized subject must suffer and, at worst, die. The demands of the colonized subjects cannot be elaborated upon by the French Communist Party because they call for the end of the colonial world, the very demand that is absent from the grammar of the worker (Wilderson 2003a). It is very clear that the demands of the colonized subject cannot be satisfied, and Césaire's resignation is having to face the fact that in the French Communist Party there was no possibility of the appearance of the human, but only a thing. The very ontologico-existential scandal of thingification still remained, and the ontological status of being a worker was just cosmetic. Having being faced by the necessity of the return, Césaire engaged in the politics of liberated subjectivity and, as the colonized subject, having to know where he stands in the decolonial struggle.

Resigning from the French Communist Party is indicative of the fact
that as the colonized subject, he took seriously what Gordon (2006)
refers to as embodied subjectivity, which marks the fact that the
enunciation of the subject is fundamental in the struggle for decolonization. Embodied subjectivity is elaborated thus:

> To intend, one must intend from somewhere. But somewhere for
> living beings is an originary point of their own unsurpassability;
> no living creature can, in other words, surpass its own location
> except as an analogical positing of that location at another point
> ('there'). This originary point is *the body*. If consciousness were not
> embodied, it would not be somewhere, and not to be somewhere is
> to be nowhere.
>
>   (Gordon 2006, 249 [emphasis original])

The return, as Césaire's resignation shows, including his indictment
of the idea of Europe, is the full expression of being an embodied
subject. As Bogues (2006, 334) rightfully points out, "the expression
of [the] radical desire ... that would create an epistemic break." The
epistemic break is not only the discursive formation, it also recon-
structs the subject and it then, if taken seriously, translates into the
grammar of being. It challenges the colonization of unreason which
masks itself as reason. The epistemic break works in synergy with
the shifting of the geography of reason. And both have the major
task of confronting the colonization of knowledge and its dehumanizing practices.

For another human to emerge, the very change of the colonized
subjects to become human beings, the episteme of the colonial
subjection with its guise of knowledge, while it is colonial knowledge,
should be challenged from its interiority and expression. To colonize
knowledge is to militate against the return. The return in this sense
would mean "cleaning up and restoring the house of knowledge
that has been knocked down by the global storm blowing from
the paradise of linear thinking" (Mignolo 2011, 94). This linear
thinking has cemented the power of the episteme and then makes
dehumanization seem reasonable through its logical and moral
justification while in fact it is unreasonableness. The expression of
the radical desire, which is foundational in Césaire's return, is the
removal of domination and its guises, to put it in place, as a matter
of necessity, the possibility of the politics of life that militate against
all forms of dehumanization.

It is important, for the conception of return to take effect, to shift the geography of reason. Shifting the geography of reason is necessary, for it serves the purpose of accounting for the subjectivity of the colonized subject. The return of the colonized subject means, as Bogues (2006, 325) correctly notes, the "human that needs to be brought to the fore out of bondage." Not only this, another human being should also be invented, the human who consistently asks the relentless question: what does it mean *to be human?* The answer to this question need not be in the utopian imagination and its teleological end, but the radical desire where the return is something fraught with the politics of uncertainty. Ontologically and existentially, the colonized subject who is dehumanized is said to be, as Malcolm X (1970) articulates, found at the bottom, not being human at all. Therefore, what the colonized subject wants is something that is answered in the affirmative. Malcolm X argues that what the colonized subjects want is to be human beings. There is a need to come to existence. To support Césaire's thinking, Malcolm X (1970, 86) is on the mark when asserting: "We have to make the world see that what we're confronted with is a problem for humanity."

As Gordon (2011) correctly points out, there is no move to some end point, but to engage in teleological suspension. It still remains a challenge to account for the conception of the return in that it is important first to account for it being located in the realm of the body and consciousness. Indeed, in the Césairean sense, to return is to free oneself – as the colonized subject – from the clutches of colonial interpellation which keeps the infrastructure of dehumanization alive. To return is the realization that the colonized subject did not exist in the ontologico-existential domain of the human, but that of the non-human. To come to that realization is to be in the domain of consciousness and to engage in the mental and epistemic return. It is to realize that the bodily return is not sufficient in that the consciousness of that body is not decolonized. The challenge that still remains with the return is whether the colonized subject, as Césaire is, will engage in the decolonial process of bringing the world to an end after having acquired decolonial consciousness.

This is only possible if humanity is outside the configurations of the modern colonial world. This essentially means, therefore, that the modern colonial world should cease to exist. From all of the above mentioned, and Césaire's critique to be specific, the human question should be understood from the vantage point of the colonized subject, and to pose such a question in confronting colonial subjection and its dehumanizing practices. It is, as a matter of fact, to account for the emergence of the human and to render *faux* humanism an ontologico-existential scandal. Césaire's return cannot be the synthetic moment yet, since this will be reducible to the *telos* – but is the process of invention in the continued struggle to become human in the dehumanizing world.

Indeed, Césaire's articulation of the possibility that authorizes the colonized subject is not only utopian and imaginary. It is the radical desire and political responsibility that accentuates the creation of the new human being and accounts for the re-definition of the human and humanism. So, in addition, this re-definition should eliminate the processes of dehumanization completely and chart the way for the world to come, the coming of which must be the concerted effort of the colonized subjects. The possibility of another world – the decolonized world where the human is human in relation to other humans – is the responsibility of the colonized subjects in that it is they who must end dehumanization. Nothing can liberate them but themselves, as everything depends on them.

In general, Césaire scandalized the question of the human by exposing the deceit and hypocrisy of the idea of Europe and its civilization. The question of the human has been taken by Césaire as something that originates from the site of the dehumanized and also is railing against the Cartesian human subject. In the ontologico-existential formation and the constitution of the subject, the Cartesian subject in the dichotomy of self–other relations determined the politics of life and even death which Césaire exposes. The impulses of reason that propel the mastery of the self, the mastery of the world, and the mastery of the "other" through the colonial subject legitimize dehumanization of the colonized subjects.

In essence, for there to be another world, there should be resurrection of the subject and fusion of such a subject with the human content. That is, the human subject *qua* the idea of Europe is not human in its own terms. It is human in so far as it dehumanizes what it renders non-human. Even humanism and the civilizing values of *faux* humanism failed the test of bringing the human to birth. In so far as the colonial subjection is concerned, there is no human in the genuine sense. In short, there will be no human in the presence of dehumanization.

At the same time, it is important to eliminate dehumanization by the colonized subjects through the resurrection of subjectivity and the possibility of giving the world the name that it is worth. Of course, currently, the modern colonial world cannot be named, since it must first be exorcized of its dehumanizing practices – the absolute end of colonial subjection. In a similar vein, colonial interpellation, which creates Césaire's thingification, perpetuates the pathological attachment that plagues the colonized subject not to have any form of relationality to the world. It is worthless to authorize the possibility or the presence of another humanity while the modern colonial world still exists. But to heed Césaire's plea for the possibility of another humanity is to take seriously the task of ending the world as it is. This is the world that is contaminated by the idea of Europe and its civilizing project which institutionalized, naturalized, and normalized the decadence of humanity. It is also to take seriously the devastating impact of dehumanization on the life of the colonized subject and to put that life at stake.

Césaire's subjectivity on the question of the human subject has been challenging, and, more specifically, has put it into the equation of colonization = thingification. Dehumanization is what presents a scandal and it is the logic on which the modern colonial world is founded. Césaire, however, neglected the critique of the colonized subject in the postcolony, reproducing the very sense of dehumanization in its conception of the return. That is, there is no clear critique of the colonized subjects mutating into colonial subjection. The latter, of course, are those who are in service of the idea of Europe wittingly and unwittingly, and their main role is to stand against decolonial efforts of bringing to birth the new human. To Césaire's credit, and contrary to what most of Césaire's critique implies for the conception of Negritude, it has been demonstrated here that it is much more radical and it still needs to be taken seriously as a decolonial critique. The diagnostic thinking of Césaire takes the question of the human subject to task, along with the world that it inhabits, which ultimately create the non-human. It is clear from Césaire that another humanity is possible in the world of the human *qua* human – the decolonized world – the world where subjects collapse as agents of being human and non-human.

3

Steve Biko as the Figure of the Outlawed

What does it mean for Steve Biko to be signified as the figure of the outlawed? This is a question worth exploring, which of course has no definitive answers, except by some form of diagnostic intervention and pinpointing some existential *problématique* of Biko in the era through which he belongs to everyone. But what is at stake here is that this question borders on the unmasking of a scandal, which is to say that there has been every attempt to erase, distort, and deny the existence of Biko, more in the light of the uncomfortable politics of writing that combated the system of racism and its logical order called white supremacy. The politics of writing, which are antagonistic in nature, are informed by the ontological questions of the existence of blacks in the antiblack world. Black Consciousness is the philosophy that shaped the political writing of Biko. It did not emerge as an historical accident, but was a necessary condition informed by the existential condition of the antiblack reality called apartheid, and enduring settler-colonialism. A view that has been fashionable in post-1994 South Africa is that Biko is located in the politics that are outside his writing, and as a matter of convenience iconicity takes precedence. Biko is a contested figure and no attempt is made here to contest Biko in terms of what he would have done were he alive. Rather, Biko is situated as a black subject and as such one who had his humanity questioned. The antiblack world is the world that is informed by its self-imposed duty to question the humanity of the black in ways that consistently dehumanize. It is the world that justifies terror in the lived experience of the black.

The concept of the outlaw is deployed here for the very purpose of situating Biko among his own – the black in the antiblack world. The existence of Biko and his philosophical thought needs to be foregrounded in the world in which he was at the receiving end of oppression and was a resisting subject that informed the spirit of militancy. The challenges arise where there is an attempt at glorification, which has a hidden agenda that negates the existential struggle that informed Biko's lived experience. What is argued for here is Biko in the mode of writing – that is, the politics of authorship. It is the very same form of writing that has put Biko at odds with the white supremacist order, and the very same politics of writing that give Biko a particular form of existence. The existence of Biko is one which was at all times political, and this is evident in his way of writing. Therefore, this intervention does not reduce Biko to the level of biography, since the discourse is pervaded with that. The politics of writing are the area through which Biko's thought can be resurrected from the whims of the liberal consensus, which seeks to reduce Biko to a mere pacifist who in effect fits very well with the post-1994 political project.

The struggle of Black Consciousness was ongoing, and its philosophical grounding was shaped and reshaped from many entries and perspectives. Its potent force still stands, on the basis that the totalizing muscle of white power still plagues black existence. Having been challenged to the point of being decimated in the political arena, it still remains a force that is a bane to the oppressive reality that still haunts blacks, even in the liberal democratic post-1994 era under the rule of the African National Congress (ANC). The resurgence of Black Consciousness has moved from the psychological and spiritual realm to even infuse political content, which takes various forms. As it is, Black Consciousness has never found any form of hospitality even in the era of black political administration, which still manages the antiblack reality that bastardizes Biko. Here, as will be demonstrated, Biko is the outlawed.

On Blackness: The Problem of the Problem

What is the problem of the problem? To try to respond to this difficult question, what can be said is: being black is a problem and to be a problem is to be black. The existence of blackness is problematic since blackness is militated against by antiblackness to the point where blackness is banished – the aberration from the norm and the thinghood of the living, which is the entity that is substitutedly dead and its life not worth accounting for. To be a problem is to be black and to be in the existential predicament caught in the negative of whiteness. Therefore, to be black is a problem on this ground – that is, the "other" of whiteness. The state of negativity, being that blackness is inferior and falls short of whiteness, is seen as a problem. As a problem, blackness is fixed into a traumatic experience of alienation, brutality, humiliation, depersonalization and even death. To see the black as a problem is to appropriate the presence and operating logic of racism. It is on this basis that racism is used as a tool to render blacks as a problem, and as a master signifier it signifies blackness as depersonalized. What renders blackness as depersonalized is the idea of race and its practising logic of racism. Racism is still present and felt by blackness, since it is intact, plagues and is directed to blackness. It is blackness, not whiteness, that is at the receiving end of racism. Biko (2004, 97) states that: "[T]he racism we meet does not only exist on an individual basis; it is also institutional to make it look like the South African way of life." And, as a way of life, it renders blackness a problem; and the manner of addressing that problem is to oppress blackness to become subjects without essence.

Most crucially, blackness exists, not only by virtue of existence *per se*, but as a problem. As a problem, blackness is structurally constructed to exist as a non-entity. This construction is made to create an ensemble of phobias, lacks and deficiencies to make dehumanization justifiable. It is this dehumanization that makes it possible for there to be no moral outrage, but rather silence, in the manner that blackness exists. Therefore, blackness as a non-entity is the racial formation created and sustained by antiblack reality, which serves the purpose of alienating and negating blackness. What then remains as the definitive factor of blackness is being systematically positioned at the receiving end of antiblackness. Biko (2004, 97) states clearly that "the system derives its nourishment from the existence of antiblack attitudes in society." Biko also states that not only is blackness considered inferior, it is also bad. This negativity of blackness is totally out of the realm of being and whiteness is the ideal to which blackness must gravitate.

The existence of blackness is made to be dependent on whiteness for survival, and whiteness is dependent on blackness as the raw material to be extracted. As a raw material, there is nothing human about blackness, it is just a non-entity. The self of blackness as the construction of whiteness is to keep the infrastructure of the negative. This negativity is what Biko pointed out, lamenting what white oppression does to the self of the black. The self of the black is self-objectified and this is done by crushing the humanity of the black by constant questioning and also by reminding blackness that it is a non-entity, as it constitutes negativity, lacks, and deficiencies. The black self as the contingent cannot be individualized in the atomic form. The black self is the self in relation to other black selves by virtue of being structurally positioned by the antiblack world. As Gordon writes:

> The self is not a complete formation of itself but a dialectical unfolding of overcoming through which selves and correlated conceptions of domination, bondage, and freedom emerge. The self, so to speak, is always struggling with its own fragmentation and incompleteness in relation to a world that resists it and through which other selves emerge through such struggles.
>
> (Gordon 2008, 84)

The self in the form of the black self is a predicament. Biko as the self is such, by the very fact of his blackness and his relationality (that which does not have any capacity) to the antiblack world. As Gordon (2008) laments, the self of blackness cannot be the self by itself; rather, it is the self in relation to the antiblack world. The existence of blackness in the antiblack world is a phenomenon that is operationalized by racism as the existential infrastructure. As More (2012, 36) asserts: "[R]acism is dehumanization and human alienation par excellence." It is only in the racist gaze that blackness is a problem, and the very fact of being a problem renders blacks dehumanized and alienated. Ramphalile (2011, 16) posits that "being black is either something that people become and/or are said to be in relation to something else, because there is no such thing as a given blackness." The positionality of the world through its antiblack genetic makeup and logic of operation is the creation of blackness. To be antiblack is to assume white essentialist position-ality, which locates blackness in the exterior of humanity. Black Consciousness was concerned with blackness at the ontological level and the central concern is still "the politics of Black being in an antiblack world" (More 2012, 24). As More states, the ontological questions are central to blackness as they raise the place of the black being in the world. But as something that is constitutive to a problem, the world, in its antiblack positionality, erases the black. But still, as a mode of persistence, Black Consciousness asks "what is the meaning of the being of a black person in an antiblack world?" (More 2012, 25). These questions are essential, as Black Consciousness à la Biko is loaded enough with ontological weight to confront antiblack racism, though in the midst of impotence the ontology of blackness pervades. They are questions that haunt the present as they continue to make ontological demands.

There are many other forms of racism that affect other races. However, they do not dehumanize to the extent to which black bodies and souls are damned. Biko (2004, 30) charges thus: "this is the extent to which the process of dehumanization has advanced." As More (2012) acutely points out, Biko demonstrated the dehumanizing effect of racism on blacks – a specific form of racism that militates against blacks in all forms of life – antiblack racism. It is this form of racism that questions and denies blacks humanity. As More elaborates:

> Apartheid racism is misanthropy, total and complete hate. It is the hatred of the being of the black victim. The original project of this hate is the total suppression of the Other's consciousness; it is the desire to annihilate and kill the Other.
>
> (More 2012, 31)

This explains why blacks, by virtue of being oppressed, are denied the insurrectory possibility. This possibility is the radical conversation that is the confrontation with death at the moment of asking ontological questions. One of these questions is formulated by Trask (2004, 9) thus: "[H]ow do we, as terminated people, understand the colour of violence?" The ontological questions are rooted in the actual political practices of Black Consciousness, and Biko as a racial subject asked distinct ontological questions. It is on this basis that he insisted that blacks should ask fundamental questions. This is because "whatever is [that] is impoverished as a remedy will hardly cure the conditions" (Biko 2004, 29). The problem is, of course, asking the wrong questions that are outside the realm of blackness – the subject that is positioned as the problem in the antiblack world. Thus, the ontological questions of the black are categorically distinct. They stem from *what does it mean* as opposed to *what is it*; and this is the case as blackness is the ontological position that Black Consciousness always asks: what does it mean to be black in the antiblack world? Also, as Wilderson (2008) frames it: "what does it mean to suffer?"

It is at the level of being a problem that blackness asks ontological questions. The asking of these questions, paradoxically, does not exonerate blackness from being a problem since the very asking of these questions is seen as something problematic in itself. This is because they are questions that disturb the status quo, and there are efforts to contain them by suppressing, denying, or averting them. This brings to the fore the understanding of blackness as a condescended and displaced category of the political (Ramphalile 2011). That is, the symbolic order of the political *qua* blackness assumes the structural positionality of antiblackness. The very asking of these questions is not for the sake of getting answers, but rather blackness engaging in the political project of subjectivity – Black Consciousness – for itself and not expecting to be understood by whiteness or demanding answers from whiteness. These are questions for those who are being wronged and it is for them to find their own answers in their own mode of articulating their own lived experiences in search for liberation. Ramphalile (2011, 20) engages the concept of dislocation *qua* blackness by differentiating "the subject as political subject and subject as subject-position" to suggest that dislocation is rupture that opens up spaces to allow different interpretations of subjectivity. Dislocation, as Ramphalile insists, conveys specific reality and, in this case, the reality conveyed by Black Consciousness is different as it relates to blacks in the antiblack world. To be precise, "[Black Consciousness] was able to develop a 'unique political idiom' informed by 'its conditions of possibility'" (Ramphalile 2011, 23).

Chipkin (2002, 569) engages the conception of blackness that is "detached from its historical referents (notions of oppression, alienation, and exploitation)," which actually means that those referents are outside the existential reality of blackness. For Chipkin, blackness is a sublime object. There cannot be anything sublime about blackness, and of course as an object, if it is caught in a perpetual existential crisis that renders it a non-entity. The sublime of blackness is of course the popular mantra that "black is beautiful," something that is problematic. The problem of blackness is that which is assigned to the body. The body of the black is a problem by being black and also in the ontological form. To think of the black subject and even to articulate such is to engage the body. It is the body that does not possess life, since what is possessed is externally owned; it is contingent on that which is outside the body. As Gordon (2008) states, whiteness by itself is never white enough as it needs black or its distance from blackness; its domination is a matter of dependency. Gordon also insists that blackness is always too black in relation to its distance to itself, but never white enough. So this means that blackness is a problem of the problem, in the sense that the nature of the problem that blackness is "caught" is unsolvable.

What makes blackness is antiblack racism, a dehumanizing project that positions black as a problem to sustain itself by feeding on black suffering. The full subject, whiteness, possesses ontology. This is a being that is not contingent upon something but is a being in itself, that is, it determines its life form through the political practice of determining and choosing. Blackness is the opposite of whiteness and its place is the zone of non-being. In such a place blackness cannot make demands that are similar to those of subjects who have ontological density, since blackness is dehumanization that creates the ontologically dispossessed subject. Blackness as the subject reduced to the level of the body is a (non)entity that is judged not ontologically but at the level of appearance. Gordon (2007) foregrounds the condition of appearance that is a form of emergence, namely black skin reflecting the ontology of non-being.

The hegemonic claim is that racism is something that is supposed to be dealt with for it to come to an end, and this is a gesture that borders on deceit. This deceit is presented thus: the end of racism has to be a collectivist effort, with those who are racist and their victims "working together" to end racism. Biko's advocacy against racism is that it has to be confronted by its victims in their own political register by exposing the liberal hypocrisy that claims equality, justice, and freedom. The liberal hypocrisy is entangled in a fundamentally racist infrastructure of antiblackness. Black Consciousness is a philosophy born in struggle in that it was fermented and brewed in the belly of apartheid. To struggle is to engage in the politics of resistance. Black Consciousness is a philosophy in that it articulates the lived experience of blacks who are in the clutches of oppression, the very negativity of antiblackness. It is a philosophy born in struggle in that the very same lived experiences and the testimonies that come with it, and to some extent, the articulation that tries to understand the manner in which oppression is constituted, are the very basis on which this philosophy rests.

Philosophy that is born in struggle is not philosophy that is detached from the lived experience of the subject, but in which the subject makes sense of the world from where it is located. The black subject articulating Black Consciousness is indeed a rebel with a cause, and of course has the aim of engaging in the politics of antagonism. Racism is understood here in terms of its antiblack posture, the pathology of which should be unraveled in the ways in which it brutalizes black life. This brutality is of course that of rendering black life meaningless. Biko's position is clear: racism affects blacks and it should be confronted by blacks themselves and on their own terms, rather than being told *what is* racism and *what it is not*.

What is opposed here is the very act of denying racism and claiming that it is not relevant. This is often advocated by whites who are not affected by racism. Racism exists and South Africa was and still is racist due to the presence of antiblack reality, where black life is still cheap. So racism should not then be understood in terms of the public posture, but the private posture and practices that are deliberately ignored. Race denialism is the elaboration of racism and this arrangement is such that racism goes from the public (apartheid) to the private realm (liberal democracy). To argue that South Africa is free due to its liberal democracy with its illusion of non-racialism is to lie and to choose to ignore the denigration, indignity, and humiliation of blackness. Racism operates in the private realm so that it cannot be pointed out, and this is the kind of racism in which blackness is made to deny there is such a thing if it dares to articulate it. It takes the form of what Goldberg (2004) calls a "lobotomizing racial violence" that detaches racism from existential realities and experiences that plague blackness. Biko's approach to racism is not that of fighting for non-racialism or, worse, what is popularly advocated – that is, the transcendence of race, where blacks are made to believe that there is no race but only humanity. The racist order that Biko confronted is still present today and, as Goldberg (2004) states, it is a racist order that immobilizes and terrorizes blackness. As Goldberg argues, this is the formalism that abandons race and leads to born-again racism.

> Born again racism, then, is racism acknowledged, where acknowledgment at all, as individualized faith, of socially dislocated heart,

rather than as institutionalized inequality. In short, it is unrecognized racism for there are no terms by which it could be recognized: no precedent, no intent, no pattern, no institutional explication.

(Goldberg 2004, 227)

It means that what exists in post-1994 South Africa is something different in relation to blackness, the latter of course being something else since there is no apartheid, with the justification that blackness cannot claim to be oppressed due to the absence of apartheid. As Chipkin (2002, 569) insists, "today blackness is more and more spinning out of the symbolic field that once gave it meaning in South Africa." It seems blackness here is not to be explained in the existential domain that permanently plagues it – antiblackness – but is posited as something wholly accountable to the symbolic order. The latter as a political register seems to assume the totality of blackness; it is an arrested discourse only explainable to the symbolic order itself. This is bad faith in that even if racism exists it should not be pointed out, since the very act of pointing out is said to be regression in the form of autochthony, reverse racism, victimology and so forth. It is in this illusionary existential schema that blackness should not in any way render antiblackness as the problem that structurally positions blackness at the pathological level. According to Fanon (1967, 32): "[R]acism is not the whole but the most visible, the most day-to-day and, not to mince matters, the crudest element of a given structure."

Fanon argues that racism mutates its melanin (the pigment that gives skin its color) to adapt itself to the socio-political condition of the context in which it finds itself. Racism tends to change its form so to create and re-create blackness to sustain itself. This is done in multiple implicit ways. In contexts where people declare that race does not exist or where racism is condemned, racism usually occurs in an institutionalized form. In this form, the logic of its operation is hidden but continues to give effect to racism. However, paradoxically, the effect will be declared not to be racism, because it is effectively normalized and institutionalized. Fanon sees racism as a systemic form of oppression of a people that is justified to such an extent that it remains a part of reality.

Blackness emerged as a matter of racial "othering," involving tormented and troubled psyches. Blackness is related to pathology, and stands in a position that renders it devoid of being; blackness operates in an antiblack world, where "the Negro, the African, the native, the black, the dirty, was rejected, despised: cursed" (Fanon 1967, 26). The way racists sophisticate bad faith is to force the victims of racism to deny their own experience and to make them believe that there is no racism, but some faults of humanity that can largely be blamed on the victims themselves. One common form of sophistication is *you are obsessed with race and this is the very same obsession that makes you have no agency and be caught in victimhood.* Another famous one is "there is no racism and we have transcended race." These might at face value appear legitimate, but they are not; and they border on bad faith since they legitimize racism and deny its victims by the way they articulate their experience that is informed by racist practices and that places them in victimhood. This is aversion, which is a flight from responsibility and which amounts to bad faith (Gordon 1995). This is the worst form of sadism, in which pain is inflicted on the victim and the victim is denied ways to articulate that pain.

The manner in which these sophisticated racist practices operate is by demanding that victims respond in a manner that they do not feel, but that the racists desire. They will even go further to claim "there is no racism, we are all humans, when I see you I do not see color, I see the human." In this mode of bad faith the white racist knows that he or she is lying and the intention is to make victims of racism regard that transient gesture of white paternalism, with its race denialism, as something permanent, whereas it is just transient at that moment of being expressed, and not transient at all since this is a lie. The violation of blacks by whiteness is the violence determined and controlled by whiteness by claiming the totality of its whole experience, even if it is felt by blackness and not whiteness itself. Why then should blackness believe in its condition in the ways determined by whiteness? Again, this is sadism in that the pain that is felt by blackness is pleasure for whiteness and at worst, whiteness elides that pain. It therefore means that for blackness to feel pain at the level of articulation is something that is criminalized. So it means that for blackness to make whiteness comfortable it must not articulate its pain, and it must live not inside its own experience but in the experience that is desired by whiteness.

The white gaze is not only a look, as Fanon ([1952] 2008) puts it; it is also violence against the black body, since this is a gaze that pierces through the black body. The whole weight of blackness presses down on blacks in a form of a neurosis – the problem of an inferiority complex produced by the white racial gaze and socio-economic realities. This gives life to structures that militate against black humanity and leaves blackness with the absence of recognition of humanity. This creates the black condition, where the ontology of blackness is objectification, since blacks are regarded as objects and not as subjects. Blackness cries out for a humanity which is denied to those who are black by an antiblack world. To understand the antiblack world, it is important to understand "its real coordinates" (Fanon [1952] 2008). Blackness has been and is still that which is objectified, because "every ontology is made unattainable" in that "it does not permit [the] understanding of the black *being in the antiblack world which is unethical par excellence*" (Fanon [1952] 2008, 82 [emphasis added]). To study blackness is to examine the ways in which blackness is interlocked and confused with emancipation instead of liberation in the postcolonial or post-liberation period. Blackness is a negation that exists as a result of the white gaze. This gaze, even if it does not recognize blackness, means that the inferiority complex is still in operation, since blacks want to be afforded concessions by whites – they want recognition and affirmation. The existence of blackness is not only problematic; it is outside the register of humanity. Blackness is pathology and the racist order of apartheid and its neo-form (the ANC is the manager of the racist order) is the reality that still haunts blackness. The ANC continues to do what its racist masters did, and that is to adopt the antiblack position. The illusive project of liberal democratic ideological orientation is informed by the malicious intent of masking racism. According to Martinot and Sexton (2003, 178), "liberal ethos look at racism as ignorance, something characteristic of the individual that can be solved at a social level through education and democratic procedure."

The framing of blackness as a problem – that is, the being which is seen in the negative sense in which the prevailing agency is to wipe out that being from things ontological – renders blackness a problem worth solving by the manner of its negation. What needs to be put forth in relation to blackness, in relation to Biko's position, is that it is an issue that is the rallying point of his political ontology. The life of the black, even in the midst of oppression that renders that life as nothingness, is challenged by Biko. This challenge is in the form of a critique, and this critique's positionality is not anti-white. The critique of whiteness by blackness carries no ontological weight and it is clear even from Biko that he did not want dialogue with whiteness. What Biko advocates is the positionality of blackness asserting itself, and this demonstrates clearly that Biko's message is targeted at blackness, hence they must be on their own. That is to say, the critique of Biko is for blacks and about blacks to understand the nature of oppression. This should not be mistaken for the view that Biko wanted to be heard and understood by whiteness, but rather as blackness affirming itself in the politics of opposition and making ontological demands. This is a political gesture in which blackness affirms itself from the vantage point of wretchedness.

Building on Gordon's ontological schema of presence as absence, Wilderson (2008) introduces three layers of black absence. The first layer is absence as subjective presence, which means that the world cannot accommodate blackness at the level of subjectivity. In terms of this layer, seeing a black is seeing a black – something that precedes humanity because the visibility of blackness is *a priori*. Wilderson (2008, 98) argues that blackness is "an ontological freeze that waits for a gaze, rather than a living ontology moving with agency to the field of vision." The second layer is the absence of a cartographic presence, which means that the life of the black is about fate, while that of the white is about freedom. According to Wilderson, the life of blacks is about "when." In other words, "when will I be arrested, when will I be stopped by police, when will I get violated and so forth. The third and final layer is the absence of political presence, which does not allow for 'the temperature of the black's grammar of suffering'" (Wilderson 2008, 99). This implies that when blacks make demands, these demands are not met, since they are rendered impossible. The agency of blacks is thus negated, since blackness is something that is absent from the political world. Wilderson (2003a) argues that blackness is a scandal in that its structural position threatens the status quo. He suggests that blackness as a subjective position presents an antagonism that cannot be satisfied. The existing structures deprive black modes of articulation; as such blacks, who are slaves, have no transactional value. Blackness does not call for taking into account, and the plague of pathologies that befall blacks in the black condition reduces them to non-entities.

The absence of ontology clearly means that there is no life at all. It is in the antiblack world that "no history of or those not remembered, whose past is not made present, whose past is deemed to have no presence" (Goldberg 2004, 227). For Chipkin (2002), blackness has no historical essence in the contemporary era due to the absence of register, which negates historicality. What Goldberg is aiming at is indeed the ontological presence and absence, the latter of course being the one that plagues blackness. The absence of history, as Goldberg states, actually means ontological absence. Here it is clear that blackness does not exist even in the contemporary, as it has no history. Blackness is therefore left with nothing to hold onto. That is to say, the ontological absence means that blackness has no ground to stand on. Biko's concern with the erasure is concerned with what reduces blackness to an empty shell. Wilderson (2008) brings to the fore that black suffering means that the suffering of blacks is the dispossession of being, making blacks ontologically absent. "From the terrestrial scale of cartography to the corporeal scale of the body, Blackness suffers through homologies of Absence" (Wilderson 2008, 99). As for Wilderson, the presence of the black is also a form of absence. That is to say, the affirmation of presence by blackness is actually the very affirmation of absence. Being-in-the-world implies that existence is a given, as the basic structure of existence is historical (Manganyi 1973). The human mode of existence is characterized by being black-in-the-world and being white-in-the-world, which suggests that there are differences, and sometimes this negates blackness. Put simply, black humanity becomes absent in the world, as the body itself carries with it the undesirable, and ceases to be part of the view and therefore has to register to the world.

What intensifies alienation *qua* blackness is the structural positioning of blackness having been at the receiving end of oppression. The antiblack world makes blacks "exist in a violent and violated world" (Trask 2004, 9). The kind of violence that pervades the antiblack world is, of course, structural violence. This means that blackness is negated by structural violence to realize its agency, and, therefore, blacks are organized by violence as the workings of race and racism take shape as something institutionalized, naturalized, and normalized. Structural violence has the crude ability to turn the abnormal into normal in the ways in which it appropriates itself to lack of life. The misery of black life that is abnormal becomes normal, and it is as if the very same blacks brought the existential misery onto themselves. Structural violence, according to Wilderson (2010, 75), "is not a black experience but a condition of black 'life'." Structural violence mutates and is hidden behind structures to make the hellish life normal. In this form of violence, the perpetrator cannot be pointed out, and what remains the sole focus is attributing blame to the victims of violence. Structural violence is effective in the sense that it attacks blackness at the level of the body by means of packaging it as the "site of a common human vulnerability" (Butler 2004, 44). This means black bodies suffer because they are of a commonality and that is being black. So the collective blame is attributed to such bodies and they are even blamed for their own dehumanization and its long-lasting effects.

The manner in which antiblackness is structurally constituted is such that it renders blackness invisible at the ontological level. In this arrangement, blackness does not exist. That is, antiblackness collapses the ontological weight of blackness to the point of absence. The absence of the ontological schema is the very thing that Biko is concerned with, the quest for humanity that is. There is a problem here in that blackness is militated against and the affirmation of blackness to become human is negated by the force of dehumanization. So the humanity lived is not humanity in the ontological sense, in that there is ontological absence. Wilderson (2008) argues that blacks do not possess a human life, but a "black life" – that is, a life that is already dead, since blacks die because they lived.

On the Mystique of the Martyr

In the condition of change and its opposition, there seems to be the emergence of the martyr, who is on the side of change – dying for the cause. Life after death as a form of excess gravitating to a meaningful desire, in which death is confronted head-on, seems appealing for the status of the martyr. This is foundational to the ways in which the politics of resistance are predicated on the making of insatiable demands. Biko seems to be located in this existential zone, in which he is a figure larger than life because he confronted death, and such death did not liquidate him, since his ideas still live on. Though this might be plausible, the danger these discourses produce is that of removing Biko from the political through erasure, distortion, and denial. Whenever Biko is evoked as a martyr (this of course being the ritual of the post-1994 September commemorations fiasco), he is no longer the black who is the bane of the racist infrastructure that puts the black in the zone of non-being. Biko is no longer the figure who grapples with philosophical meditations that seek to chart a way for liberation. What then pervades is the romanticist version of a martyr who lived, fought and died for freedom, and, of course, the accommodationist project that is the constitutional democracy of the post-1994 era.

Biko is stripped of all the revolutionary and philosophical tools, and this is done by projecting him as a sort of martyr. The figure of the martyr is problematic in post-1994 South Africa, more so if such a martyr is Biko, who is unwanted by the practices of the ANC. These practices are antiblack and they do not in any way coincide with Biko's philosophy of Black Consciousness and his revolutionary subjectivity, which was channeled into realizing liberation, not cosmetic emancipatory reforms and their modicum of freedom. This projection of Biko as a martyr in many ways makes Biko a figure that he is not and never has been. What this means is that the projection of Biko takes the form of a mythical figure – the politically impotent subject – negated to the point of being left to the whims of various contestations that militate against Black Consciousness and render it irrelevant, while pretending to commemorate it as such. It is this figure of martyrdom that is irrelevant to the reality that Black Consciousness faces today.

The politics of martyrdom in relation to Biko raise the dead subject and the one that cannot speak from the grave to the realm of consciousness. If Biko is a martyr it means that he is dead. If Biko is a revolutionary and philosopher it means he is alive, and as Mngxitama et al. (2008) assert, that he lives and continues to haunt the present. The ideas of Biko are still relevant and they do not need any form of martyrdom that will require renaming public spaces and streets and erecting statues and monuments. On the contrary, the Biko who is advocated here is the one who is a black subject in the struggle for liberation or black subjectivity and for blacks to have the ontological status in their own political register. As such, Biko is a living subject due to the fact that the ideas are the ones relevant and most pressing in the present, and they are worth being engaged, criticized, and updated in the light of the existential conditions that befall blackness. It also means that to be a subject, and a black one for that matter, is to be troubled in the realm of martyrdom. To be a black subject, Biko is not then a martyr. The notion of the martyr *qua* blackness is not only a myth but an oxymoron. The martyr is a dead subject and prior to being dead possessed ontological density. Biko, being black, did not possess ontological density, and therefore, the result is self-explanatory – Biko cannot and will not be a martyr.

Most crucially, to state it point-blank, blackness is that which is socially dead, and in death it is the *dead dead*, meaning that death has already entangled the black body even in its life. No form of life in the ontological sense has prevailed in blackness. It is problematic therefore, and at best scandalous, to think of life where there was no life and where there is no life. The martyr is dead and in death, the martyr is a martyr. There is no life in blackness and the sacrifice of the black subject in pursuit of liberation, though fighting oppression, is not worth noting as something of the status of martyrdom, since this will mean that the legacy of such a figure lives on. In this case, Biko's legacy has not lived on as the very same struggle he engaged is the one being grappled with. South Africa is still antiblack. It is essential to position Biko outside this iconography of martyrdom since he is a socially dead subject. Biko occupies the existential configuration of what Patterson (1982) calls "social death," where the subject is dead while being alive. For Patterson, the desociali-zation and depersonalization of black subjects render them dead. This death is in the form of the death of the subject and the death of subjectivity, all that are reinforced by subjection that determines the forms of life. Wilderson (2003b, 23), drawing from Patterson, defines social death as "[a] metaphor *that* comes into being through violence that kills the thing *which is the black subject* such that the concept might live" [emphasis added]. For Wilderson, social death is a scandal that is hard to articulate in the absence of structures that should support the positionality of the black subject. The position-ality of the black subject is the spectre that still haunts, due to its disarticulated historical groundings.

Biko as a revolutionary subject informed by Black Consciousness breaks totally from this myth of martyrdom when his political stance is not that of the moral discourse, but the struggle against antiblack racism initiated by blacks themselves. This struggle was necessary as Biko faced the ontological problem of antiblack racism that required a revolutionary stance and philosophical articulation. This is political action that does not require any form of martyrdom status, but political commitment, since the ontological struggle is still continuing. If the figure of the martyr was to be put in place and Biko were regarded as such, it would mean what Biko struggled for has been achieved. It also means that blackness cannot be explained and understood in its pursuit of self-realization through having to cling to the figure of the martyr. There is no worthy ancestry to hold on to in this existential crisis of blackness; the will of the dead went with the dead, who are not spared either but are still militated against even if their lives have been liquidated. What is socially dead cannot pursue the struggle in this political arena of erasure, which then justifies them being regarded as irrelevant. It is on this existential plane that they should not be remembered in the posthumous status with those who are existentially in social death. It is in this reality that the martyr is to be rejected at all costs since this means burdening the dead with a responsibility that does not concern them. The martyr, as noted earlier, is part of the human and in death they assume transcendence that can be claimed and justified on ontological lines that are absent from the socially dead subject – the black.

The politicization of blackness is all that is left and this does not rely on having to evoke the figure of the martyr. Biko here is the politicizing subject and should not be remembered through annual commemoration, but should be engaged in the everyday practices of political life. This negates the preoccupation with the figure of the martyr, since such a figure in the present moment of the political will stop any form of thought at the level of subjectivity because memory will prevail. There is not even a need to mourn, but to continue the struggle against the politics of sentiment and romanticization that border on the obscenity of forgetting. The figure of the martyr is a depoliticized figure. This is based on the logic that it is death in a form of becoming. It is in this logic that the politics of becoming are those of seeing and being destined for the future – "the future" as in having another life. How can that which has never been become transformed to that which is to be?

Therefore, it means death is transacted with life in the quest for martyrdom. There is nothing extraordinary about the death of Biko, and it should not be romanticized in any form. The black body is denied and suppressed – its very own crisis being the demand of humanity. In doing so, this crisis is ignored and the state of death intensifies. This is a form of elimination and destruction. The ontological dynamic of obliteration pervades, and in no way can there be any form of martyrdom. This is the body that cannot transcend death – the end of life – to another form of paradise. The black body's ontological status is penetrated to such an extent that it penetrates the state of ontology to understand the non-ontological status of the black body. Gordon (1995, 104) argues that: "[F]rom the racist standpoint, the black body as embodied in lack is a body of raw desire emanating away from itself." The black body is the body that is wrapped in desire to frustrate desire (Gordon 1995). And still, this reveals the state of understanding martyrdom, and martyrdom cannot originate even if the black body were to kill itself. More troubling: What is death to what is already dead and what significance, or value perhaps, does that have?

In other words, to be a subject is to live and to be an object is to die. The destruction of the black body has been a given, the black body being the possession of the empire. The ontological difference of blacks differs from any other form of body for the black body is that of the extraordinary affair. According to Gordon (1995), there is absence of being or ontology in the black. Suicide bombing for and/or against that which does not exist or lacks human essence reaches another meaning of death. This is not the meaning of something emerging, but the amplification of what is being normalized – that is, the death of the black is normal and does not rouse any form of agency. This is the death of the already dead and this also implies that the martyr cannot be a thing or being that has not existed. The absence of ontology means the condemned of the earth, who are absent in the world. A martyr is a *mythe fixe* in stature, that which is depoliticized.

The Outlawed in the Racist State

In what follows, the figure of the outlawed in the clutches of the racist state will be engaged and the legitimacy of the state in creating criminality, whereas it is criminal itself, will be questioned. According to Althusser (1971, 137) "the state is explicitly conceived as a repressive apparatus." If the conception of the racist state is to be understood in this light, it means that it is worse than the state that Althusser had in mind. Warren (2018, 62) is right to ask: "How exactly does the law produce and reproduce forms of terror that are ontological – meaning laws that sustatin the metaphysical holocaust?" Indeed, Althusser is closer to the conception of the racist state when he regards the state as the "repressive machine." But Warren (2018), in precise terms, shows how the law is grounded in the very idea of ontological diference. It is this difference that makes the black to be a thing, nothing, none-thing before the law. It is the ontological difference itself that sustains the law as Warren states, and this is the manner in which blackness is excluded from the domain of being. This is the basis through which the state metes out oppression. To ensure its repression, the state in the Althusserian sense takes the form of Repressive State Apparatus and also the Ideological State Apparatus. The former functions by means of violence, while the latter functions by means of ideology. The racist state – that is, the apartheid state and also the post-1994 liberal constitutional state – constitutes both functionalities, since they are antiblack. The co-functionality of violence and ideology keeps the naked force of the racist state intact in order to justify itself. The racist state therefore assumes the high moral ground by criminalizing those who resist its practices. To resist such a state is to then become the figure of the outlawed, and Biko is one such subject. The outlawed subject is defined by Anidjar thus:

> [T]he outside of law as that which exceeds the law, excluded from the law by the law, and understood in a manner more general than individual or specific individuals or outlaws, but rather as a *special* figure, the name even of a domain or sphere located out of the law.
> (Anidjar 2004, 41)

The racist state is its own problem. Its functionality (violence and ideology) is highly likely to produce its own fantasy and obsession – the outlawed – its own problem. In this instance the racist state does existentially negate the ontology of blackness, in that there is no way that blackness can claim resurrection and affirm demands to be human. Of course, the racist state in its functionality does not want or anticipate the creation of the figure of the outlawed. It is the state that requires obedience and complicity. Returning to Althusser's Repressive State Apparatus and Ideological State Apparatus, the representation of the outlawed takes the form of language. The racist state represents and is represented in positive terms in its justification of the outlawed and this, in the form of language, (re)produces violence and ideology. The outlawed, the obsession and fetish of the racist state is defamed, conspired against and criminalized through the medium of language. This language as the regime of truth is in fact a symbolic order that is absolute and beyond challenge. To challenge such language is to play in the domain of the outlawed, if not becoming outlawed at all.

The outlawed are people who are said to have no interest in playing by the rules of the state (Barnard 2008). The outlawed existence, imagined or real, is something that justifies the excess of power of the racist state, power that at times can be pursued and exercised to suspend law. The outlawed, from the articulation of the racist state, is an entity non-existent at the ontological level, which is to say that the outlaw is not a human being. The construction of the outlawed and Biko in this regard is the expression of the racist state itself – its practices (violence and ideology) – to negate the essence of what it casts out of humanity – the black. Also, with regard to apartheid as "a crime against humanity" it is essential to add that it is a sadistic conception of the state, one that is ontologically corrupt. The sadistic trope of apartheid and its ontological corruption, as opposed to viewing it as a crime against humanity, is something that Biko aimed at. That is, these two conceptions unravel the racist state and they are the terms through which the racist state should be engaged. It is these two conceptions that lie at the heart of the construction of the outlawed, and Biko's body was judged on the grounds of the full might of the racist state in its obsession with the outlawed. Biko is the outlawed and, as Anidjar (2004, 42) shows, "the outlaw, is the inhuman." The construction of the outlawed is the signification of the racist state upon the raced black body, in this case Biko, in the realm of blackness. The blackness of Biko strips him of all that is human and is signified in ontologically void terms as the outlawed. This form of signification is embedded in racist *telos* within which the racist state expresses itself in the largesse – the law. The understanding of the racist state in this register is to account for the fact that what it appears to be is not what it is – that is, the crime against humanity is some form of moral blameworthiness that needs to be resolved by some ethical demands. This is not the racist state that Biko the outlawed subject engages, but one that needs to take account of sadism against blacks and ontological corruption that de-ontologizes blackness.

For the racist state to refer to Biko as a terrorist is a very symbolic order of language and as such is the self-justification of violence and ideology. This language of the racist state actually means that the outlawed should be eliminated, as the apartheid state did to Biko. The naming of the outlawed by the racist state creates the anti-sublime substance that is barricaded and targeted as an enemy (Coleman 2003). The injustices committed in the naming and identification of the outlawed cannot be regarded as injustices. The naming of the outlawed is violence and no matter how criminalized that violence, it cannot be brought against the state – that is, the racist state cannot subject itself to the laws it makes. Language is here a racist signifier that makes a threat to the racist not to allow any outlaw, since the outlaw will contaminate the very racist infrastructure that sustains the racist state and its asymmetric ontologies.

In acting against the outlawed, the racist state is itself an outlaw, but is not represented as such since it is the racist state that possesses the language of who is an outlaw and who is a citizen. The racist state is what Agamben (2005) regards as the state of exception, where the state can make, repeal and suspend laws at absolute will. "Outlawing is outside law, since it contravenes the ethical imperative to see the invisible, and also inside law, since it enables and conditions this very imperative – the censure is at the very heart of law" (Warren 2018, 71). It is in this state of exception that the outlaw can be constructed from the wildest fantasies of its logic, and in this case – Biko as a terrorist who is perceived as a threat to the apartheid order – a disorder par excellence. The racist state *qua* state of exception has the prerogative to move, remove, and erase what it languages as the outlaw. The construction of the outlawed is the active process that is "activated, reformulated and remade" (Anidjar 2004, 39). Biko takes the racist state to task by making it the outlaw, and this act makes the state intensify its justification through ideology and violence. Biko nevertheless stands in forceful opposition by insisting on exposing the racist state for what it is. The act of language requires silence on the part of the outlawed, meaning that the outlawed has no language against the racist state. Only the latter has such a language due to its possession of violence and ideology. In addition to silence, the racist state requires obedience and complicity, and this is something that Biko defied as he pursued the opposite line of the political, the outlawed, but not the outlawed that he chose, the one that the racist state attributed to him. The elimination of the outlawed by the racist state is seen as a good deed of preserving of good over evil.

The outlawed is seen as the enemy of the state, and the convention of the state in the act of war where it is challenged by another state or states, changes and not even in a civil war fashion, but where the state engages in conventional warfare against its own citizens. But by the mere fact that the outlawed is outside the conception of citizens, it is outside the state, meaning that it is situated within the state but, paradoxically, outside it. What is argued by Coetzee (2007, 4) is that "[t]he law protects the law-abiding citizen." Being outside the state, the justification of the racist state *qua* law solidifies the basis of conventional warfare. This of course cannot be an ethical or moral crisis since the outlawed is not a citizen and not the responsibility of the state, but something to be erased by the state. This is because the outlawed, in the sight of the law of the racist state, is the enemy of the state. Coetzee (2007, 4) amplifies this by saying "there is no law to protect the outlaw, the man [sic] who takes up arms against his [sic] own state, that is to say, the state that claims him [sic] as its own." What does not appear in this account is a case where the state is not being armed against, but arms itself against its citizens and arbitrarily refers to them as outlaws. This is to say that what is not engaged by Coetzee is the conception of the racist state.

The conception of law, no matter how empty it is of justice, is something that the racist state is obsessed with. The existence and maintenance of the racist state is reasoned on and derived from law – that is, the law is the informer and the racist state informs the law. The presence of law permits the "reason" of the racist state. It is the racist logic that is based on injustice, deceit, oppression, and dehumanization. Indeed, what can such a state be if not the apartheid state, and also the present state under the mask of "new South Africa"? It is in South Africa where the racist state should be understood on the basis of the past and the present entangled. This should be understood in relation to the existential predicament called blackness. Blackness in apartheid was not in power and it was oppressed, and blackness in the "new South Africa" is at the helm of political power and is still oppressed. In this present regime, blackness is in full service of the white racist order. The racist state is a clear testimony that it has metamorphosed, since blacks are still a defeated group, with few at the master's table.

The racist state creates oppression and alienation in order to create the outlawed. Biko found himself in this existential position but he did not give in, and the rebelling spirit is the very thing that makes him the outlawed. Why is Biko the outlawed? The cogent answer is that Biko is black and on top of that he refused to be disciplined by the racist state. This is evident from the philosophical meditations of Black Consciousness, which oppose the conception of the racist state. The racist state for its survival needs to negate the outlawed. The outlawed here is understood in the realm of the raced body – the black body in the antiblack existential condition – the body of Biko outlawed by the racist apartheid state and bastardized by the post-1994 "new South African" state with its antiblackness. Biko as the outlawed subject is a creation of the racist state. In no way did Biko refer to himself as the outlaw; he was created. The racist state tries to convince society that what opposes it is a greater evil that must be exorcized and destroyed.

It means that through language, the outlaw is from the beginning excommunicated and marginalized. Even before Biko was signified as the outlaw under Section 6 of the Terrorist Act, he was already an outlaw due to the fact that blackness is the outlawed subject and subjectivity.

This is the nature of the apartheid state that black rule under the ANC has reformed, rather than destroyed. Such a reform is a modicum of change, one that does not seek to destroy the foundational and constitutive basis of the racist state but to continue with its sadism and corruption in a form of a neo-apartheid project. In this project the black face is in power and blackness has to face the very same ontological position and existential struggles. By the mere fact that Biko was outlawed by the racist state (apartheid), he is still not exonerated by the post-1994 state that continues the othering of blackness as its white masters did. The black reality is still that of landlessness, indignity, humiliation, and suffering, the very corruption of the being of blackness and, to be frank, the erasure of being. The logic of the racist state is making sure that nothing challenges it. For the possibility of the racist state being challenged or its paranoia about being challenged, it creates the self-justification of acting on whatever means necessary in the liquidation of the outlawed. The same can be said of the post-1994 liberal constitutional state, which is against blacks. By putting blacks in the same existential crisis, it dehumanizes them as apartheid did and as the post-1994 "new South Africa" is doing.

Biko is still in the same scale as those who are constructed by the racist state's fantasy as non-humans. In no way did the racist state's fantasy think that Biko fought for what is just. Biko, the outlawed *qua* non-human, does not count for anything. Indeed, the racist state cannot be expected to understand Biko's plight since he is diametrically opposed to the fantasy of this state. The manner of opposition is coined as antagonism, which then creates the figure of the enemy of the state. The outlawed is not a legitimate level of citizenship. To be the outlawed is to be exterior to the state and, at worst, its enemy. "The enemy, the other, would also be the excluded one" (Anidjar 2004, 37). The outlawed as the enemy of the state is a mythical and obsessive construction of the other – a fetish actualized to reality – the very *imaginaire* and perfomativity of sadistic violence. The outlawed is a fugitive whom the state must hunt, track, capture, torture, prosecute and even kill. "If the enemy comes to be as that which is excluded from the law, it is also because the enemy exceeds the limits according to which the law seeks to situate, localize, and ultimately seize him [sic]" (Anidjar 2004, 40). So, the outlawed is the enemy of the state and the latter is unlikely to make concessions to what it regards as a threat to it (perceived or real).

The qualification, therefore, exists (by means of law) to criminalize the outlaw, where the imposition of law should be applied to the outlawed, even if this has to be arbitrary. The law has the power to define legality and illegality, to determine admission and prohibition, to offer rewards and punishments, and also to determine life and death. The outlaw is obviously on the negative side of the law and there are no concessions that can be made in such a subject position. In short, the law is the power that determines, defines, and prescribes *what is* and *what is not*. This is the power that means law is law, the absolute bounty of the racist state from its accumulation and extraction from the lives of black bodies.

The law determines the fate of the outlawed. Even if this means killing the outlawed, under law this is not lawless but lawful. What is revealed here is that the outlawed has no recourse in the face of law. Even if the outlawed can have or demonstrate legitimacy that amounts to some form of legal status, or something that can put the law into question, the very existence of the outlawed in the face of the racist state rules out the possibility of taking a stand against the law. The outlawed has no chance of becoming compatible with the racist state. For the outlaw to be compatible means that the racist state will lose its form and character – that is, the law. The law is there to render the outlawed the outlawed, the subject that is liable for disciplining and penalty. For there to be the construction of the outlawed, the law must assume full presence and functionality as the creator of law. Illegality is formed from illegality. As Anidja (2004) points out, the law is where the enemy is identified and executed. If the racist state is law, it is criminal on the basis that it criminalizes blackness, not because of the transgression of law but because of blackness. So, by the way the law of the racist state positions blackness it is criminal, but the paradox is that those who make and enforce law can never be called the outlawed, even if their criminality is excessive. By the manner of their constitutiveness and privilege they are law, and what is law cannot be outlawed. That is to say, the law cannot be outlawed even if it acts like an outlaw.

The Tyranny of the Paradigm of Policing

The way blackness is positioned in relation to the state apparatus –
and more specifically one of its arms that is the point of focus here,
the police – has been problematic. To police is to control black bodies
that are already implicated as being criminal. The police do not have
a relationship that is of service to blacks; the relationship is that of
force. The police should not be understood in isolation, but as the
constitutive part of the state apparatus and its structural mechanics
that are antiblack. According to the power vested in them by the
state, police can employ the means of violence. Martinot and Sexton
(2003) argue that the state gives the police permission to brutalize,
hunt and even kill fugitives who happen to be black. As the state
apparatus, police are the structure of wanton violence "whose source
is the paradigm of policing" (Martinot and Sexton 2003, 172). The
paradigm of policing is the paradigm of the state. Both Martinot
and Sexton strongly argue that police violence is the institutionalization of white supremacy. The paradigm of policing allows police
to be violent, and the nature of this violence is both systematic and
systemic. This is not the violence of the police *per se;* it is that of the
antiblack world against blacks.

> Those who wish to command must constantly invoke violence, if not
> directly, then in displaced or mimic form. It is the invocation – above
> all, by those entrusted with the *impossibility* of enforcing the law –
> with which we are concerned here: its rough play, its predilection
> for criminal fantasy, its response to the vicissitudes of state power.
> (Comaroff and Comaroff 2004, 809)

South Africa is a police state, and even under the black government
the police have been antiblack. The security branch – that is, the
police *qua* military arm of apartheid – existed above the law and were
a deadly force against those who opposed and resisted their dehumanization by apartheid. As Comaroff and Comaroff note, the security
branch was seen as the ethical enforcer of the state in that it defended
the state against evil, namely terrorists, treason, and savage insurrection. The paradigm of policing is a racist project and blackness is
its main target and its concern. Blackness is always suspected, and
this is because blackness is criminalized and must be policed. To be
policed is to be subjected to constant violence, and this violence means

the condition of being solely identified with criminality. Blackness is placed in the wrong place in the world, and this justifies the logic of the world to be antiblack. The paradigm of policing is antiblack in the sense that blackness is a problem, a deviance to be disciplined. So, it is also in the paradigm of policing, where blackness is a pathology to be dealt with; this means dehumanization of blacks. To be against blacks by violating the existence of blacks is to be antiblack.

There is no law, and there never has been, that is made specifically to protect blacks. Blacks, being vulnerable due to their existential nakedness in the form of absence in the ontological schema, are the subject exposed to police violence. The very form of self-defense by blacks from the paradigm of policing is a crime. The attempt of blacks to resist police violence is criminalized, and this resistance can be used as a means to accuse blacks of being violent toward the police, thus providing a justification for the violation of blacks by police. This paradigm enacts itself by perpetually putting blackness in a state of fear since it is the paradigm of terror. In this state of affairs, blackness, by the very nature of being criminalized, is always on the wrong side of the law, which the paradigm of policing enforces on behalf of the state apparatus. To be on the wrong side simply means that the paradigm of policing should enforce discipline. This is in the form of the law of imposition, a law that can even be improvised by the police in their role of enforcing law upon that which is outlawed. As Biko (2004) states, the paradigm of policing is indeed a tyranny, in that the police possess and execute power as they see fit. The police use phallic power "to determine the lives and deaths of others" (Comaroff and Comaroff 2004, 807). The existential condition where blackness is located in all this is where police impunity reigns, and the nature of law is that which does not apply, since there is no law that can serve the outlawed. The tyranny of the paradigm of policing is that police violate the existence of blackness. Police are, as Martinot and Sexton (2003, 171) state, "duty bound by impunity itself." This means police are the law and the law is the police. Martinot (2003, 211) amplifies this by saying that "any police directive translates into law." Trask (2004) adds to this by stating that police in their impunity have power over blackness. They have, as Trask (2004, 11) notes, the "[p]ower to define and confine." As testimony to this, Biko was attacked by the multifaceted nature of violence, to which he did not concede, but against which he acted with formidable force. Biko's life "was cut short by a cruel act of violence" (Lalu 2004, 108).

The rule of law and the maintenance of law and order in the structural positionality of blackness as the criminalized other (the outlaw) brings to the fore the ethical crisis that shows the sadistic relations of violence. The paradigm of policing is war, and it is coined as such, in that its efforts at making its violence evasive and in projecting itself as a moralizing factor – that is, "the war against crime" and "war on drugs" – are violent statements that can be easily used to justify or actually to mean "war against blackness." In point of fact, that has been the order of things, as war is incessantly declared against blackness. The rule of law and the maintenance of law and order within the paradigm of policing are fraudulent when blackness is introduced. They are scandalous, and fall within a skewed conception of communal life, in which the notion of community is the displacement and dispossession of others; and the police ensure that this Manichean reality is kept intact (Maldonado-Torres 2008). If the rule of law and maintenance of law and order are central in the paradigm of policing, then it means that there cannot be any ethical nature when it comes to blackness. The paradigm of policing is said to serve and protect society by maintaining law and order. Police are in the matrix of violent social (dis)order, and, as Comaroff and Comaroff (2004, 803) point out, "police come, in the public imagination, to embody a nervous state under pressure." In this state, the police response to wanton violence is the excessive maintenance of law and order. This ethical pronouncement, which is, of course, a scandal, is made to conceal the structural operations of the paradigm of policing. It is in this scandalous condition that blackness is fixated by the obsessive imaginations of the crime that needs police, and, for that matter, a militarized police force.

Police violence, as the existence of white power against blackness, projects itself as that which cannot be criminalized, for it in itself militates against that which is criminalized. Biko (2004) is correct in stating: "In South Africa whiteness has always been associated with police brutality and intimidation." It is, therefore, expected that there will be no criminalization of police as the servants of the white supremacist order, because of the ethical scandal of the rule of law and the maintenance of law and order. In a state that is antiblack, it is clear that what is being served and privileged is whiteness. As such, police under this white supremacist order are also its extension. They are under the white supremacy that ignores and negates the ethical demands of blackness. There cannot be any ethical demands for the police, but the call for the police to cease to exist, since they have the very brutality of blackness.

> The dichotomy between a white ethical dimension and its irrelevance to the violence of police profiling is the very structure of racialization today. It is a twin structure, a regime of violence that operates in two registers, terror and seduction into the fraudulent ethics of social order; a double economy of terror structured by a ritual of incessant performance.
>
> (Martinot and Sexton 2003, 176)

In no way in the realm of policing does blackness assume the terrain of justice. The actual reality is that blackness is the very entity that is at the receiving end of the paradigm of policing, which is tyranny. The life of blackness cannot be associated with the value of justice, since it is already criminalized. Police assume the positionality of law as they determine criminality in their practices, and this is done in an arbitrary fashion, since the law ceases when blackness is confronted. So, it means that there cannot be justice for blackness as long as the paradigm of policing still exists. If the paradigm of policing is informed by antiblackness, it cannot be expected to act in the interests of blacks, but rather against blacks. The racial structure of antiblackness creates blameworthiness and sees blackness as criminal. Whenever the paradigm of policing encounters blackness, prosecution starts. Police are, in the paradigm of policing, what Maldonado-Torres (2008) refers to as a "community of masters" who determine the fate of those they dehumanize. This means that the paradigm of policing is controlled by police as a community of masters. The community of masters also assists in racial oppression, since they are the major tool of the racist order. "The unethical excess of signification is, therefore, tied to the project of creating a world to the measure of a 'community of masters'" (Maldonado-Torres 2008, 240). The very logic of a community of masters as subjects on the side of the racist order facilitates militancy of the existence of other subjects they deem criminal. For Maldonado-Torres, the value of police as a community of masters is to ensure that control, domination, and dehumanization are kept intact.

To police is not only to violate black bodies, but to affix blackness to the ontological status of being a problem. Blacks are criminals and police antagonism toward them is justified, since what is policed is a problem. To deal with a problem in this instance is to eradicate it. Biko (2004, 82–83) states that "police only need to page at random through their statute book to be able to get a law under which to charge a victim." To police blacks means to keep them at bay and to re-entrench them in a pathological state of existence. The paradigm of policing in this case should be understood as the relational capacity, something that collapses when linked to blackness. Blackness is embodied in a criminalized existence and the role of the police is to bring blackness to justice. This then means that when blackness is in an encounter with the police the prosecution has already started. The black body is itself a crime and it must be arrested, harassed, interrogated, and even executed. This is because blackness is lawlessness that invites police violence. This means that there should not be any form of resistance, but instead obedience from those who are violated. It is clear that the paradigm of policing is racist. Blacks are a crime and it follows that they are criminalized. This criminalization is rooted in the infrastructure of racism. To police means to racially target blackness. To be criminalized means that all acts of existence that pertain to blackness are crimes. Blackness is suspicion and whiteness is not. It is in the racist logic that the paradigm of policing is rooted, and this creates the criminalized and the pathologized. This means police practice is informed by the paradigm of policing and the manner in which it positions blackness is fundamentally racist.

To ensure black oppression, police must justify their employment to their masters by brutalizing black bodies. Police serve the evil system that oppresses blacks. As Biko (2004, 83) states, "[T]he philosophy behind police action in this country seems to be 'harass them! harass them!'." In Biko's thinking, police are nowhere closer to being part of law and order. Police are, in all ways, violence. They are, contrary to their propaganda, lawlessness and disorder. This discharges their racially motivated violence with honor. For, they know that their violence is the ideology of the racist order they serve. This violence is racist, since it is targeted at blacks. If police are part of the racist order they are not there to maintain law and order, but to enforce racist practices and to keep oppression intact. The lawlessness and disorder of police is such that it is from the place of blackness. When it relates to blackness the paradigm of policing cannot be that of service, but is that of force. Violence must be there to make sure that blackness is contained. Blackness is erased from that which should be served. To bring Biko into this, he was structurally positioned and he was killed by the police. As such, there should be no way of expecting the paradigm of policing in relation to blackness to be reconciled. Police serve the racist order and they must be a force against blackness, which is structurally positioned as criminality and pathology. It is the racist order that killed Biko – the police.

What does Biko mean when he says there is no such thing as the black police? Yet, serving the racist order, the order that is against blacks, there can be no such thing as the black police. In short, how can something that is antiblack be black? The very fact of black police violating a fellow black under the tyranny of the paradigm of policing is self-annihilation. When blacks serve a racist order of police that is against blacks, they are engaging in bad faith. As Gordon (1995) argues, bad faith is a flight from freedom and responsibility. It is in the context of bad faith where black police situate themselves at the side of the oppressor to oppress their fellow blacks. This means that they do not want to confront their own oppressors, but rather to assist the oppressors further in oppressing their fellow oppressed. Bad faith as an option is an escape route, but is the very option that is captivity, since blackness is still caught in the clutches of oppression. The black police try to run away from being victims of oppression and want to be its perpetrators.

Moreover, Biko's conception of the police and the paradigm that is tyranny should be thought of along the lines of bad faith, since the oppressed want to become the agents of apartheid that works against them. That is to say, in serving the racist order they are oppressing themselves. What is in the psyche of the black police is suppression of the conscious to isolate the self from reality. In the "new South African" political situation blackness is still profiled as criminality and still vulnerable as a victim of police brutality, and, more clearly, blackness still fits the profile of the criminal. In no circumstances will police raid or stop and search white people or have arbitrary access to their properties by means of raids. Their crime-combating operations leave the white *residentia* at the wayside, and these are areas that must at all costs be protected from potential criminals who are blacks. The racist logic of police in terms of profiling blackness is also evident in suspecting blacks to be foreigners, which is the reason why they must be stopped and asked to produce passports; the very act being like the apartheid passing of laws. If the people do not carry such documents, they will be arrested.

When black police brutalize other blacks, they do this with the intention of claiming superiority. According to Biko, police operate on the basis of putting blacks in perpetual fear. As Biko (2004, 83) states, "If you cannot make a man respect you, then make him fear you." The manner in which police conducted themselves in the murder of Andries Tatane and Mido Macia is the paradigm of policing in its obscene form. These two events clearly symbolize the manner in which the ontological content of blackness is an oxymoron. Andries Tatane, who was thirty-three years old, led a protest in demand of basic services in Meqheleng, Ficksburg, just for black people who were living in undignified living conditions. He was killed when police assaulted and shot him; he collapsed and died on the scene and this incident was shown in live footage. This happened on 13 April 2012, and the video footage went viral, exposing the brutal manner in which he was killed. Although this caused a brouhaha, nothing was done, as it was a black body put to death by the police. This event caused outrage where police used their paradigm of policing, something that absolves them from any kind of responsibility. None of the police could point out who shot Tatane, and their ridiculous logic was that all police were wearing helmets, so that it was difficult to point out who was responsible. Tatane's death is not extraordinary; it is the black condition, the living of everyday life. It is a life that police can take at will when they are confronted by a criminal subject that is black, and killing the black does not matter since the black is a crime. The wanton violence that surrounds and makes the black body captive to it is dramatized by the paradigm of policing. Tatane was murdered by the police, and, of course, the arrest of the police as murderers was deemed impossible and has proven to be such. The "lack of evidence" is the jurist's semantics and, on the basis of such technicism, the case will be thrown out of court. In that way, justice will be done; here, of course, justice is a semantic game among jurists where technicality takes precedence. The death of Tatane was brutal and happened in public view, but still there had to be an "investigation" into his murder. What then to expect? Even if there was an investigation, it would be of no help because the life that was put to death was not worth investigating. In other words, black life does not matter and the violence that puts it to death is left untainted. Even though there was outrage at the death of Tatane, life went back to normal because the black died and no level of moralist political rhetoric that claims to condemn police violence will help. The black died, case closed!

Another case is that of Mido Macia, a 27–year-old taxi driver from Daveyton, Ekurhuleni. On 26 February 2013, Macia was assaulted and fastened behind a police van that dragged him along the street. Macia died on 1 March while in police custody. When the post-mortem was conducted it revealed that he had sustained head injuries and internal bleeding as a result of this treatment. Police claimed that they would conduct their own second post-mortem, and, of course, this one contradicted the findings of the first one. In both cases (Tatane and Macia) what emerges is that police brutality is the killing of the black, and this is a form of ritual. "This ritual is performed in public" (Martinot 2003, 205). In the case of both Macia and Tatane, police were suspended; a banal outcome that clearly demonstrates that they will get away with murder and return to their jobs after the case is concluded. What to expect when the black dies? Nothing! Blackness does not correspond with justice, so justice is always denied since blackness is criminality.

Biko could not escape the paradigm of policing, and his life was liquidated by it. Biko was arrested, driven naked for hundreds of kilometres, interrogated for many hours, assaulted, and put to death. This, of course, was the act of the police, who had the black body to objectify. Objectification is breaking the black body and destroying it from the bone to the marrow and even to the soul. The paradigm of policing has been that of blacks dying in detention, as with Biko, and after that there is no justice. The fatal injuries that Biko's body sustained during his detention are still a mystery. "Beatings and other torture resulting in deaths were safely, symbolically, locked into a protective conspiracy between police witnesses and the state" (Wilson 1991, 72). Tatane and Macia, like their predecessor Biko, were killed by the police, and the result of this killing means there is no justice. Police got away with murder. The two cases, Tatane and Macia, show what police brutality is when it comes to the black body. This is interesting in that it was black police officers against blacks. I have drawn examples of defenseless victims to show how police violence was indeed excessive and sadistic. To claim that police transformation is a concern borders on the obscene, in the sense that they are still the instrument of violence. It is not enough to change police and call for them to stop brutality, enforce human rights, and adhere to the Constitution, without really thinking about the end of the paradigm of policing – that is, the very ending of policing itself. The very nature of the police has been violence against blacks, so that violence has to end:

it cannot be changed. What should exist is the end of policing – the very thing that is violence itself. The destruction of the racist state will mean the destruction of the police, and the racist paradigm that informs it.

White Liberals in Black Affairs

One of the main important and historical significances of Black Consciousness is the de-linking from white liberals. What remains known and banal is that white liberals become worried and cry for Armageddon when blacks assert their own political register, meaning, of course, that the liberals lose the power of being able to control and manage blacks. By the very fact that whiteness created blackness, it saw itself fit to speak and act on behalf of blackness. So, if blackness has to undergo self-definition and self-construction, it has to de-link from whiteness and to chart its own political register. Biko (2004, 68), as the outlawed subject with a capacity to judge, asks: "[W]ho are the white liberals in South Africa?" In the very same subject position of a judge he answers in a pointed and affirmative manner thus:

> It is a curious bunch of non-conformists who explain their partici-pation in negative terms; that bunch of do-gooders that goes under all sorts of names – liberals, leftists, etc. These are the people who argue that they are not responsible for white racism and the country's "inhumanity to the black man" [sic]; these are the people who claim that they too feel the oppression just as acutely as the blacks and therefore should be jointly involved in the black man's [sic] struggle for a place under the sun; in short, these are the people who say that they have black souls wrapped up in white skins.
>
> (Biko 2004, 69)

Biko's exposé of the scandal of white liberals meddling in black affairs is profound. This is an indication that whites should keep out of black affairs, since their participation is problematic; blacks and whites are not on the same relational side of oppression. The scandal of white liberals meddling in black affairs is by its very nature oppressive, since blacks are made to be absent because whites act on their behalf. Being acted upon essentially means that blacks are denied engaging oppression in their own terms, and therefore it stands to reason that the participation of white liberals in black affairs is something that borders on hypocrisy. As Biko (2004, 70) points out: "[M]ost white dissident groups are aware of the power wielded by the white power structure." This awareness actually means that white liberals know where they stand, and that standing is, of course, different from that of blackness. As Hudson (2012, 4) argues, "there is asymmetry – 'whiteness' is the master signifier and it has both white and black subjects in its grip." For Hudson, whiteness possesses wholeness, self-control, and sufficiency and has something to hold on to – and that is blackness. But blackness as something held by whiteness has itself nothing to hold on to; it is *without*.

White liberals stand on the side of privilege that is provided by the white power structure, and that is why there were no radicalized demands for the end of the white power structure. The argument here is that white privilege is tied to whiteness as an identity, and white privilege should be understood, from the positionality of black subjects, side by side with their own dispossession. White privilege benefits from black dispossession, and it is in the condition of dispossession that black subjects depend on whiteness for survival. Therefore, even if there is some sort of dependability between white subjects and black subjects, what must be made clear is that this dependability is asymmetrical. The racist logic of white privilege and black dispossession remains profound, and this is something that whiteness will never end, since this would be the very ending of whiteness itself. So, if this asymmetry were to be obliterated, it would mean the obliteration of whiteness itself. Whiteness as a dense ontological position operates on the basis of solidarity. Biko (2004, 98) confirms this: "[T]he overall success of white power structure has been managing to bind whites together in defense of the *status quo*." If the political act of speaking on behalf of blacks were to be eliminated, this would be detrimental to white liberals, so they have to engage in hypocrisy; knowing that if blacks were to speak for themselves they would raise discomfort by antagonizing the white power that intrinsically serves white liberals.

> Why do they persist in talking to the blacks? Since they are aware that the problem in this country is white racism, why do they not address themselves to the white world? Why do they insist on talking to blacks?
>
> (Biko 2004, 70)

The location of blackness outside whiteness in terms of the politics of opposition is the very thing that white liberals do not want. The very co-opting of black radical demands within the white liberal consensus is the very absence of blackness. This is because white liberals determine what blackness can and cannot do. It means that blackness has to obey white liberals. The very act of blackness acting by itself is something that white liberals did not see coming. When blacks were tired of white parenthood, tutelage, and control they were accused of being ungrateful by "putting the white liberals out of work" (Manganyi 1973, 17). It was, of course, not expected for blacks to act on their own and to take charge of their own affairs. Biko's criticism of white liberals still stands. As Manganyi insists, the kind of reaction by white liberals to blacks liberating themselves is to be expected, as white liberals are preoccupied with narcissism, a form of self-love in which whites think that blacks are nothing without them.

> Finding their way their own way was itself an act of liberation, but it was also a pragmatic expedient against, it was thought, the diversionary effect of white leadership, and even participation, in black movements. Here, again, the movement presents itself as a secession from a world that rejects, or frustrates, or cannot comprehend its concerns and needs, but the secession precedes the shattering of that world and the creation of another.
>
> (Nolutshungu 1982, 152)

The rejection by blackness of white liberals is the self-definition and self-construction of blacks for themselves and in themselves. That is to say, blackness posits itself as the antidote to the paternalism of white liberalism and the totality of whiteness, and by asserting the negation of whiteness as the standard bearer of values. As such, there cannot be Black Consciousness if blacks are acted upon by whites and are given an ontological outlook that is alien to the existential conditions of blackness. The role of white liberals was to ensure that blacks are engaging in politics which are outside their lived experience, the very act of alienation. In doing this, they ensure that whiteness affirms its totality against blackness. This also explains why blacks cannot be left on their own to determine the political terrain in their own terms, but are rather disciplined by liberal vices to keep engaging in a false political terrain.

The self-definition of blackness and its self-constriction called for blacks not to be acted upon by white liberals. Blackness was the negation of the negativity of whiteness, and, as Manganyi (1973) states, that blacks have to change the negative sociological schema imposed to them by whites. The assertion of blackness by Black Consciousness means that blacks "implicitly rejected the conventional racial nomenclature, particularly the label 'non-white'" (Nolutshungu 1982, 151). The main reason for this rejection was that blackness is something that is the negative of white, and, for the positive value to be achieved in blackness, whiteness should be aspired to. It is on this very basis that white liberals arrogated themselves as spokespersons of blacks and believed that blacks should mimic them.

Blacks are in themselves blacks and by definition those who define themselves outside the self-imposed normative framework of whiteness. Blackness cannot be imposed by white liberals who are not at the receiving end of oppression. "The black people share the experience of having been abused and exploited *while this is not the case for white liberals*" (Manganyi 1973, 19 [emphasis added]). Blackness on its own determines its own political register and political demands that white liberals will resist, since they have a lot at stake and a lot to lose. The political register of Black Consciousness means that blacks did not want to define their demands and grievances through the language and categories of their oppressor, since this is not liberation at all (Nolutshungu 1982). This is very important, in that blacks themselves made their own discovery in terms of the route that can chart the terrain of liberation and action for themselves. The political register of Black Consciousness means that blacks make their own demands and in their own terms, since the oppression that afflicts them concerns them and not white liberals. Biko totally expels white liberals from black affairs when he writes:

> The liberal must fight his [sic] own and for himself [sic]. If they are true liberals they must realize that they themselves are oppressed, and that they must fight their own freedom and not that of nebulous "they" with whom they can hardly claim identification.
>
> (Biko 2004, 72)

This very act of expulsion is that of creating the sites of imaginaries that blackness must engage. The problem, as Biko states, is racism that affects blacks. Racism does not affect white liberals, since they are located at the very structure of whiteness. This structure does not have any negative consequences for whiteness, but it has the opposite and dire effects in relation to blackness. "The biggest mistake the black world ever made was to assume that whoever opposed apartheid was an ally" (Biko 2004, 68). It is here where it is clarified that blacks are in fact on their own, and the struggle is theirs. This affirms the irrelevance of white liberals, since their very participation, as stated earlier, is the oppression of blacks.

There is a tendency for white liberalism still to refuse to bow down to Biko's expulsion. In this situation, whiteness still re-affirms itself and does not heed anything that renders its participation in black affairs a scandal. Whiteness adheres to the call for ethical demands of belonging to the black struggle, and seeing that as an ethical act for the collective good. The issue of whiteness has been taken by whites themselves, and in no way is it suggested here that it will remedy the existential conditions of blacks. As such, whiteness should be on its own, where whiteness speaks for itself. If it does not speak for itself, whiteness will be caught in what Alcoff (1991) describes as the problem of speaking for others. As Alcoff (1991, 6) warns, "speaking for others is arrogant, vain, unethical, and politically illegitimate." So, the positionality of whiteness is not in any way fit to speak on behalf of blacks and dictate to them how they should and should not engage the issue of race. This even includes how blacks should engage the post-1994 reality, since the reality of whiteness and that of blackness is not the same even if the idea of the rainbow nation can be propagated. The premise made by Alcoff is essential in this regard:

> Rituals of speaking are politically constituted by power relations of domination, exploitation, and subordination. Who is speaking, who is spoken of, and who listens is a result, as well as an act, of political struggle. To the extent that this context bears on meaning, and meaning in some sense the object of truth, we cannot make an epistemic evaluation of the claim without simultaneously assessing the politics of the situation.
>
> (Alcoff 1991, 15)

So it is important to emphasize that whiteness must speak of itself and for itself. If whiteness speaks for blacks, then it entrenches itself and negates the lived experiences of blacks by imposing its own distortions on what is fair and just to blacks. Whiteness by its very nature is the antithesis of blackness. The phenomenology of blackness is collapsed by whiteness. It is still contended here that Biko's criticism *à la* Black Consciousness is still relevant and still stands, even in the post-1994 era. Whiteness, by redeeming itself and affirming itself as the ethical practice of critiquing white privilege and racism – that is, whiteness as anti-racist practice – cannot be different, even in its mutation of total complicity with white liberals who were at the receiving end of Biko's expulsion. Even the harsh criticism of white anti-racists against whiteness, its racist infrastructure and racism should not be seen as an ethical demand or ethico-politico practice from the vantage point of blackness. The position of white anti-racist practice seeks again, like the liberal hypocrisy, to speak on behalf of blacks, providing a caveat that its positionality is that of totality. Its ethical demands apply as if they have black demands at the center, whereas this is not the case. This positionality is fundamentally rejected if it is in that posture. What it should assume is the positionality of whiteness for itself and by itself. The critique of whiteness by whiteness should not be seen as that which will produce outcomes that will apply and be beneficial to blackness.

What is of interest is the appropriation of Biko by the post-1994 white anti-racist project. As Hook (2011), who is white of course, states, the name of Biko has become the master-signifier in South Africa. Biko is, according to Hook (2011, 19), "an emblem of credibility, as a marker of moral, political and cultural capital." The status of Biko in these forms is not that of the revolutionary *per se*, but that of the martyr with some form of historical currency. This status is problematic in the sense that Biko belongs nowhere in the terrain of blackness making radical demands that even expose the very scandal of white liberalism and its radical version of the white anti-racist project. The Biko being argued for here is the one who is outlawed and the one who, in the register of white liberalism, is a black – the bane that exposes white invisibility in the structure and function of oppression. In terms of the invisibility of whiteness, Mngxitama writes:

Whiteness is so pervasive it has become invisible, that is to say normalized – the "normative state of existence." This normative state of existence is also a powerful tool of silencing. "Why can't we all just get along?" someone asks innocently, while another claims that "colour is just skin deep, we are all human beings ultimately." Blacks are under pressure to accept this, in fact we are heroic when

we accept our common humanity, and thereby fail to bracket off
whiteness and make obvious what it actually is.

(Mngxitama 2009, 16)

Hook (2011) attempts to expose the visibility of whiteness that hides
through invisibility behind the anti-racist posture. The visibility of
whiteness exposes what whiteness is, and that is the very thing that
whiteness can be separated from – that is, what Hook refers to as
values that border on brutality, inhumanity, and capacious violence.
Of course, these are kept by whiteness when it projects itself as the
standard of beauty, virtue, and morality that blackness must aspire
to. As in the liberal political practice, blacks are supposed to engage
oppression passively and through the eyes of whiteness. It is Biko's
critique that renders white liberalism visible, and therefore it is the
contention here that the white anti-racist project should be stripped
of its hypocrisy in claiming to fight on behalf of the black. It should
be located within whiteness only, and for the interests of whites. As
Hook (2011, 24) puts it, "Biko's arguments offer whites no distance
from whiteness, no possibility of dis-identification."

Truscott and Marx (2011) accuse Hook of homogenizing
whiteness and also its anti-racist strategies. They argue for the
emphasis of understanding "the ethical paradox post-apartheid
whiteness must traverse" (Truscott and Marx 2011, 482). It needs
to be highlighted that Biko's criticism of white liberals and their
expulsion from black affairs was a confrontation with whiteness in
totality. The positionality of Biko as the outlawed subject was not
an interest in trying to understand the complexities and the differences of whiteness, but seeing whiteness as an affair problematic to
blackness. The problematic of whiteness in its anti-racist project is
the very nature of controlling blackness as something that should
not imagine itself outside whiteness. What Truscott and Marx fail
to acknowledge is that whiteness in relation to blackness assumes
homogeneity. That is, whiteness is superiority while blackness is
inferiority, and these are dichotomies that reproduce themselves
in invisible forms as they are not verbalized as forms of discursive
practices. This is to say that the white anti-racist project, as with
white liberalism, still oppresses blackness because it wants to act
on behalf of it. In their insistence on the heterogeneity of whiteness,
both Truscott and Marx (2011, 485) state that there are other
forms of white anti-racist efforts that need to be acknowledged "as
a step in the right direction." This is true, but only in white political

circles, and not in the black existential crisis in which blackness must wage its own struggles against racism and the ontological weight of whiteness. However, it is important to note that this closing remark by Truscott and Marx is troubling in the sense that it seems that whiteness is the solution, and it needs to be followed in the so-called right direction. The righteousness of such a direction seems scandalous in the sense that it is not clear where the direction is heading, by whom and for whose benefit. It is only acceptable here if such a right direction excludes blacks, who have a different utopic register.

The very white anti-racist project is a white project, and, even though it aims to absolve itself by writing off its whiteness, it is still white. In no way should there be a dialogue, since blackness is still outside the realm of power relations that affirm whiteness. As Wilderson (2008, 101) states, "white politicos had been radicalized by Black Consciousness' criticism of their liberal hypocrisy." It is only when antagonized that whiteness will claim credibility by distancing itself from the brutality of what whiteness is. This is done deliberately to render whiteness invisible and to still emphasize it as moral virtue. Vice (2010) asks a question on how whites live in South Africa, which she refers to as a strange place where whites are products of apartheid and still benefiting from it. Vice (2010, 331) claims that "the problem in white South Africa is not just with being *white*, but being white *South African*" [emphasis original]. But then the opposite is true in that being white is to be structurally positioned in relation to the accumulation and preserving of privilege. This cannot be seen as something problematic since this is the betterment and protection of white privilege. Whites do not feel bad that privilege is bent in their favour and blacks are left wanting, and their existential condition is a crisis. Vice is wrong to assume that privilege is something that contaminates whites and thus they must have a sense of shame and guilt. White privilege is not a moral burden, hence the reaction of white subjects when it is threatened. According to Vice, white privilege is non-voluntary in its origins, and it creates a situation where white subjects can choose to embrace or reject it. This is what Vice proposes as a way in which whiteness can rehabilitate itself from its contamination by white privilege:

> One of the tasks of white people is to engage with their selves, and if the theses of habitual white privilege and moral damage are correct

there is certainly enough work to do. Our thoughts are heavy with whitely assumptions, and so they would be morally risky, at best, to utter publicly in as racially charged a space as South Africa. Given the necessary self-vigilance and double thinking imposed by knowledge of whiteliness, being careful in this context does not seem cowardly or disengaged. Rather, the care stems from a recognition of the moral complexities and potential for mistakes, which would entrench the very habits from which one is trying to become disentangled. We would, instead, express our attachment to justice through a commitment to a private project of self-improvement, recognizing the moral damage done to the self by being in the position of oppressor.

(Vice 2010, 334–335)

What Vice proposes does not engage with how privilege is dismantled, but it is the moral exercise of making whiteness more humane. It does not matter whether whiteness engages or disengages, but it is important to stress that this does not say anything about how the privilege should be destroyed. For Vice to call for whites to refrain from airing their views and withdrawing from the political discourse is something that absolves whites from responsibility. The form of life that Vice is proposing for white subjects is to live as quietly and decently as possible. The white privilege that informs part of the existence of whiteness is left largely intact, so that it reproduces itself. No matter how intensified the criticism of whiteness is, it cannot bring it to an end since that is the end of whiteness itself. In simple words, white anti-racists cannot commit suicide. Doing away with oppression of blacks simply means destroying white privilege. Of course, this is often rejected even by those who claim to advocate the white anti-racist discourse. Whiteness in post-1994 South Africa will always fail to moralize itself credibly because the scandal of black subjectivity, where blacks speak for themselves, is the collapsibility of whiteness and even its anti-racist project. This is because the situation in which black subjects speak for themselves and call for the destruction of white privilege is seen as problematic.

The argument here is that white subjects should not, in the anti-racist effort, join black subjects in the struggle. This may sound separatist, and in fact it is due to the opposition to integrationist tendencies that Biko expressed by virtue of the fact that demands of black subjects should not be negotiated and mediated on their behalf. What is essential is that the anti-racist efforts of whites should be fought by whites themselves in recognizing their own privilege and injustices. But then this should not be a moral crusade in which doing so will mean that they are doing it on behalf of black subjects or exonerating themselves from whiteness. If they continue to do so, they will realize that they are fighting on the wrong side as they have been doing in the past (Alcoff 1998). Whites are compelled not to recognize their privilege and as such see themselves as a normal part of being white-in-the-world. Mngxitama writes:

> But even recognizing privileges of whiteness serves to self-perpetuate the inherent goodness of whiteness. It enacts self-critical evaluations which lull blacks into a meaningless celebration of the self-revealed evils of whiteness. This says, "Look, we know we are benefiting from your oppression but at least we are kind enough to admit to it." It assuages the consciences of (liberal) whites as they continue to enjoy the privileges which come with white skin.
>
> (Mngxitama 2009, 15)

This means that whiteness has the power to silence, and it means that in doing anti-racist work it absolves itself and also silences the demands of black subjects. As Leonardo (2004, 137) posits, "the conditions of white supremacy make white privilege possible." So, without engaging the total makeup of what constitutes whiteness, this will be of no help, even if it means making white subjects aware of their privileges. This is what Ahmed (2006) refers to as the non-performativity of anti-racism. This proves the impotence of the white anti-racist project and exposes that it does not have the capacity to end what sustains it – white racism, white power, and white privilege. According to Ahmed (2006, 105), "performatives succeed when they are uttered by the right person, to the right people, and in a way that takes the right form." Therefore, it is clear from this perspective that white anti-racist efforts should be for whites and in no way should they be advocated as if they are serving the interests of blacks. "White support for anti-racism is often similarly flawed: driven with supremacist pretensions and an extension at times of the colonizer's privilege to decide the true, the just, and the culturally valuable" (Alcoff 1998, 7). Matthews (2012) encourages white anti-racist work in the recognition of past injustices and persisting inequalities and also encourages whites to join the struggle to achieve social justice. Matthews (2012, 172) also warns thus: "anti-racist work may actually result in the perpetuation rather than the erosion of white privilege." White anti-racism, from

Biko's positionality, is something that is not worthy of redeeming itself for the greater good of blackness but for itself, and it should not be expected to. This largely explains why white struggles are irrelevant to black affairs. The de-linking that Biko called for is not just a race project but an ethical project, in the sense that the white presence in black affairs is unethical. The expulsion of whites by Biko is an ethical practice and should be necessitated as blacks are on their own.

The Politics of Black Solidarity

The foundational and constitutional basis of black solidarity is that blacks are on their own and they must in their solidarity liberate themselves from the clutches of oppression. Blacks are on their own by virtue of having antiblack racism targeted only at them, and they have nothing to hold on to since there are no institutions that support their plight. Blacks should by all means determine their own trajectories in the struggle against oppression. As Biko (2004, 74) amplifies, "[T]he philosophy of Black Consciousness, therefore, expresses group pride and the determination by the blacks to rise and attain the envisaged self." It therefore means that black solidarity does not emerge for its own sake, but is informed by the conditions in which blacks find themselves, the primary one being antiblackness, which structurally excludes blackness from the realm of ontology. For black solidarity to be limited to the psyche is to neglect the very fact of the embodiment of blackness in its totality, where black solidarity is the making of ontological demands. Black solidarity is informed by the liberatory demands of those who are at the receiving end of oppression and who bring that end by themselves. It is a form of solidarity that calls for the articulation of ways in which blacks call for the reality that seeks to do away with oppression. In addition, as Shelby (2002, 236) argues, it "is based on the common experience of antiblack racism and the joint commitment it to an end can and should play an important role in the fight against racial injustice." Biko supports black solidarity and he asserts that:

> The quintessence of it is the reali[z]ation by the blacks that, in order to feature well in this game of power politics, they have to use the concept of group power and to build a strong foundation for this. Being an historically, politically, socially, and economically

disinherited and dispossessed group, they have the strongest foundation from which to operate.

(Biko 2004, 74)

Black solidarity is the solid commitment to resistance of white domination and oppression (Ramphalile 2011). Hook writes:

We need to read Biko's Black Consciousness as *a radical humanist politics of solidarity* that operationalizes blackness and concomitant notions of identity and culture around the political objective of liberation rather than simply as psychological ends in and of themselves.

(Hook 2012, 26)

Self-definition of blacks is the very basis on which Black Consciousness is founded and it is a philosophical outlook. "On their own" means that blacks take ownership of themselves by means of black solidarity. Black Consciousness is a collective, the very basis of black solidarity. It means that blacks must make every effort to overcome the oppression that affects them, and if there is no black solidarity where there is oppression of blacks it means that blacks must therefore become complicit and do nothing about their condition. As Gordon (2008, 88) asserts, "[O]ne group wants to claim benevolence to those whom they dominate, and the other must seize its freedom." In addition to this, More (2009, 21) poses a question: "How should black people, for example, respond when they are grouped together and oppressed on the basis of the contingency of their physical characteristics?" It is important to point out that black solidarity emerges because blacks are oppressed on the basis of being black. Identity is a nodal point of black solidarity. Oppression operates on the basis of identity that is antiblack toward blacks and, as such, blacks as a result mobilize themselves on the basis of identity, black solidarity. As Shelby (2002, 233) posits, "Blacks can strengthen the bonds of sympathy and loyalty that will enable them to overcome the barriers to collective action." Black solidarity is self-justified due to the positionality of the world, which is antiblack. This structure and logic of antiblackness not only attacks blackness at the level of singularity, but also as a collective identity. The collective response of black solidarity is necessary for blacks to confront antiblackness. This is enough to explain the basis of the antiblack posture of the world, and its structures and processes that place blacks in perpetual oppression.

Black solidarity emerges because of the oppression of blacks and it is "an effort to liberate blacks from the burden of oppression" (Shelby 2002, 231). Oppression is targeted toward blacks to deny them liberation. Therefore, Black Consciousness as the basis for group solidarity and commitment is not accidental, but the constitutive part of reality. There is no way blacks can attain liberation without engaging their existential reality, which is plagued by oppression external to their bodily experiences. Blacks are oppressed because of the fact of their raced bodies, which are racialized and have certain notions imposed on them. It explains well why the world assumes the antiblack positionality, which clearly explains why blackness is militated against.

> It is important to see that an oppression-centered black solidarity is not a matter of being antiwhite, or even problack, but of being anti-racist. Consequently, solidarity with other racially oppressed groups, and even with committed anti-racist whites, is not precluded by it. Thus, progressive individuals, regardless of their "race," ethnicity, cultural identifications, or natural origin, have no reason to oppose black solidarity once its basis and point are properly understood.
>
> (Shelby 2002, 260–261)

Though this is laudable, the problem is that antiblack racism places blacks on their own. It is only blacks who are at the receiving end of antiblack racism, and they are the only ones who can save themselves and, if not, they will be acted upon by whites who will dictate to them what is good for them.

> The point is obvious: black people must lead and run their own organizations. Only black people can convey the revolutionary idea – and it is a revolutionary idea – that black people are able to do things themselves. Only they can help arouse in the community a continuing black consciousness that will provide the basis for political strength. In the past, white allies have often furthered white supremacy without the whites involved realizing it, or even wanting to do so. Black people must come together and do things for themselves. They must achieve self-identity and self-determination in order to have their daily needs met.
>
> (Ture and Hamilton 1969, 46)

If blacks abdicate responsibility and leave everything under the control of whites, who they deem their allies and comrades, things will not move. The results are, of course, that there will be no change, or it will be cosmetic in nature. Black solidarity against antiblack racism cannot be shared and all-inclusive on the basis that blacks are most likely denied their own lived experience. "For instance as victims of antiblack racism, blacks are, and experience themselves as, invisible; to see that black is to see every other black" (More 2009, 25). The experience of invisibility is drawn from the ways in which blackness is that which has no life and is, as such, a non-entity that does not deserve to make political demands. According to More, inertia, alienation, separation, and power-lessness are the very basis on which black solidarity comes to being, since it aims to overcome those very existential pathologies. This is precisely because oppression keeps these existential pathologies intact and denies blackness any form of political resurrection. As such, it stands to reason, as More puts it, that black solidarity does not emerge out of racist intentions, but against oppressive conditions that deny blacks any form of existential freedom. If the problem is race or racism, a racial response that is not racist but formed on racial grounds should be expected.

The proposition here is that blacks should be in charge of their own solidarity. Biko (2004) affirms black solidarity to state its intentions of ensuring a singularized purpose in the minds of black people and to make possible their total involvement in a struggle that is essentially theirs. The lived experience of blacks demands that they engage in a black solidarity strategy that constitutes the aim to liberate themselves. It is their struggle and it is by themselves that they must chart its terrain and in doing so, they should determine the very manner in which they will engage it – and that is black solidarity. It is clear that liberation should be pursued by those who want to be liberated, and for that to be actualized they should liberate themselves. This then explains the fact that those who sympathize with and want to participate in black solidarity should not dictate to blacks who need liberation how they should engage in this political practice. The reason for this is that black solidarity "seeks to talk to the black man [sic] in the language that is his [sic] own" (Biko 2004, 34). This is essential, as blacks are on their own and they are on their own in pursuit of liberation. They are, on their own account, making sure that there is a possibility of becoming human as antiblackness structures them out of humanity.

Anti-solidarity sentiments and political formations suggest that black solidarity is racist, immoral, and should be rejected. The solidarity of blacks, black bodies in unity against that which oppresses them, is something prohibited to the point where it is criminalized. To point out from the onset with regard to black solidarity, more so post-1994, is that it is criminalized. The criminalization is sensationalized in the manner of referring to blacks engaged in the politics of solidarity as suffering from victimhood. The resistance against black solidarity is that blacks are not allowed to be their own, but to be the mimic of something that they are not. It is only through the politics of solidarity that blacks engage in political practice, and there are often accusations that black solidarity is indeed reverse racism. What is not questioned is what exactly blacks are resisting and what makes them express themselves in the form of black solidarity. By extension, it is not asked that black solidarity is formed as the natural response to what attacks blacks as a collective. That is, the collective attack on blacks triggers a collective response: black solidarity. It is important to note that black solidarity finds itself in the middle of the politics of censure. As Parry (1999, 218) points out: "[S]uch censure is surely depended on who is doing the remembering and why." It is clear from this instance of asymmetric power relations and the violation of the ontology of blackness that blackness will be denied the privilege of remembering from its vantage point being at the receiving end of antiblack racism. In addition, blackness is denied the ability to remember what it is, to remember what oppresses it and also to imagine the possibilities of how to liberate itself. According to Biko (2004, 42), the politics of censure are "intended to get black people fighting separately for certain 'freedoms' and 'gains' which were already prescribed for them long ago." To censure blackness in the realm of politics of solidarity is not only to gag but to erase the politics of possibility.

According to Mbembe (2007, 137), Biko "believed that black solidarity would one day make it possible for members of all races to live together free in one nation." What seems problematic here is that solidarity is resisted by members of all races, including some who are black. It also means that black solidarity is not in the service of all members of all races, as Mbembe would like us to believe. If that was actually what Biko aspired to, then there would have been no need to criminalize black solidarity. Mbembe also makes another assertion that claims that Biko's defense of black solidarity was not predicated on race. According to Mbembe (2007, 140), this defense was about "eliminating unjust racial inequalities, and improving the life prospects of those racialized as blacks." The contention here is still that Biko's defense of black solidarity is that which is predicated on race, since it was blacks who were oppressed as a collective solely on the grounds of their race. To extend the point further, Biko was not a non-racialist, since this is predicated on the very integrationist political arrangement that Biko wholly rejected. Black solidarity will obviously be criminalized in the non-racialist order and naive claims that there is no race or racism are the order of the day. It is in the non-racialist order of the liberal constitutionalist South Africa that saw the banning of the Native Club in 2006 and the Forum for Black Journalists in 2008. Mbembe rightfully points out that:

> Today blacks in South Africa have political power. Their ability to effect meaningful social change is substantive. They can no longer act as if they were totally powerless. For black solidarity to serve as a political and moral resource in the post-liberation era it needs to be refined not only to deal with new social realities but, even more importantly, to conform better to democratic principle.
>
> (Mbembe 2007, 144)

Though blacks are in political power, their power is not problematized by Mbembe and it is a form of power that still manages and perpetuates the antiblack reality. In fact, the political power of the ANC is not the kind that serves the interests of the black majority. This is political power that is devoid of any form of power in the real sense, but that is symbolic in nature. It is powerless power, since the ANC government cannot meet the demands of the black majority and finds it convenient to dehumanize blacks continuously in the service of white supremacy. The majority of blacks are still left in existential want and deprivation, in which democratic change and its miracle of the rainbow nation are still a rumor; or, if the rainbow nation is a destination, it is still a mirage. As it stands, there are conceptions of blackness that need to be sketchily highlighted, such as the conception of blackness in which those who are in political power will benefit at the expense of the black majority who are still trapped in the existential crisis: that is the black condition. The latter are, of course, still powerless, and they are the ones who feel the barbarity of antiblack racism, also managed by blacks in power on behalf of white supremacy. The democratic principles that need to be conformed to are problematic since they are founded on the antiblack reality, and they are, in a number of ways, beneficial to those who are privileged and simply useless for those who are dispossessed. The very same principles are devoid of social justice and are powerful enough to maintain the racist infrastructure of apartheid by means of economic might, land ownership, and property rights.

Black solidarity as Biko espoused it still yearns for a victory that is liberation and not conformity to defeat, which is the liberal democratic principles that are foundational to the post-1994 reality. The version of black solidarity that Mbembe (2007, 147) advocates, however, is the one that espouses "moral commitment to racial reconciliation and equal justice for all." This form of black solidarity is itself a defeat, since it takes the illusionary posture of the post-1994 negotiated settlement with its myth that South Africa belongs to all, but in fact blacks are still excluded under the watch of the black ANC government. "How can those who suffer from racism hope to succeed in their liberation by utilizing the very same false instrument of 'race' used by their oppressors?" (More 2009, 37). It needs to be noted that the false instrument of "race" connotes the idea that race does not matter or it does not exist, as espoused by Appiah (1992). This proposition by Appiah is problematic by its very nature of being far from antiblack reality. This is the reality that is being erased, and it affirms the reality that is actually outside the realm of blackness. Appiah criminalizes black solidarity by rendering it blameworthy of being racist. It is problematic then to render black solidarity racist whereas by its very nature it is impotent in the face of antiblack racism. In no way does black solidarity, and Black Consciousness in this case, aim to be racist. This is far from reality, in the sense that the aim is to liberate blacks from racism. Therefore, to be liberated from racism does not require one to be racist.

> Black consciousness and solidarity must be seen by us as phenomena that are positive in themselves. This means that they are desirable even outside considerations involving white domination and racialism. References to these developments as racialism became meaningless in the face of this recognition. Nobody should ever have any right to tell anybody else that he [sic] should not be aware of himself [sic] as being. Black consciousness and solidarity as expressed in the present should also mean something in addition. They should mean continuity with the past and the future.
>
> (Manganyi 1973, 20)

Antiblack racism is solidarity in itself since it works as a collective power in which the majority of blacks are embodied, and they are racially marked on the basis of their body. It is not through spirituality that blacks are judged as "the other," but through the very fact of being racialized – that is, their body as appearance in the antiblack world.

Problematizing the hegemonic discourse and the totality of white power is indeed the work of oppositional practice that is grounded in "subjectivity, identity, agency and the status of the reverse-discourse" (Parry 1999, 215). In its form and content, this is what Black Consciousness, the philosophy that Biko advocated, is, the very thing that is nothing else but black solidarity. It is the political practice that is still blossoming and continuing to resist in the middle of the stubborn hegemony that denies any form of blacks as a collective to become politically organized. Black solidarity *qua* Black Consciousness "seeks to channel the pent up forces of the angry black masses to meaningful and directed opposition basing its entire struggle on realities of the situation" (Biko 2004, 33). The realities of the situation do not demand anything from blacks but their collectiveness as they are structurally objectified as a collective. Black solidarity, if it were possible and not inflicted by antiblack racism (its hegemonic mask of liberal consensus), would perhaps have created "a structure of feeling [that] would have enunciated a black grammar of suffering" (Wilderson 2008, 112). Black solidarity is yet to emerge, the one which Manganyi (1973) calls for in which blacks are not dictated to in terms of their political register. What this political register agitates is the very fact that black solidarity is yet to stand the test of time as in the past, present and future. Blacks are yet to be liberated by the very political imagery of Biko *à la* Black Consciousness in the realm of black solidarity.

Authority to Judge

The positionality of Biko in his political work is that of assuming the role of judge. The complexity arises about the positionality of the judge, in the sense that the figure of the judge here is somebody criminalized. What judges the outlawed subject is that which the racial subject seeks to judge. That is to say, blackness should have the capacity to judge what brings it exploitation, alienation, and dehumanization. In this instance, to judge is to possess authority, something that is denied to the black subject, since its position-ality is that of being judged. Obviously for one to judge, one must have the authority to do so. It is sufficient to say that Biko had the authority to judge and this is rooted in his position as the subject at the receiving end of oppression. Indeed, it is uncommon for the subject at the receiving end of subjection to have the authority to judge, but in the case of Biko things were different, since Black Consciousness philosophy was the authority through which he made pronouncements and judged the lived experience of the black. Therefore, it is essential to state that Black Consciousness is the authoritative standing through which Biko assumed the position-ality of the judge.

Biko's positionality *qua* judgment is not judgment *per se*, but that which is informed by the oppositional spirit. It is through the prisms of Black Consciousness that blackness was affirmed as the oppositional force toward the white oppression. It assumed a clear stance, as can be seen from Biko's judgment. The judgment that confronts blacks is that they are not judged as humans, but as blacks. Then this renders them mere outlaws who are at the margins of the configuration of the racist state and its logic of white supremacy. Biko is judging the system that always puts the humanity of blacks in perpetual doubt and under question. Blacks are judges by the mere fact of racial ordering. The politics of judgment in the oppressive condition are not informed by justice in so far as they concern black subjects. The oppressive condition means that judgment judges blackness outside justice. Therefore, judgment directed toward blacks is arbitrary for the reason that it serves oppression and denies blacks justice. The denial of justice is the very form of judgment that claims to stand on the moral ground of justice. When blacks are outside justice, its principles will not apply, meaning that blackness cannot be reconciled with justice, but with its very antithesis – injustice.

Biko engaged deeply in the formation of meaning, something that led blackness to (re)define and (re-)discover itself. There is no closure, but the continued search to make ontological demands. The ontological demands cannot be made by the mere gesture of giving, since this is not enough; nothing can be given in the struggle for liberation. The ontological demands made by Biko are grounded in this question: "what does it mean to suffer and to be black in the antiblack world?" Demands made by Biko are in themselves political judgments, what Wilderson (2010) refers to as insatiable demands. These are demands predicated on the liberation of blacks. For blacks to march toward liberation they must make political demands. These demands are not demands in the simple sense of the term, but demands that are turning reality upside down. To demand is to live, to live is to render dead that which brings obstacles to the possibility of living. Biko as a resistant subject defies the status of the martyr, which is something that teleologically suspends him. Biko continues to call for black liberation, since he did not pronounce the *telos* of Black Consciousness, and this is something that still makes him the outlawed subject, since the call for black liberation is something that is criminalized as it disturbs the racist system and its logical order of white supremacy. Therefore, Biko demands liberation of the black and calls for the death of white oppression and for liberation that is genuine and just for blacks. Blacks, when liberated, should not be accommodated by whiteness; they should be liberated on their own terms.

4

The Prison Slave Narrative: Assata Shakur and George Jackson's Captive Flesh

If there is a right to exist, this right is on the wayside for those who are incarcerated and haunted by the stigma of being captive flesh. The jailing of the black body and that of the political prisoner, to be precise, attests to the ways in which the power of the carceral apparatus is exercised upon the body. The might of the carceral state is seen in the ways in which it creates a binding (non)relationality where whiteness feeds itself on the dehumanization of blackness. Black bodies are incarcerated by virtue of their existence in the world that is antiblack. The will to live is militated against, and blackness, in resistance to this, is tenacious in exercising that will.

It is through writing that Assata Shakur and George Jackson assert the will to live through the politics of writing, which can be understood as the narrative of the prison slave. What does it mean to be a prison slave, and is it possible to have this existential embodiment? This question is fundamental to understanding the ontologico-existential condition of the prison slave as the fugitive figure as nothing but that which deserves violence and, if need be, death. The prison slave is seen outside the domain of life and if there is life, it has to be lived through survival. It is upon the will of the carceral state in the capacity of the *master politicos* to determine the life and death of the prison slave. What arises from the narrative of the prison slave is to reclaim life and to assert the will to live life through existential struggle. Prison slave's agency is restored permanently, but there are also various forces causing its disruption. In short, they resist and they are also resisted upon through the mightier degree of breaking their resistance. To uproot antiblackness, which in the *longue durée* of slavery right through present day mass incarceration – the continuity of the racist infrastructure that affects and afflicts blackness – has been the animating force of Shakur and Jackson writing. Both do not negotiate with racist prison and tyrannical juridical order. Their writing, as prison slaves, is the writing that calls for the end of politics and the beginning of other politics where life, rather than death, is the motif.

What does it mean for the prison slave to be free? The symbolic order of antiblackness and its carceral apparatus do not allow any sense of freedom for the prison slave. The latter should be held captive and brought to justice (which is tyranny, with the ultimate result of death, if necessary). Therefore, there is no freedom for the prison slave. It then becomes something of interest for the prison slave to engage in the practices of freedom, which is seen in Shakur and Jackson, who do not allow their minds, bodies, and souls to be incarcerated even if their bodily flesh is confined by concrete and steel. It then explains why to escape is seen as a necessity and as the actualization of the practices of freedom. This means that both are informed by the spirit of resistance of the fugitive slave and the resistance which has been the political subjectivity of the Black Panther Party and Black Liberation Army, as well as other resistance struggles that wanted the end of white supremacy. This resistance is important in that it refuses to enter into a dialogue with the oppressor and what is called for is for subjection not to exist.

Shakur and Jackson are prison slaves in their modes of being and subjectivity. As a result of the fact that they are black, they are violated and they keep on fighting the very structures of violence. It is this limit that sparks revolt and provokes them to assert their humanity by rejecting whatever captures their flesh, including its psychic mechanisticism, and then authorizing themselves by insisting on not being incorporated into the narratives of justice and by challenging justice, as it were, in the racist infrastructure of antiblackness. Perhaps it is important to highlight that the prison slave's struggle is not that of the individual, and in the case of Shakur and Jackson it is related to the politics of collective activity that resist the violence of the state directed at blackness. As fugitive subjects, Shakur and Jackson are bound by a similar fate of being prison slaves and their politics being fought against. Thus, in authorizing themselves and in relentless pursuit of their politics, they escape from prison, with different outcomes, namely, that of exile (Shakur) and death (Jackson). These outcomes bear similarities, in the sense that the violence that is directed and applied to the prison slave's body renders such a figure a fugitive. The demand to be free is frowned upon by the carceral apparatus as a cardinal violation. For justice to be served, according to the narrative of the carceral apparatus, the flesh of the prison slave should remain forever captive, even in death.

The Prison Slave Narrative

One of the fundamental aspects of the prison slave narrative has to do with the politics of writing that forms the basis through which the carceral state is not resisted, but confronted. The prison slave's writing is not only a testimony; it is the articulation of existence. It is the writing that comes from the perspective of the brutalized body that is captured, its soul being the potent force of resistance. Personal experience of capture in the narratives of the prison slave is necessary to understand the manner in which the flesh that is captured writes itself and its relationality with the world. Indeed, the manner in which the black body has been structured to be under systematic, systemic, and continuous attack has to do with the articulation of these experiences. "The carceral, the imperial, and the industrial were intertwined in the biopolitical regulation of black life, the expansion of capital, and the production of blackness, whiteness, and white supremacy" (Dillon 2012, 119). These technologies of subjection that form the meta-structure of the antiblack world should be understood as the carceral regime. In this regard, the prison slave as "[t]he writer seems compelled to assume the role of the witness" (Gready 1993, 490). The very fact of bearing witness is the claim to the narrative of the prison slave, which is the counter-narrative of the meta-narrative of the antiblack world.

> Of the most basic functions of these narratives is to communicate the horror and degradation of being incarcerated. But they invariably go beyond the walls of the prison to address social ills.
>
> (Miller 2005, 15)

Foucault (2003) argues that writing is the great political instrument that is centered on the systems of power. This system of power, to assert itself, does not stand in relation to the realm of the sovereign might but stands in relation to the infrastructure of antiblackness. Writing will not only involve the efforts to describe what Foucault terms "apparatuses of domination;" the writing of the prison slave is also the unmasking of antiblackness *in toto*.

> Then the prisoner writer gazes back upon the strategies of power; then the prison writer attaches the body – subjugated by torture, surveillance, and other forms of legitimized and illegitimate punishment to dominant powers.
>
> (Larson 2010, 159)

Foucault (1977, 189) asserts that "[a] 'power of writing' was constructed as an essential part in the mechanism of discipline." It is the writing that is embodied in the ritual that Foucault (1977, 184) terms "the examination" – "a normalizing gaze, surveillance that makes it possible to quantify, to classify and to punish." The body in incarceration is subjected to the power of writing, with its rigidity of the examination that Foucault insists is a ritualization of the incarcerated body. This is the ritual of power, the power that claims to be sovereign over that which it renders captive and that exerts itself through writing – that is, the power of writing seeks to be a totalizing narrative – the truth in the absolute sense. That is what the power of writing and the examination ensure. Foucault (1977, 196) writes: "The registration of the pathological must be centralized."

> The examination leaves behind it a whole meticulous archive constituted in terms of bodies and days. The examination that places individuals in a field of surveillance also situates them in a network of writing; it engages them in a whole mass of documents that capture and fix them.
>
> (Foucault 1977, 189)

The examination, which is the embodiment of the power of writing, happens in the prison context as Foucault rightfully argues. But then, what about the power of writing and the examination that takes place in both the prison and on the streets? To capture the flesh of the prison slave means that the power of writing and the examination is not only quantifying, classifying, or archiving, it is death itself. The prison slave is subjected to the modality of power with its dehumanizing practices – the power of the writing and the examination as the vices that render the captive flesh constitutively dead. The captive flesh is that which is captured from inception, pregnancy, birth, life, and death. That is why, for Shakur (1978, 13), "prison is not that much different from the street." For, as Dillon (2012) notes, the street is the extension of the prison where black life is possessed through various technologies of capture.

Gready (1993) deploys Foucault's concept of the "power of writing" in the ways in which the prison slave is being written. As Gready rightfully notes, the power of writing resides in the carceral apparatus. The power of writing is embodied in multiplicity of forms "to isolate, to discredit, to destroy, to rewrite everything and everyone to serve a political end" (Gready 1993, 492). It is the narrative of resistance where the prison slave militates against what Foucault refers to as the power of writing that is done by the state. The prison slave's narrative militates against the meta-narrative that propagates the falsity that slavery is just an event of the past and has no relevance in the present.

It is the continued reality that still positions black in the condition of antiblackness. Therefore, the present afterlife of slavery has everything to do with slavery itself. In amplification:

> An engagement with slavery's afterlife means that we must make sense of what we know and how we know it, who we are and how we got here. We must also grapple with that which never was. This means looking at dust for a trace of the past and connecting the present with the absence of memory. Slavery lives on in what we can see and feel, but also in what feels like nothing, in the absence left by millions who lie at the bottom of the ocean or under rows of cotton or rice.
>
> (Dillon 2012, 121)

For this, the existential continuum is still, the political present that still has blackness and the prison slave as "the stateless, the socially dead, and the disposable" (Best and Hartman 2005, 5). Therefore, the prison slave, in demanding justice, is writing through the frustration of legislative defeat and, in point of fact, there is no legislation that is pro-black because the whole apparatus in which justice resides and the ethos of the state are antiblack.

If to be a prisoner is to be contested through writing and to be vigorously (re)written as Gready claims, then it is important to understand the manner in which this writing takes place. There is no difference between the actual document that is filled with ink and the prisoner writer, in that the writing that is done there in prison is similar to what is done to the incarcerated body. "The prisoner writer is a heavily documented and materially mapped writer" (Larson 2010, 146). Foucault's (1977) concept of "the examination" shows the way in which the state writes the prisoner, subjecting the body of the prisoner to the excess of writing. It is then true that prison writing is not writing for its own sake and, more importantly, the narratives of the prison slaves are informed by an intentionality to write against the excess of writing done by the carceral state. The prison slave is not written in excess just for the sake of writing. Its physicality is eliminated through this excess of writing done by the carceral state. The manner in which Shakur and Jackson write, as prison slaves, is contrary to the view below:

> It is the arena of "rationality," rather than the body, that stands as the primary realm of human agency, superintending an engagement with the world that ultimately constructs physical and social realities. These predominant metaphors, although reliant on the physical, suggest a transcending of the physical.
>
> (Barrett 1995, 423)

There is no way this is applicable to the prison slave narratives. Shakur and Jackson's prison writing is politically infused and conscious. There is no way the captive flesh can be in the arena of rationality and transcendence of the physical. The writing comes from the body and it is rational in its sense against the irrational, which claims to be rational. In short, there is nothing rational about the racist infrastructure of the antiblack world and its extension of the carceral apparatus that Shakur and Jackson are writing against. Therefore, the notion of being rational is determined by that which is irrational itself. Thus, there is no rationality. The bodies that are put on trial by the carceral apparatus and that are the captive flesh of the antiblack world cannot claim transcendence, as the body is the site of the political and the conscious. Human agency is the site of the white terrain and the prison slave narrative is writing what whiteness does not want to come in contact with. Blackness wants liberation, which whiteness refuses, and the writing of the prison slave is not there to pander to white sensitivities but to unmask the antiblack world that is privileging whiteness.

The conditions of incarceration are dehumanizing to the prison slave, who "chooses writing as his or her method of resistance to those conditions" (Larson 2010, 144). The prison slave narrative is political in nature and its advocacy for the affirmation of life exposes the existential horror that haunts blackness. In view of the fact that it is writing marked by incarceration and the antiblack world, it goes into the throes of the existential abyss. This writing is both confined to the lived experience of incarceration and is the actual articulation of the dehumanizing practices that afflicts the black body. It is the self coming into being from the perspective of those who are ontologically and existentially faulted taking it upon themselves to militate against the forces that crush all forms of life. It is writing from the concrete, steel, and electrified fence, using the last breath as if it were the last. Shakur and Jackson are not only writing from, but writing against "the concrete and steel that contains their bodies" (Larson 2010, 146). The form of writing that Shakur and Jackson engaged in not only bears testimony to, but is also used as a weapon against the power of the warder, the carceral state, and the whole antiblack world. Their narratives contained in the texts, which stand as manifestos of black life, serve as treaties that reclaim the violated life of blackness.

> Prison writing is a genre bound not only by its subject and authors but in its expressive tropes, and those tropes at once determined by, actively resistant to, and thus indicative of both global and local conditions of composition.
>
> (Larson 2010, 143)

This resistance came into being as a result of the manner in which the carceral apparatus violates, in a banal way, the very existence of blacks. The brutality discharged at black bodies is such that the state does not have the duty to protect its citizens, but to remove blacks from the realm of citizenship, so that extra-juridical means can be used. In other words, the excess of law is those who are written outside the law. As such, what they deserve is nothing but the wrath of law mainly because of their criminality of being. "The law defines the human and so to be outside the boundaries of the law is to be exposed to a form of illegal barbarism that renders one inhuman" (Dillon 2013, 188). They are both outside the human status and insert themselves in the struggle *to be* human. But it is important to note that Shakur and Jackson do so of their own accord, as they are not buying into the American Dream and the liberal consensus that is, in fact, the ideological interpellation of the state of incarceration and the ethos of antiblackness. Shakur demands of her own accord and does not seek any accommodationist gesture from the carceral apparatus. This is clear in the encounter below with the warder, Mrs. Butterworth:

> "When can i be unlocked from this cell and go outside in the big room with other women?"

> "Well, I don't know, JoAnne. Why do you want to go out there?"

> "Well, i don't want to stay here all day, locked up by myself."

> "Why, JoAnne, don't you like your room. We had it painted just for you."

> (Shakur 1987, 47)

This encounter signifies violence in the sense that the needs of Shakur are downplayed through the weight of patronizing language. The warder speaks to Shakur as if she is a child. The warder even goes further by stating that Shakur is locked up for her own safety. The issue here is making the prison slave like the cell in which he or she is locked. Since the prison cell is the container of the black body, it is illogical for the prison slave to like what contains him or her. The same applies to Jackson who, according to Conniff (2005, 155), "is never content merely to meditate in his cell as he formulates his ideology; all along, his self-education is wedded to revolutionary action." Having spent most of his prison years in solitary confinement, Jackson (1970, 123) has this to say: "Locked up 24 hours a day now. It's all right, though – gives me plenty of time to do my work. My cell faces north, and there is a window in front of it. Plenty of fresh air comes in my cell." The flesh is not having fresh air on the paternalistic gesture of the warder who patronizes Shakur on her cell being beautiful and expecting her to like it. Clearly, it is Jackson who does not adapt to prison and, of course, fresh air is necessary. It is Jackson (1970, 144) who charges: "Confinement in this small area all day causes a build up of tension." Therefore, how can there be the expectation for Shakur to like her cell because it was painted especially for her?

The painting of the wall is intended to crush the spirit that informs the prison slave's narrative. It represents the erasure of all the efforts that are waged against the regime of incarceration. "While prisoners had little or no control over the manner in which they were captured and fixed in official writing, other written forms, from scratched messages on cell walls to the writing of autobiographical accounts, provided a way of regaining control" (Gready 1993, 492). The meta-narrative of the power of writing by the carceral apparatus is confronted with the writing of what it (re)writes. The language of political good is as good as the violence it metes out to black bodies. Shakur and Jackson do not trust the prison warders; their belief is that the warders serve the very system that dehumanizes blackness. Consequently, warders cannot be in a common struggle with those they are dehumanizing. In short, the prison slave can in no way be expected to embrace what renders the black flesh forever captive. Because this is the worst form of ontological violence, it has to be rejected by all means – hence Shakur's rejection of the warder's gestures.

It seems, then, that the warder knows what is good for Shakur and finds it fit to act upon her. What is striking indeed is that Shakur is supposed to like the cell because it has been painted specially for her. But it is clear that there is nothing special about it for Shakur. Shakur, in vigilance, is able to see behind the pretentious nature of the prison warder and refuses to separate the warder from the larger institution of structural violence that creates the black condition. The painting of the cell might have been nice, but it was an act of erasing what had previously been written on the wall. The warder creates the impression that there is something new to the cell, whereas there is nothing new to it.

The very fact of painting is violence. The violence of painting appears gruesome when Jackson recounts an event of a fellow prison slave who drew on his cell walls, and who called him to his cell to see the artwork. From Jackson's account, it is clear that his breath was taken away by the artwork of the night sky, and he appreciated that the fellow prison slave was a good artist. Jackson (1970, 273) says: "When he finished the last stroke the pigs moved him to another cell and painted over it; gave him a bad-conduct report, and made him pay for the new coat of paint." This shows the extent to which painting of the cell is violence. The decision to paint over the artistic effort of the prison slave clearly shows the extent to which the power of writing by the warder is done through the erasure of that which it inferiorizes.

The walls have been recently painted. Undoubtedly they once had names on them, messages, words of encouragement, dates. They are now bereft of any vestige of testimony.

(Timerman 1981, 3)

The painting of the cell represents the power of writing by the carceral apparatus, which erases the markers and traces inscribed on the cell walls. Shakur is denied the right to see who has been there before her and what they wrote, what was going on in their minds and, moreover, how they engaged in the practices of freedom by writing against what rendered their flesh captive. What renders the flesh captive is the fact that the existence of blackness is, according to Dillon (2012), foreclosed by being policed and then imprisoned. In recounting the pain of the captive flesh, Timerman (1981, 32) writes: "It is a pain without points of reference, revelatory symbols, or clues to serve as indicators." Shakur wanted to be let out of the cell; she did not make the demand because of the ugliness of the cell. The pain she articulated was not taken seriously. For the warder to respond to this demand by focusing on the beauty of the cell is immaterial. The painting of the cell walls and Shakur's desire to get out are irreconcilable, and the gesture of the warder borders the absurd.

By centering antiblack technologies and discourses, Shakur challenges normative conceptions of space and time to demonstrate the ways that neoliberalism's carceral technologies track, manage, and immobilize rebellious or surplus life – a process that is driven and informed by technologies inaugurated under the Atlantic slave trade. *We were, and still are, in a much more terrible jail.*

(Dillon 2012, 122)

The prison slave also writes back counter-narratively by exposing the deeds of the carceral apparatus in the context of incarceration and also in relation to sociality writ large. For Gready (1993, 493), this "is the attempt to proclaim an oppositional 'power of writing.'" It is the writing that is opposed to the officialdom of the carceral apparatus. The writing of the prison slave is in confrontation with the might of the carceral apparatus. The prison slave writes against that which is against his or her body. The daily challenge of survival because life is under siege means that writing is not a luxury but a race against uncertainty of life itself. It is a political act, not only of resistance, but also of the will to fight. To be under siege does not strike fear, but calls for, in the subjectivity of Shakur and Jackson, the rage and determination to face brutality while standing.

Foucault has also shown how the power of writing and the examination individualizes those who are subjected to this power. This is true in terms of the body of the prisoner who was free before incarceration as opposed to the prison slave whose captive flesh is incarcerated indefinitely. Shakur and Jackson are not individuals – they have no personas – and what they have that makes them fall outside the individual and to be collapsed into the amorphous of blackness is their captive flesh. They are not in the commands of the power of writing and the examination, they are nothing but black. So, then, the prisoner and not the prison slave, the white subject and not the black subject, the free person and not the fugitive is the one who is subjected to what Foucault terms "disciplinary power." Foucault argues that disciplinary power is exercised through invisibility and makes its subjects visible; they are subjected to the spectacle of power itself. What more about Shakur and Jackson, who are made invisible? Clearly, the prison slave cannot be captured by Foucault's account of disciplinary power, since it does not account for the ontologico-existential horror of blackness, which is in prison and on the streets. Disciplinary power cannot account for the accumulation, fungibility, and gratuitous violence that is directed at the prison slave (Wilderson 2010).

The power of writing came from the carceral apparatus through naked censor and the intention to control the thought of the prison slave. This also takes into account the fact that Jackson's letters were subjected to rigorous censorship by prison officials. It is the power of writing – the meta-narrative of the carceral apparatus – the authoritative power that prohibits speech and its ultimate aim is nothing but thought police. In this instance, thought police would mean, as a matter of fact, that the prison kept the body of Jackson captive – it saw fit to render his writing captive. To censor means that the power of writing from the meta-narrative of the carceral apparatus is under threat; it is subjected to challenge through the counter-narrative of the prison slave. In his prison narrative, Conniff states that Jackson appears to be explicitly political and ideologically charged and never appears to depict himself as politically naive. This explains the profound influence of Jackson's writing and the manner in which he is distinct as "a thinker capable of articulating a moral and political framework that could focus resistance to the kind of violence and repression *of the antiblack world*" (Conniff 2005, 148 [emphasis added]).

Indeed, Shakur and Jackson did not see a prison slave's narrative as the writings of the individual. They were writing from the standpoint of being violated blacks who, in solidarity, were writing in relation to other blacks. They waged the ontologico-existential struggle against antiblackness. In Shakur and Jackson's prison narratives the duty to write is not the writing of the self in relation to the self, but of the self in the collective of the humanity of black. It is the writing of the collective in the sense that the form of oppression that they both faced affects the multitude of blacks. The ground for political contest cannot then remain closed, for the narrative of the prison slave is a tenacious force that persists, despite the mighty effort to stop it from writing itself instead of being written by the carceral apparatus. Shakur and Jackson assume authority to challenge the sacred nature of power. They challenge the excess of power, which is arbitrary, that is aimed at breaking the spirit of the prison slave. The writing of the prison slave, as is evident in the narratives of Shakur and Jackson, does not turn its back. Instead, it continues and dares to challenge the carceral state and the infrastructure of the antiblack world. The narratives of the prison slave serve as the counter-narrative of the meta-narrative of the carceral apparatus. It is then clear that it is a fiercely contested space, which is definably marked by power, however asymmetric. The incarcerated body is militated against exceedingly if the carceral apparatus sees itself being threatened by the counter-narratives. This is clear in the encounter between Shakur and the prison warder, Mrs. Butterworth.

Shakur challenges the self-arrogated authority of the warder, who addresses other prisoners as girls and refers to them by their first names, while she demands to be addressed as Mrs. Butterworth. She addresses Shakur by her first name, JoAnne, and when Shakur asks her name, she refuses to give it. Shakur even asks her if she is ashamed of her name and the warder's response is as follows: "No JoAnne, I am not ashamed of my name. It's a matter of respect. I am the warden here. My girls call me Mrs. Butterworth and I call them by their first names" (Shakur 1987, 47). This shows the crushing weight of white supremacy: where the white woman has her own girls, she is the maternal figure – a mother and her perpetual children. It is Shakur (1978) who states that the warder refers to women inmates as girls and this does not erase the violent relation between the warder and the prisoner. The warder assumes the position of superiority and that of being better than those who are imprisoned. Mrs. Butterworth claims superiority over Shakur and the other prisoners. A form of respect that is condescending is discernable when Mrs. Butterworth refers to them as "my girls" and calls them by their first names, while she is still "Mrs. Butterworth." Respect means only Mrs. Butterworth must be respected, and for her to say: "It is a matter of respect" and to exercise the authority to call the prisoners "my girls" is an act of arrogation, in that it borders on a type of colonial relationship. Respect, in short, is for the warden to speak of "my girls" and to call them by their first names, and for her to be called "Mrs. Butterworth." Shakur dismantles this white supremacist respect and in the following exchange, things unravel:

> "Well, you haven't done anything for me to respect you for. I give only respect only when they earn it. Since you won't tell me your first name, then I want you to call me by my last name. You can either call me Ms. Shakur or Ms. Chesimard."
>
> "I am not going to call you by your last name. I'm going to continue calling you JoAnne."
>
> "Well, that's okay by me, if you can stand me calling you Miss Bitch whenever i see you. I don't give anybody respect when they don't respect me."
>
> (Shakur 1987, 48)

Indeed, this is the end of dialogue. There is nothing that can be negotiated. The encounter shows Shakur's rejection of respect as a colonial signification and imposition. She restores respect to what it is, that is, something that is mutual and reciprocal. The power of the warder is challenged; she is not allowed to reign supreme over Shakur. This stance is affirmative in the sense that it is informed by courage and determination. It represents the exercise of political will *stricto sensu* and the unwillingness to be in bad faith. Not only can Shakur's political will be limited to her standing up to the warder, but her modes of writing as a prison slave. The prison slave writes from a degraded position of humanity, a position of being dispossessed and having nothing to hold on to, where only the revolutionary spirit serves as a reservoir of hope. "As the prisoner reckons a voice, a sense of self and world, gains a restoration of worldly self-extension, the equivalents of their captors contract, and are given perspective" (Gready 1993, 522). It is important to remark that the power of the prison slave's narrative is not a given. It is the political act that is met with the brutality of the carceral apparatus. The logic of domination that underpins the meta-narrative of the regime of incarceration does not want any form of contest. While the captive body is written, in defiance, this body writes against the carceral apparatus, which sees itself as power in the absolute while the prison slave is nothing.

The writing of the prison slave centers on what Shakur and Jackson call "our politics, our political consciousness, and our actions" (Buck 2000, 28). This comes from political commitment and there is a price to pay. The prison slave has to be undeterred in order to stay strong from the blows that come from the might of the carceral apparatus. The emphasis on justice is not that Shakur and Jackson are calling to be heard by the carceral apparatus, but are calling for justice in the terms that are outside the clutches of the carceral apparatus. The act of writing by Jackson and Shakur is itself justice, in that they write against injustice. "The very effort to write is thus an act of political resurrection, a re-envisioning of the narrative of justice" (Larson 2010, 147).

Shakur and Jackson bring to bear the question of what it means to suffer, and they do not allow themselves to be muzzled. The writing of the prison slave is infused with the ontologico-existential question that presents a scandal to the antiblack world. These are questions that are persistently posed to put weight onto the antiblack world. These are questions that are not to be entertained by the antiblack world. They are questions that are calling attention to the plight of the prison slave and that are fundamental to understanding the black condition. In the form of writing, the prison slave narratives of Shakur and Jackson bring the monologue of the antiblack world to an end. By articulating the black condition, they are articulating what Wilderson (2008) terms "the grammar of suffering" in narratives that end the dialogue; that has nothing to do with meeting the insatiable ontologico-existential demands of the prison slave that the carceral apparatus cannot engage in because it would be its demise. The grammar of suffering attests to the fact that prison slaves always write with their backs against the wall – their writing is the act of resistance in their own terms, terms that are not structured by the carceral apparatus.

The prison slave narrative is not a nostalgic attempt to reach the purity of the past. It is not a cause for restoration, as there is nothing left, and to do politics from nothing is the clear mark of uncertainty. The prison slave has a life that has been dispossessed, and the demands of the prison slave are to want dispossession to be obliterated, including possession as it is. In writing, what comes into being from the prison slave is the perspective of blackness as the corporeal account of "issues of power and powerlessness" (Barrett 1995, 415). Prison writing is a question of embodiment where the body that is writing is structured at the receiving end of antiblackness and speaks its truth. The prison writing of Shakur and Jackson exposes the darker side of the antiblack world and bears witness to the carceral practice of the black body in relation to the carceral apparatus and its non-existence through its humanity being put into question. Prison writing is, according to Barrett (1995, 422), "the facticity of the body." Thus, Shakur and Jackson write from their bodies to break the strictures of the carceral apparatus.

> We can then attend to the ways the dispossessed responded to what was stolen from them by escaping the terms of what they were imported to be and by crafting new modes of being, often repossessed from scraps of what they were invested with.
>
> (Kazanjian 2014, 281)

The prison slave narrative does not have a triumphant spirit, for there is nothing triumphant about blackness in the struggle to be free. The indomitable will to wage the ontologico-existential struggle against injustices directed at the captive flesh says a lot about the testimony of blackness and the horror by which blackness is dramatized. This testimony is not one that convinces, but that stands in its own right and is in no need of being legitimated as the acceptable truth by the carceral apparatus. It serves as the direct critique that unmasks the injustices of the antiblackness and as a bane to the carceral state, which needs the liberal consensus to sustain itself and to write off the prison slave narrative. The manner in which Shakur and Jackson structure their narratives is to end the carceral state and not to ask for it to reform so to accommodate the demands of those who are wretched. By unravelling the systematic subjection that confines their bodies, they do not allow their spirit to be confined and disciplined by the dictates of the carceral state. Both Shakur and Jackson are, in the main, fugitive slaves who are not willing to bow down to the system that oppresses and dehumanizes them. Their refusal to give up on their will to be free shows their tenacity in staying dedicated to their cause. Yet they do not claim to be triumphant at this time of pursuit, as this will just be an illusion, because the captive flesh wallows in legislative defeat. Shakur and Jackson see their cause as worthy and as one that will not be crushed by the weight of subjection, which serves as the foundational logic of the carceral state. Using their last strength and whatever is at their disposal, their defiant spirit keeps them alive.

The political communiqué, as Wilderson (2014, 176) defines it, refers to "that text which the revolutionary offers the world to make his/her thought and actions legible to all, if only acceptable to some." It signifies the articulation of the prison slaves' demands and, however insatiable these demands may be, they are made as they inform the prison slave narrative. It is in this breath that Shakur and Jackson should be understood in their prison slave narratives, which are the textual embodiment that not only gives an account of black life, but also the wanton violence that surrounds it.

The narrative of Shakur and Jackson is the articulation of the black existential anguish that has no linguistic currency. It is not translatable and its absence of effect testifies to the disembodiment of blackness, which is a state of nothingness. Having made their narratives into a political communiqué, it remains incomplete as demands of blackness are made in the void. As Wilderson (2014, 176) states: "[I]t can only succeed if its author has a 'right' to authorization." Wilderson is skeptical on authorization, due to the ontological status of blackness. How will it be possible for the criminalized, colonially stigmatized, structurally violated, and socially dead to have authorization? Since blackness is denied authorization and authorship, there is, by implication, the production of the text – the political communiqué. This is because the idea of textual production means having the political communiqué, which is essential for what Wilderson (2008) terms "the grammar of suffering." The slave narratives of Shakur and Jackson are not the result of the plight of being assimilated into the human family, and by virtue of their fugitive subjectivity their narratives become "symptomatic of an undertaking that threatens authorization itself" (Wilderson 2014, 177). Clearly, the slave narrative, in the quest to articulate the grammar of suffering, presents the end of dialogue and de-authorizes the consensus of the carceral apparatus that wields a monopoly of authorization. It is the consensus that appropriates the narratives to cement its meta-narratives. The slave narratives are not created in an attempt to appeal to the sensibilities of the antiblack world, but to provide a damning critique of it, and are not created in order for the antiblack world to change, but for it not to exist at all. For Wilderson, blackness is not the object of certainty, but the subject of it. There is no way that blackness will emerge in the *humanitas* index if the antiblack world ceases to exist.

What is clear in Wilderson's intervention is the manner in which the institution of slavery has reduced blackness to the bodily site where violence can be exercised at will and with impunity. Shakur and Jackson struggle for liberation in a committed way, without knowing the outcome, as Wilderson (2014, 184) states, "the outcome is not known." They have no futurity to romanticize about and can only call for the present to come to a halt. The prison slave narrative is the political communiqué of uncertainty precisely because it has to do with institutions that elaborate and support antiblackness and that militate against blackness. It is the narrative that is incommunicable and, as Wilderson (2014, 191) notes, it is fraught with "mechanisms which are not available for the Slave." The notion of time and space – temporality, so to say – does not apply to the prison slave who has no relational capacity and who is barred from the realm of existence. There is no moment where the prison slave is relieved from subjection, constituting a state of permanence where the life of blackness is always weaved into structural violence. This is the existential horror of incommunicability; the political communiqué is not made by Shakur and Jackson as a tool that will have a moral appeal or empathy for the plight of blackness. The incommunicability of the political communiqué is not only forced speech, but to bring to witness the extent through which black suffering is too much to bear. The political communiqué is in the belly of the tyranny of justice, but is not structured by it.

The Tyranny of Justice

With all the glory and high standing of the justice system, the very presence of the prison slave is in contradiction with the justice system. This also extends to the moment of resistance of the prison slave, which attests to the incoherence of the symbolic order that is nothing but the law and order of the antiblack world. The narrative of the prison slave is an exposé of the injustice of the justice system.

First and foremost, the justice system that is relationally structured to blackness is antiblack. Therefore, it is naive to expect justice from the antiblack institutional relationality. In considering the manner in which the racist gaze is fixed upon the black bodies of Shakur and Jackson, what stands out is that they are regarded as extremists who must be subjected to constant surveillance. They are, as the stereotypes anomies of society, portrayed as those who are outside the citizenry – the very image that aims to distort and to disfigure their persona and politics. Both Shakur and Jackson are arrested by the phantom language of the colonial stigma that inscribes their fugitiveness (Dayan 2002).

Blacks have been at the receiving end of injustice. The meting out of injustice is the relational practice of the carceral apparatus with respect to black bodies; it seems fit to violate black bodies. These are criminalized bodies and even if they are killed, it is in the best interests of justice. The prison slave is caught in the state of injury and it is, as Best and Hartman (2005, 1) argue, "too late to imagine the repair of its injury." This injury is irreparable in that the damage has already been done and there can be no restoration. To understand the predicament of the prison slave is to problematize the present mechanism of justice including its pretentious rhetoric of justice. This is used to put off the mark the prison slave and its incapacity to account for that repair of slavery. Best and Hartman (2005, 2) pose a fundamental question: "How does one compensate for the centuries of violence that have as their consequence the impossibility of restoring a prior existence, of giving back what was taken, of repairing what was broken?" The call for justice by prison slaves and blacks in general falls into the terrain of inaudibility and thus leads to the non-availability of justice mechanisms, since blackness is a phenomenon outside the *humanitas* index.

> All of our shouts reached them muffled from a great distance, almost from another world. They hardly disturb those hard of ear and of heart, those about whom we know, from a thousand testimonies, that they have a good laugh when, among themselves, like a good, crude joke, they utter the expression "presumption of innocence."
>
> (Derrida [1995] 2002, 126)

Justice for blackness is non-existent. The values that come with justice and that are attached to the American citizen cannot apply to blackness by virtue of being criminalized. The American citizen is the figure of whiteness, the one who does not have the pathological attachments that are directed to the black body. The legitimation of whiteness through expulsion and exclusion of blackness means that whiteness is governed through civil law, and, for that matter, as Dayan (2002) states, whiteness possesses civil bodies. If justice serves the rest of humanity and everyone is equal by being legal persons, it is clear that blacks do not fit into this category. By not being legal persons, they do not fit into the legal sphere at all as they are in the domain of the prison slaves. That which is legal collapses in front of the prison slave and the injustice will pervade itself in excess. The status of the legal person does not disappear in front of the prison slave; it is the status that has never been there. The tyranny of justice hides behind its façade of rational basis, impartiality, and fairness, which is deadly to prison slaves. Not having any form of legal standing and falling outside the juridical order, Shakur and Jackson are on the offensive, since they will in no way be exonerated from the clutches of the tyranny of justice.

The prisoner's slave identity is constructed out of the hatred turned into fantasy, the excess of power to which Shakur and Jackson have been subjected. As prison slaves, the fugitive identity is there to legitimate the fascist character of the police. The fugitive character of Shakur and Jackson took a formidable emphasis. As Fisher (2002) notes, the slave's resistance opens up the possibility of being politically significant. Bukhari (2003, 10) gives a telling personal account when he writes: "It is one thing to hear about the underhanded things police do – you can choose to ignore it – but it is totally different to experience it for yourself." This awakening to the reality of being black in the antiblack world is experienced by those who are black and for nothing but being black – a crime. As Best and Hartman (2005, 9) state, "police violence and brutality create the identity of the fugitive." It means that Shakur and Jackson are the products of the racist juridical infrastructure and their politics are a commitment to free themselves from the fugitive identity, which means that they can be killed at will in the best interests of justice. They both call into question not only police brutality, but also the whole carceral apparatus that the police are accountable to. Making the decision to face police brutality and all the injustices directed at the black body, Shakur and Jackson clearly expose how police brutality manifests and encroaches on the livelihood of blackness. Bukhari (2003) refers to a "political direction" to understand the ways in which consciousness of the prison slave comes into being and how political commitment is the route of no return, precisely because what matters is to see the end of injustice. Political direction means, then, that Shakur and Jackson's politics are on the route of no return.

According to Dayan (2002, 54), "the felon rendered dead in law, takes place in a world where the supernatural serves as the unacknowledged mechanism of justice." There is no justice for the prison slave, leading to Best and Hartman strongly arguing that such a figure is dead in law. The law cannot account for and serve the best interests of what does not exist in its ambit. The law, argues Dayan, is the mechanism that materializes dispossession. Punishment and prison mean that the incarcerated body is both property and dispossession. It is, therefore, the very same law that is the result of the institutionalization of what Shakur and Jackson term the carceral apparatus, which in turn is the state that creates its fugitives. The sovereign nature of the warder is the extension of the antiblack world, which is based on denigration of the humanity of the captive body. Best and Hartman (2005, 9) posit that in "the propagandist account of the dangerous fugitive, the purpose of the narrative is to justify the police power, to justify the exercise of power to kill." Society is led to believe that there is no police violence, but the violence of the prison slave whether in the streets or in incarceration. What is exposed here is what Ferreira da Silva (2014, 121) rightly notes is "the collapsing of justice that exposes the violent face of the state." The violent and deadly force of the state with its sadistic impulses is expressed and directed to the captive flesh of blackness.

> Racial violence, unleashed in the in/difference that collapses administration of justice in/to law enforcement, immediately legitimating the state's deployment of its force of self-preservation, does not require stripping off signifiers of humanity.
>
> (Ferreira da Silva 2014, 158)

Clearly, away from the societal eye, everything is permissible; power is the actualization of sadistic relations, the realization of fantasy. If the fugitives are not their own creation, as no one would choose to live under siege, it is then clear, as Fanon (1970) argues, that blackness is designated to be a phobic object, which is the anomie for the white gaze. And, as a result, the hyper-creation of genocidal impulses is infused into the violent and sadistic practices that are directed to that which is eliminated from the *humanitas* index. "The image of the 'blackened' person, disabled but not necessarily dead, remained a more terrifying example of punishment than that of the executed body" (Dayan 2002, 59).

Since the black body is captive flesh, warders subject the body that is incarcerated to their mercy. For the warder to claim power over the incarcerated body, this body must reciprocate what Larson (2010) dubs the "monologue of power," which disables civil persons and invents legal slaves (Dayan 2002). The monologue of power is in the hands of the warder who is the extension of the carceral apparatus. The despotic nature of the reign of power is to render the body of the prison slave into that which is expelled and excluded. The body of the prison slave is that which is devoid of what Dayan calls "the purity of blood" and the prison slave is not governed by law, but by the "death of law." Because the purity of blood stands in opposition to the filth of blood, prison slaves, by the fact of their blackness, are subjected to what Dayan terms the "racialized fiction of blood, moreover, supplementing the metaphoric taint, not only defining property in slaves but fixing them and their progeny and descendants in status and location" (Dayan 2002, 59). Blackness is the figure of the degraded ontology, due to not falling in the purity of blood. This is the structure of sadistic relations, as the warder is a sovereign beast who confers allowance and restriction, will and prohibition, peace and violence, and life and death. The incarcerated body belongs to the warder inasmuch as the body of the slave is the property of the master in the plantation. The power of the warder is the embodiment of the sovereign beast. The warder is a sovereign beast in that s/he has many sources of power and this power can be practiced or improvised to sadistic proportions. The power of the warder is a fetish, in that it is exercised at the micro-level of institutionality (the prison), but it is informed by the larger racist infrastructure from which it derives the source of being sovereign (the antiblack world) – the one who territorializes and whose prey are not certain when they will be predated upon. The prison slave as a fugitive means the prey that is on the hunt even in the condition of capture. As Larson (2010, 144) notes, the warder "operates doors and gates, grants and withdraws privileges, and metes out punishment; and all the activities are carried out within the walled and fenced perimeters of the prison ground."

Shakur and Jackson refuse to be dependent on the warder. They are steadfast in their commitment to liberation and are not willing to sell out. The law of the arbitrary is what Shakur and Jackson come into confrontation with. The elasticity of justice is the very violence that structures them in the antiblack world. It is even in the domain of justice that warders as sovereign beasts have the prerogative to exercise their power in sadistic ways, in that they are the law makers in prison. "The dominant characteristic for the political prisoner, was exactly about violence" (Gready 1993, 495). The manner in which the body, mind, and spirit of the prison slave is subjected to violence is to rid it of any sense of resistance. The prison slave, through the embodiment of captive flesh, is subjected to the hyper-legality of the law. The law can stretch to its excess, that is, illegality, to make it relational to the prison slave. So, in the relationship between the law and the prison slave, there is no law.

> The incarceration exists in all legal, extra-legal, and political forms: political prisoners, men and women unjustly jailed, and men and women who pose a real threat to the citizens who enjoy a right to personal and public safety.
>
> (Larson 2010, 145)

The carceral apparatus justifies its power as being in the interests of the citizens. However, the self-arrogated claim of being in the interests of the citizens cannot be left unproblematized, taking into account that the very carceral apparatus violates its citizens. In the antiblack world there are those who are inside and those who are outside, the latter being at the receiving end of violence and dehumanization. The citizen is not the one who is subjected to the antiblack world. By implication, wittingly or unwittingly, the warder who quarantines the prison slave also does the same to blacks who are outside prison. Since they are not citizens, prison slaves and blacks in general pose a threat to citizens. The politicization of Shakur and Jackson is seen as a threat to the carceral apparatus, which is the guarantor of the institution of slavery at large under its antiblack posture of maintaining law and order.

> Lawyers and judges confronted slave resistance by promoting stories about the origin and development of slave character and behaviour that removed rational agency from slaves. In this way the law created an image of blackness as an absence of will, something which Shakur and Jackson were subjected to by being libeled against by the state apparatus.
>
> (Gross 2002, 319)

What politicizes the tyranny of justice is that Shakur and Jackson were members of the Black Panther Party and that Shakur was also affiliated with the Black Liberation Army. Both are political prisoners who suffer the fate of what other members of these movements went through by means of arbitrary arrests, being jailed on trumped-up charges indefinitely and being subjected to many more violations legitimated by the carceral apparatus. Though the courts were and are spaces that adjudicate legal matters pertaining the legal person, they are not, on the other hand, legitimate spaces where the plight of the prison slave can be deliberated. For, there is nothing legal about the persona of the prison slave; the courtroom is the space where such a persona is weighed down by criminality that does not depend on any verdict. Making reference to Jackson's death, this is what Angelou (1975, 4) says: "The silence was shuttering. The crowd held the quiet as if the silence itself was body of Jackson." This silence is shuttering. Even the state that killed Jackson could not account. It refused to take responsibility for his death. However, for Angelou, and most blacks in the forefront of the existential struggle against antiblackness, this is no surprise. Indeed, writes Angelou (1975, 4): "Only surprise was absent."

> American justice provides answers when American law has none. When it becomes impossible to stand a man up in court and frame him for murder, when it becomes impossible to release that man because of his courage and his single-mindedness in making no compromise with oppression, it becomes necessary to eliminate him.
> (Dhondy 1971, 1955)

The contradiction of the legal person needs to be understood from Esmeir's (2006, 1546) perspective that "[a] person is, therefore, at once a human and yet-to-be human, a member of universal human kind and its dehumanized figure." The contradiction is true only for those who are legal persons and whose humanity can take different forms, with the possibility that there is a remedy for every existential injury, as being dehumanized is temporality. This means that their humanity is not taken outside the legal framework. Their humanity is always recognized, hence they are legal persons. Also, importantly, blackness having the figure of the *exteriori* does not feature in a "human," a "yet-to-be human" and a "member of the universal humankind." That which is blackness – the prison slave who is the *exteriori* of the *humanitas* index – cannot be a legal person in the world that has written blackness outside the legal framework. Blackness, in short, is not the figure of the law, that is, the legal person. Esmeir demonstrates how legal status provides the basis for legal standing and the basis for there to be a legal person who has entitlements, duties, obligations, and rights that are provided and protected by law.

By being in the courtroom and facing the judge, the dissolving of the persona is something that is also outside the courtroom. The law of persons is used *mala fide*, in that it is used to make that which is criminalized stand trial, where the verdict is premeditated, not only by the court, but also through the largesse of the carceral apparatus. Therefore, the courtroom is a space without blackness and there is no way the court can be expected to act in the interests of those who are black in the face of the antiblack world. The fugitive characters of Shakur and Jackson are illegality, and the court is the space of the tyranny of justice. As Koerner (2011) states, both Shakur and Jackson engage in fugitivity as the affirmation of politics that resist capture, and the refusal to bow to injustice. They refuse, in totality, according to Koerner, the "terms of captivity" and they carry the long history and memory of what was done to their ancestry. So, both Shakur and Jackson know that they are confronting, and they use their "blackness and writing" as Koener signals, to reformulate the terms of liberation. Indeed, to Shakur and Jackson, the court is a middle passage to the regime of incarceration – the route of no return. By being in the courtroom, the prison slave is "against the law" and, as Gross (2002, 299) states, "unrecognized by law." With no juridical standing, Shakur and Jackson stand in relation to the historical continuities of slavery.

> It was a cardinal rule of slave law in every state that slaves could under no circumstances testify against a white man; this rule applied to out-of-court non-hearsay as well as live testimony. The rationale for the rule was simple: slaves were mendacious and unworthy of taking the oath to testify; their words could not be the basis of liability or culpability of a white person.
>
> (Gross 2002, 316)

This does not end in slavery: it is a continued reality; blacks are still criminalized and cannot have their narrative in court. Shakur and Jackson cannot testify against the white man owing to the carceral apparatus and its tyranny of justice. Because of the fact that both of them have been implicated for violating the white man, they, as prison slaves, have no say and will not have a say. They have transgressed the white flesh and they must pay with their lives. Both Shakur and Jackson stand at the receiving end of the passion of hate. This does not deter their will to resist and to express love to those to whom they pay allegiance and to whom they have an affinity, that is, black people.

The Loving Subjectivity

Shakur and Jackson are informed by love and their ethical stand is radical and unique in the sense that they articulate ethical questions to scandalize the carceral state. Both of them think, write, and act out of love because, as Maldonado-Torres (2008) states, they are enraptured by it and their mode of articulating the political becomes a "loving praxis" that is foregrounded in the politics of critique. The critique of Shakur and Jackson is not a vitriol of propaganda or hate speech as the antiblack world states, but the rooted core of blackness and its loving subjectivity. Their fugitive spirit upsurges their intolerance for anything that tampers with loving subjectivity, and their precarious existence as prison slaves does not tamper with their love for humanity. The expression of loving subjectivity "expands the intensity of antagonism" (Wilderson 2003b, 22), and what is found in Shakur and Jackson are the symptoms of race and resignation. Their loathing of antiblackness and their persistence in their loving subjectivity of blackness means that the expansion of the intensity of antagonism is a necessity. Not that this borders on the politics of self-sacrifice: it is not a choice, but a necessity to ward off all forms of subjection. As prison slaves, Shakur and Jackson make ontologico-existential demands not as human beings, but as those who want to become humans because they are being dehumanized. Their demands are not treaties, as treaties exist among humans only and in the absence of dehumanization. What is at stake is life itself, and the expansion of the intensity of antagonism obliterates treaties in that the ontologico-existential scandal of the prison slave is introduced. As Maldonado-Torres (2008, 97) acutely notes, the loving subjectivity is the "consistent expression and in the love of dehumanized human beings." There is no form of articulation taking place and there is no ontological currency of being a sovereign subject. This subject only exists in the world of a human;

hence the treaties are the appropriate tools for humans. Not having the entitlement of sovereignty and being plagued by the absence of ontological density, the prison slave is nothing but a non-being of blackness. What, then, does it mean to express a loving subjectivity from the precarious ontologico-existential condition? Shakur's poem *Love* speaks of the centrality of love from the throes that thwart it:

Love is contained in Hell,
cause love is an acid
that eats away bars.

(Shakur 1987, 130)

The political expression of Shakur and Jackson affirms the loving subjectivity. They make it explicit in their prison slave narratives that they love black people and in their desire for a better world they want to see the liberation that will come into being after the end of the antiblack world. Their love goes uncontested, as they have given themselves fully to the struggle against all forms of oppression that affect blackness. This is the extent to which their loving subjectivity goes. This is not love for its own sake, but loving subjectivity, which Maldonado-Torres (2008, 141) terms "an uncompromising affirmation of love." It is a radical expression and it is the love of the cause. That is why even in life-threatening situations this love cannot be compromised. This love means not accepting any dehumanization of blacks and to stand in fierce opposition to the hate of the antiblack blackness. Being uncompromising clearly shows the political commitment of the narrative of the prison slave.

I must follow my call. It is of great importance for me that you understand this and give me your blessing. I don't care about anyone else. I don't feel I must explain myself or be understood by anyone else on earth.

(Jackson 1970, 121)

Jackson also elaborates elsewhere:

I must follow my mind. There is no turning back from awareness. If I were to alter my step right now I would always hate myself. I would grow old feeling that I have failed in the obligatory duty that is ours once we become aware. I would die as most of us blacks have died over the last few centuries, without having lived.

(Jackson 1970, 139)

This is nothing but a fierce political commitment, and asking for the blessings of his father does not mean he is asking for permission. Jackson has started with the cause and apart from the issue of him not having to explain himself to anyone; he has taken the route of no return, since there is no turning back from awareness. This awareness is consciousness, which comes from being politicized by his ontologico-existential condition and having to wage a struggle against the antiblack world. For there to be loving subjectivity, there should be respect.

> You can't claim that you love people when you don't respect them, and you can't call for political unity unless you practice it in your relationship. And that doesn't happen out of nowhere. That's something that has got to be put into practice every day.
>
> (Shakur 1987, 218)

For the love of the people and the love of justice, it is on these grounds that revolution takes place and is pursued until the realization of genuine liberation. Without love, there is no need for the struggle. This is not empty love, but a fundamental love that solidifies bonds of those who are oppressed and who are dedicated to ridding themselves of the infrastructure of oppression. The ethos, spirit, and commitment of love lie at the heart of Shakur and Jackson. Both are deeply engaged in politics that are informed by a love of black people. As Ferreira da Silva (2014, 158) states, it is the love of the black body that "stands before the horizon of death."

Making reference to Jackson, Dhondy (1971, 1955) writes: "The guardianship of his life has been passed on to the will and consciousness of the black people." Corrigan (2009, 2) also describes Shakur as "a self-sacrificing revolutionary guerrilla and mother leading a liberation movement against racism, brutality, and the prison industrial complex." Shakur holds love in high regard, while, for Jackson, love has a contradictory element. Jackson treats love with suspicion and there are certain times where he embraces it and there are others where he disparages it. With regard to the latter, Jackson (1970, 58) writes: "I must rid myself of all sentiment and remove all possibility of love." What makes Jackson's stance toward love to lend itself to complication is that love exists, but wanes in the antiblack world that is structured by gratuitous violence. This also relates to his conception of the soul, which he considers to be abstract. But Jackson does not rule out love in its entirety. Many of the letters he writes to his mother are signed "Love." This love is not only directed to his mother, but also to all those to whom he writes and to whom he has an affection. It is the absolute expression of love when Jackson (1970, 95) says: "I have a plan, I will give, and give of myself until it proves our making or my end." This is the commitment tied by the revolutionary intent, its expression and actualization being nothing but love in itself.

What is of interest is that love emerges from the throes of absolute absence that does not allow its possibility. For the mere fact that the existence is hellish, this love is the force that inspires commitment to liberation. "This form of love is not the narrative of love as encoded in the West: it is another kind of love, a synchronic process that punctures through traditional, older narratives of love, that ruptures everyday being" (Maldonado-Torres 2008, 141). Shakur and Jackson feature well in Sandoval's articulation of love, the love that creates subjects who are engaged in a radically consistent opposition – the subjectivity of love that seeks nothing but injustice articulated by prison slaves themselves. The existential category of the political that Shakur and Jackson create is a being who has nothing to lose and everything to gain as far as the struggle for liberation is concerned. This is love in its potency. It is that which cannot be incarcerated by concrete and steel. Of course, this is not love in the sentimental and romantic sense. Rather, it is fury that informs the persistence of revolutionary ideas and struggle. It is a love of humanity that is channeled against the existential plight that befalls black bodies. Shakur and Jackson are angry in the subjectivity of love, in that things are not supposed to be as they are and there should be fundamental change. Shakur (1987, 175) rightfully notes that: "[W]e have accepted too much of the negative lifestyle and a negative culture and have to consciously act to rid ourselves of that negative influence." The politics of Shakur and Jackson are informed by a concern, and most of all, a love for black people. In this radical stance, both are negatively represented so that the colonial stereotypes that portray them as monsters eclipse whatever possibility there is for them to be revolutionaries of love. Shakur (1987, 181) writes: "The first thing the enemy tries to do is to isolate revolutionaries from the masses of people, making us horrible and hideous monsters so that our people will hate us." This causes those who are fighting against injustice to be seen as perpetrators of injustice, and in order for the status quo to remain, they should be complicit in bad faith. This means the distorted notion of love, in terms of which those who are oppressed should love their oppressors, must prevail.

For Sandoval, the assertion of "hope" and "faith" in the potential for the utopian good is what informs the whole topography that marks love as the political register. The assertion of hope and faith is clear when Shakur (1973, 16) states: "Black brothers, black sisters, I want you to know that I love you and I hope in your heart you love me." Shakur opens her open letter to black people with this expression of love. Love is fundamental to Shakur, in the sense that it serves as a bond that keeps her and black people together. Hence, she refers to blacks as brothers and sisters, and she states that she loves them and that she hopes they love her too. In this instance, with reference to love as the assertion of hope and faith, Shakur's desire is a utopic register and, as Sandoval asserts, it breaks through restrictions to create understanding and community. The utopic register of subjectivity of love is not a *telos*, but the rupture that opens up vistas and horizons. As eloquently put by Sandoval (2000, 140): "It is love that can access and guide over theoretical and political '*movidas*' – revolutionary manoeuvres toward decolonized being." The subjectivity of love is the politics of creation and resides in the idea that nothing depends on uncertainty, but this does not mean the elimination of love – it is the driving force. This revolutionary commitment is the desire for genuine freedom. As Shakur (1987, 175) asserts: "Our desire to be free has got to manifest itself in everything we do."

The prison slave narratives of Shakur and Jackson are informed and rooted in desire. "Desire is the upsurge of the loving subjectivity" (Maldonado-Torres 2008, 158). This desire *to be* does not present itself as the transcendental subject, but as the political in the making. The very form of affirmation is the desire to live and not to survive, the desire to become human, but not according to the dictates of the master since the desire of the prison slave is not to get recognition but *to be* on his or her own terms. This means that there is a need for radical constitution and to be reshaped by the consistent expression of loving subjectivity that is not grounded on the abstract of the universal, which is politically charged but without any radical content of being.

This then propels the politics of affection, largely because both Shakur and Jackson are affected by the need for mutual re-affirmation of being black. In other words, the conception of being is not being in itself, it is being in relation to others where existence is mutual re-affirmation. Jackson (1970, 113) thus warns: "Before we can ever effectively face down the foe, we must have long since learned to share, trust, communicate, and live harmoniously with each other." The loving subjectivity comes into being through the ethos of communal spirit that is informed by the common experience of being at the receiving end of the carceral state and to gesture toward the forms of lives that are aimed for the better world, and the place of being in relation to other beings. Indeed, everything starts with the self and the self must re-affirm itself with love and in relation to others. Jackson (1970, 137) writes: "It is said and with some justification that the greatest battle is with oneself, so if I can gain a victory here the real work shouldn't be too hard." Shakur (1987, 203) amplifies this sentiment: "Revolution is about change, and the first place change begins is yourself." The self must come closer to itself, but not in a form of narcissistic identification. Rather, there must be a love of the self and the rest of those whose lives are at stake and who are pursuing the same cause of liberation.

Shakur, in her letter, identifies herself as the "field nigger" who is relentlessly in pursuit of genuine freedom. She has vowed to fight all forces of antiblackness and it is clear from her subjectivity of love that she will stop at nothing to make this realizable. Shakur (1973, 18) makes the following call: "We must gain our liberation by any means necessary." The radical spirit of being human is what is essential for understanding the conception of life. It is to stand in opposition to that which militates against the conception of love. The love reinstates dignity to their bodies, and engaging in love is the practice of freedom. Shakur and Jackson are concerned about the existential plight of blackness and the commitment to liberation. For Maldonado-Torres, the pathos of love, which is evident in the prison slave narratives of Shakur and Jackson, affirms the ethical stand against antiblackness. The uncompromising expression of subjectivity of love made them hated by the antiblack world. Their love is not that of complicity or bad faith. This love makes the demand that blacks become the agents of the kind of world that they want. The making of these demands does not mean that they must be met, because Shakur and Jackson are not naive enough to expect justice to be served or for it to prevail.

It is the love that represents the greatest threat to the antiblack world which is nothing but the antithesis of love, as its leitmotif is nothing but absolute hate. There is no subjectivity of love in the antiblack world, it is the world of deceit and trickery. In the world where blackness is the "phobogenic object" – the black body – the passion of hate directed toward blacks who must be eliminated. The universal framework and its propagation of one humanity is the mask of the passion of hate that still informs the antiblack world, including its fiction of love. If love is propagated in the service of humanity, it is still fraught with the logic of exclusion. In addition, if this love is expressed toward blackness, it is nothing but crude paternalism. The love that informs Shakur and Jackson is love for freedom, love for the self, and love to hate all forms of subjection. Love binds, as it is an unbreakable thread – a bond of solidarity. If the loving subjectivity does not serve as the tie that binds, there will be defeat. The mode of this defeat comes through the classic divide and rule.

> It is terrible that we have all been so divided. The social order is set up as to encourage this, the powers that be don't want any loyal loving groups forming up. So they discourage it in a thousand subtle ways.
>
> (Jackson 1970, 142)

Both Shakur and Jackson are concerned about the manner in which the divide and rule strategy has been serving oppressors well. "Divide and rule in its simplest form is standard police procedure" (Jackson 1970, 187). Those who are oppressed have been entrapped in the psychic structure of repeating the very mistake of being what their oppressors want them to be. In order to overcome the divide and rule strategy, Jackson proposes the following: "We must organize our thoughts, get behind the revolutionary vanguard, make the *correct* alliances this time. We must fall on our enemies, the enemies of all righteousness, with a ruthless relentless will to win!" (Jackson 1970, 234). This is clear in Shakur and Jackson and the manner in which they refuse to compromise and to make themselves and the cause they are fighting for to be a united front that will give meaning to the cause of liberation. Nothing will deter Shakur and Jackson as they are fired up by loving subjectivity. This subjectivity centers on blackness itself and the expression of blackness as that which reaches to the realm of existence and that which has to confront the carceral state with its epistemology of law that is antiblack.

Love is the end of the prison gulag. The prison gulag is not built on justice, but on hate. As such, the prison gulag represents the infrastructure of hate, and the end of the infrastructure is the end of the prison gulag. The hate that is embodied by the prison gulag is not accidental, it is deliberate. The presence of the prison gulag is not only institutional, it is ontological, hence it is informed by the genocidal impulses that are directed toward the black body as the subject of elimination. For the prison gulag to end, what will come into being is the presence of the loving subjectivity of the prison slave. The prison gulag is the territory of the colonial master and if it were to come to an end, there would be no place for the colonial master to reside, even to the extent that the colonial master would cease to exist – the effort of the prison slave acting of his or her own accord.

For there to be a prison gulag, there has to be a prison slave. The end of the prison gulag does not necessarily mean the end of the prison slave; instead, it means the end of the pathological life that produces the prison slave – the life that is the deliberate design of the antiblack world. It is, therefore, important to regard the prison slave narrative, as a textual practice, as not being confined to prison and as a larger critique of the antiblack world. For the mere fact of being called prison writing these are writings in the belly of the beast not as finality, but the world that the beast is a product of – the antiblack world. For, sociality cannot be understood only in relation to the regime of incarceration it produces. Because prisons are kept away from the social environment of which they are a part, members of the public should leave the regime of incarceration to its own whims as far as the legitimation of power excess and the non-accounting of its captive flesh are concerned. The inner workings of power improvised, adulterated through sadistic violence, and the rituals of phallic power are kept away from the public, since those who are incarcerated are liable for the punishment they rightfully deserve. If the prison slave narratives of Assata Shakur and George Jackson talk directly to the lived experience of being black in the antiblack world, surely there is a call for the end of the prison gulag, which will only come about if the antiblack world ceases to exist.

5

For Mabogo P. More:
A Meditation

The struggle for life is paramount in the preoccupation of Africana existential philosophy with the ontological and existential conception of being-black-in-the-antiblack-world. This is not accidental, but a form of necessity where philosophical interventions are the ways of imagining the idea of another liberated world in which blacks are human – the world where humanity at large lives. The lived experience of those who are existentially wronged is where Mabogo P. More's philosophical intervention sets in. To examine More's philosophical contribution is to locate him in the Africana existential philosophy tradition, the philosophical authorization that he rightfully claims. This is the philosophical context in which More locates himself as he grapples with ontological and existential questions of blackness.

This insertion of *to be* in blackness is important for a number of reasons. One, blackness has been ontologically structured to be in exact directionality with the ontological structure of antiblack racism so to become the figure that is purely dehumanized. It is in this structuring that the logic of antiblack racism is epistemologically ruptured to cement the racist logic through reason and stereotypes. Two, the existential condition in which blackness finds itself is far removed from what can accommodate those who have human status. This reinforces the pathological existence in which blackness does not live, but survives, and what remains is the fact that blackness is still a death trap. Three, the antiblack world expels blackness from the realm of existence and the logic that prevails is that of bad faith, where there is a pretence that blacks do matter. Lastly, the question of becoming human is a necessity, and blackness will wage a relentless existential struggle in pursuit of the state of becoming human in its own terms.

If the philosopher exists in the colonial state and is on the existential site through which the violence of the colonial state is directed, then philosophical preoccupations will be different. The philosophical themes of the philosopher who is violated by the colonial state will call for different modes of philosophical reflection. It is clear from More's philosophical reflection that the themes that inform his oeuvre are indeed the questions of the existence of the black subject.

The key philosophers with whom More engages in his works are Jean-Paul Sartre, Frantz Fanon, Chabani Manganyi, Steve Biko, and Lewis Gordon, to name just a few, all of whom belong in Africana existential philosophy. The works of these philosophers continue to imagine another form of life and another world outside the existential abyss of subjection. There is a need to confront the lack or absence of political imagination which has created the de-politicized subjectivity and has even claimed that philosophy has nothing to do with race. This is to counter the discourses that propagate the existential flight from the race question. Thus, this breeds bad faith, which yields the sedimentation of antiblack racism and complicity. More's philosophical contribution is key in showing how liberation has been betrayed, and it is here that the frame of analysis will be deployed to account for the conceptual fidelity of liberation and distinguish it from emancipation. What will then be contended with is how in More's work the existential horizons are articulated and what kind of world is being imagined.

The Existential Struggle as Philosophy

For there to be philosophy there must be a philosopher. And in no way can a philosopher, let alone the practice of philosophy, exist in a vacuum. The kind of philosopher that is argued for here is one who engages with philosophy born of struggle (Harris 1982). This, then, means that a philosopher of this calibre is the figure who engages in philosophy not just for the sake of philosophy *qua* philosophy. Rather, the philosophical is the very existential condition through which the philosopher tries to make meaning from life and to advocate existential struggle if that life is subjected to what Hartman (1997) refers to as "scenes of subjection." This kind of philosophy is not only that of the resisting subject or the subject who engages in what Mbembe (2002) refers to as "the modes of self-writing," where those who are resisting subjects are accused of engaging in "faked philosophies." This philosophy is the will to live and waging the perpetual existential struggle against any form of subjection. The will to live is therefore the very thematic area of Africana existential philosophy.

More is a philosopher determined by the existential conditions. By virtue of being black, he is in the existential abyss of blackness and is also vexed in the antiblack world. He is not the philosopher as a transcendental subject, nor is he engaging in the transcendental philosophical themes that are divorced from the existential crisis of blackness or the lived reality as such. Even the larger narrative arch of the universal, cosmopolitanism and post-racialism are not appealing in the sense that they are alien to the lived experience of being black-in-the-antiblack-world. More refuses to be well adjusted to the philosophical status quo, and chooses to stand on the existential site of blackness – to be the philosopher who stands in close proximity to being black in the antiblack world. That is why More's philosophical corpus is concerned with the lived reality of blackness in the antiblack world. By manner of existential location – being black in the antiblack world – different existential questions, which are in themselves existential, will be animated. This is not accidental, and it is to be expected that blackness in the positionality of subjection must ask fundamental questions that have to do with such an existential position.

> Black philosophers, within the context of worldwide white supremacy, share a certain *Othered* experiential reality, or social ontology that shapes aspects of their being-philosophically-in-the-world. This means that even if one chooses to be a philosopher, one's choice within a certain context is influenced by the existential and social situation in which one finds oneself. In an antiblack world, the racial context or situation may determine to a large extent the kind of philosopher a black philosopher becomes and the kinds of problematics such a philosopher deals with in his or her philosophizing endeavors.
>
> (More 2018, 109 [emphasis original])

If the philosopher is the distinguishable subject, the liberal individual and the purveyor of that which is in the mind and divorced from the body, what then appears is the opposite. That is, More is a philosopher of existence and simultaneously the embodied subject. If there is what preoccupies the philosophical themes and concerns that More is dealing with, one thing is for certain: the existence of blackness is hellish. The existence of blacks in a world that is hostile to their existence is what matters most. That is why it is impossible to find amiss in More's interventions the place of blacks in the world that displaces them systemically and systematically. The world is antiblack, and the existence of blacks is called into question (More 2008; Gordon 2000a; Maldonado-Torres 2008). To really account for More as the philosopher of existence is to evoke Manganyi's existential-ontologico meditation of *being-black-in-the-world* and by extension, as More makes clear, the figure of *being-black-in-the-antiblack world*. It is in the latter ontological realm that the place of blackness is punctuated as the ontological figure that is rendered placeless by the antiblack world. It is also in this ontological realm that More (2012) brings to the fore the fact that ontology and politics are inseparable. Thus, the phenomenon of embodiment becomes profound.

To exist is *to be*, and blackness in its becoming is in this ontological realm in that the condition of becoming is negation of blackness through dehumanizing practices brought about by antiblack racism. In militating against this ontological infrastructure of antiblack racism, Biko's intervention comes as the quest for a true humanity. The fundamental preoccupation of philosophy of existence as More asserts it is *to be*, and it is here that blackness becomes human in its own terms, its subjectivity not being externally mediated.

More is concerned with the lived experiences of being black, and also the manner in which blackness asserts itself in this world structured by antiblack racism. The ultimate goal is not to minimize racism, but to wage the ontologico-existential struggle for it to end. This is necessary in that the philosophical tradition from which More draws – Africana existential philosophy – is pursuing the ontological questions that center the lived experience of blackness in the antiblack world. These are ontological questions which were and are still in the canon of Sartre, Fanon, Manganyi, and Biko, to name just a few. Because these questions still do persist, it is at best absurd to suggest that they are archaic and therefore irrelevant.

If the preoccupation with *being* is ontologically grounded with the question of becoming – *to be* – then what it means to be human is somewhat irrelevant, as opposed to what it means to be black in the antiblack world. The dehumanized are asking the question of the dehumanized, and denied existence in order to become human and on their own terms. The being of the black is struggling to become human, to be free and to live. More does not see *to be* as a form of free will, but rather the struggle of life and death. It is the ontological condition that demands the existential struggle in that the assertion of blacks' will to live creates paranoia in the infrastructure of antiblack racism, which feeds itself through the de-ontologization of blackness. So, then, blackness should rebel in pursuit of its will to live – *to be*. This is evident in More's philosophical interventions, which clearly show that blackness is not the ontological extension of something exterior to it; instead, it is its own interiority, its own being in the struggle to become. The rebel character of blackness is not for its own sake, for blackness is militated against. Blackness is relegated to what Fanon (1970) terms the zone of non-being. It is More who makes explicit reference to why this is the case, why blackness is reduced to such an existential abyss.

It is clear that the struggle *to be* is to shape existential struggles against antiblack racism, and the one that is clearly advocated in More's work is the transformative philosophy of Black Consciousness. This struggle is necessary, as blacks are denied their right to be and status of being human throughout their life. That is why antiblack racism finds it justifiable to treat blackness at the ontological level of a thing. Césaire (1972) adds that this creates thingification out of blackness. It is clear from this philosophy that the ontological position of blackness is not a given, but a deliberate man-made dehumanization practice, which must come to an absolute end. The dehumanization of blackness is akin to the practices of ontological corruption that are constitutive parts of dehumanization.

From the account provided so far, it is clear that More is a philosopher who confronts the fundamental question of the infrastructure of antiblack racism head-on. The problems of existence, as Gordon (2000a) asserts, have relevance to More as the philosopher who confronts freedom and damnation of blacks. It is to be in this philosophical positionality to affirm the mantle of being the philosopher of the human, to be in the quest for philosophical commitment and doing philosophy of existence. More's observation is important in order to understand his philosophical commitment:

Despite the increase in race consciousness, philosophers in general, but South African philosophers in particular, have generally sadly ignored discourse on racism when analytic skills and philosophical reflection are most needed. Some of the reasons for this silence have to do with the fact that for some philosophers, philosophy itself, and its practice have been complicitous in racism.

(More 2005, 4)

More cites the fact that philosophy has always seen itself, methodologically and epistemologically, to be the discipline in which race is treated as an *exteriori*. But for More to be a philosopher who takes on the question of race and racism, his philosophical practice must be the one which bears testimony to the lived experience of the black in the antiblack world. It is, therefore, vital to understand the infrastructure of antiblack racism in order to understand what racism in the antiblack world as experienced by blacks fundamentally is.

The Infrastructure of Antiblack Racism

The end of racism is not the removal of statutes which are racist. It is not changing street names, and using the same facilities that previously required separate use or were differently delegated. It is not outlawing racist language, remarks, and stereotypes. It is not the propagation of non-racialism and claiming oneness and seeing no race but humanity. Racism is specifically pinned down to its most crude form – antiblack racism – the form of racism that puts the humanity of blacks into question. "While for the black the white is another human being, the structure of antiblack racism on the other hand is such that for the antiblack racist, the black is not another human being" (More 2012, 27). It is the racism that fits in the equation of antiblack racism = dehumanization. Antiblack racism is the form of racism that has to do with the manner in which the black subject is made to be in the abyss of homology of absence. To be in this ontological abyss is to be dehumanized.

So racism is a context marked by a paradox of being a human relation of inhumanity. It is a human act of denying the humanity of other groups of human beings. This human act can be structural (institutional) and situational (between individuals) ... But more, that racism involves dehumanization situates it as a form of oppression.

(Gordon 2000a, 85–86)

The structural relationality of the black to the world is the state of nothingness. If racism is to be understood in relation to the position-ality of antiblackness, then it is appropriate to account for the ways in which it dehumanizes blacks and relegates them to the existential abyss of things *qua* things. Racism, More (2008, 51) contends, "is not discrimination alone, but also the power to control the lives of those excluded." More is, in fact, amplifying Biko (1978, 114), who avers: "Racism does not only imply exclusion of one race by another – it presupposes that the exclusion is for the purposes of subjugation." Antiblack racism is directed at black bodies by virtue of their ontological powerlessness and all the institutions that this power rests on serve the purpose of subjugating black bodies. Antiblack racism is when whites have sovereign power over the totality of black existence and define how life and death of blacks happens. More amplifies this through explicating what apartheid fundamentally is. He writes:

> As a concept, "apartheid" functions much like "consciousness." One cannot simply be "conscious" without being conscious of something. Consciousness is always consciousness of something; it is intentional. The apartness of apartheid is the separation of races of people. Prima facie, the doctrine "apartheid" holds that each race has a unique destiny, history, religion, culture, values etc. and that for this reason they must be kept apart ... However, in practice and in theory, apartheid is a colonialist, capitalist, religious, and racial ideology designed to ensure the domination and subjugation of the majority of black people by the minority white European settlers. It is this meaning that constitutes the identity of apartheid with colonialism.
>
> (More 2014, 3–4)

One thing that More brings to our attention is the fact that antiblackness in South Africa, as a colonial state, has its roots in the beginning of the settler–colonial encounter (1652) and not apartheid (1948), the latter being the continuation of the former. Apartheid, as the infrastructure of antiblackness, is intrinsically linked with colonialism and is its continuation. It is important to highlight that the end of apartheid (1994) does not mean the end of the infra-structure of antiblack racism. Post-1994 as a neo-apartheid project is founded on what Hartman (1997, 5) refers to as "the savage encroachments of power that take place through notions of reform, consent, and protection." What remains a reality is the manner in which black existence continues to be militated against through wanton violence. Blacks are violated simply for being black.

The antiblack draconian laws that targeted blacks "legali[s]ed the separation of the races in almost every sphere of existence" (More 2014, 5). Therefore, to specifically locate the site of antiblack racism and its mode of expression and taking power over blacks into account, it must be stated that racism affects blacks. The latter are its victims, and they do not have power over whites, post-1994 notwithstanding. Apartheid *qua* antiblack racism has no human element, and for there to be life, it can only extend in so far as it is whites only and there should be no blacks. It is a form of racism that bans life and it creates a world, as Gordon (2000b) argues, as a better place without blacks. For whites to live, blacks must be excluded from life itself and to be relegated to the realm of perpetual suffering and even death.

If antiblack racism is structural, it is not based on the notion of time and space; that is, what ontologically incarcerates the black subjects is not racism which has passed: it is the afterlife in the modality of the present. The social death of blackness is something that the infrastructure of antiblackness needs to be understood. That is why, as More (2017) punctuates, racism has to be understood as hierarchized power relations that stand to subjugate and inferiorize the black into dehumanization. Apartheid is a regime of death, and its colonial continuities are the very infrastructure of antiblackness. As a regime of death, it manifests itself through the power that confers nothing but death. That is why More, taking a Bikoian cue, deems apartheid an evil system in absolute terms.

Apartheid was the enforcement by a minority of Europeans of a policy designed to keep in conditions of slavery or neo-slavery the majority of the black, consisting of black people. Committed to establishing and intensifying absolute white supremacy, the apartheid Nationalist Party government enacted a series of racially discriminating laws, including the Group Areas Act, mandating residential segregation; the Immorality Act, forbidding interracial matrimony; the Population Registration Act, the pillar of apartheid legislation which classified people according to their race and ordering; the Bantu Education Act, enacting separated and unequal education for different racial groups; the Prevention of Illegal Squatting Act, preventing unemployed African work seekers from living in white cities and towns; the Native Resettlement Act, for the coerced removal of Africans to the bantustans; the Land Act of 1913, the appropriation of African land, giving 87 percent of the total land to white people and 13 per cent to Africans; the Influx Control Act, regulating the influx and labour of Africans in white urban areas. All these Acts – together with thousands of proclamations, regulations, by-laws and government notices – were collectively a method of compartmentalizing the settlers and the natives, forcing apart the racial groups and instituting white supremacy in South Africa. In the apartheid world, therefore, race made all the difference, because it determined one's mode of being and perceiving; one's being-for-others; one's relation to objects, space and time, and one's opportunities – in short, one's being.

(More 2017, 131–132)

Apartheid is the negation of being. It operates on the basis of excess of power, the very form of constraining life and warranting death to blacks. As Bogues opines:

> At the sites where violence operates as power, not only is death perpetual motion, but the regular crushing of animated life. Thus death has a political purpose where it becomes the ultimate negative ground of the human. To put this another way, a regime of extreme violence has to enact regular practices of death because its purpose is the absolute negation of the human life-form in its plurality.
>
> (Bogues 2010, 74)

Apartheid, as the infrastructure of antiblack racism, rests not only in institutions and oppressive structures, symbolic orders, ideologies, myths, stereotypes, and prejudices. Apartheid *qua* infrastructure of antiblack racism has the world as its bedrock – the antiblack world. The antiblack world is fashioned in such a way that it militates against the existence of blacks. For blacks to be militated against means that the world does not want them, and it expresses its abhorrence to blacks through structural violence. As an invisible form of violence, its effects are seen as nothing but inevitable, the existential state of naturalness of blacks as the figure of the pathological other. If structural violence is pointed out by its victims, they become vilified as being trivial and blameworthy of something that has nothing to do with their existential suffering.

Structural violence is a strange form of relation in that it is the form of violence that does not take the humanity of blacks into account. It exists and operates freely with impunity and without any form of ethical accounting because it violates nothing but a thing.

"Re-presentation," argues Marriott (2000, 3), "is what brings the spectacle of injury and death to an end." This is not the case for blacks who are in the clutches of dehumanization. According to Manganyi (1973, 7), "a tolerable environment maintains a distinction between 'the people' (whose rights and existence are recognized) and the 'non-people', whose existence and rights are not seriously considered." In this regard, "the people" are subjects, while the "non-people" are things – the pattern which fits well with the making and the operation of the Manichean structure. The manner in which structural violence tears their ontology apart becomes a phenomenon without analogue (Wilderson 2010). The manner in which those who articulate and identify it becomes meaningless in that they do not matter and they would have no sense of symbolic re-presentation. It is the violence that does not trigger terror in the explicit sense of the term, or it is the violence that is recognizable. The mere fact of its being hidden serves as justification that it does not exist, and if it is said to be a problem that plagues blacks in the antiblack existential condition, then in its defense it marks the complainants as trivial, baseless, and crude; it is immaterial in that what the complaint is all about is illegitimate in nature. It matters not that structural violence is a destructive force that is felt in the lived experience of blacks. It is a form of violence that is not physical, but mechanistically inherent in social forces ranging from poverty and disease to racism and mortality (Farmer 2002). Structural violence is the violence that is not visible; it is hidden in structures. It prevents those who are affected by it from seeing, naming, describing, and explaining it, as it is institutionalized, naturalized, and normalized in everyday existence.

In point of fact, the very aim of structural violence is to dispossess blacks of their sense of being. It is to leave them in the status of things. Blacks, by virtue of antiblack racism, become not only its victims; they are rendered things in the realm where there is no life to account for. Their very status, which is nothing at all, since not to exist in the world and not to have any form of life is to be structurally positioned as that which deserves death, is a given. As Farmer (2002) affirms, the existential condition of blacks under structural violence amounts to the life of familiarity with death. Death is nothing, and this means that it has never been any death. That is to say, death cannot be attributed to a thing, since a thing is devoid of life.

To be a thing means to exist in a terrifying excess of blackness; in what Fanon (1970) calls a phobogenic object. As Hudson (2013, 266) notes, blackness is "the subject of anxiety for whom the symbolic and imaginary never work, who is left stranded by his very interpellation." To be black is to elicit phobias, to be in the racial *imago* of being negatively connoted, intruded upon, intruded, and fixated in the state of being a thing (Marriott 2007). For Marriott, to be black, to be a thing and to be a flesh is to be hated from within and from without. It is from this racial *imago* that to be black in the realm of thinghood and the death of the black are not synonymous with that which should be mourned. To be black is fidelity to death because the existence of blackness is that of social death (Patterson 1982). For social death is relevant for a thing – a flesh – that cannot be mourned because it never existed. "Blackness, I repeat, is a right to death in which dying has no value and is no longer sovereign" (Marriott 2007, 227).

In other words, structural violence is rendered non-existent, and surely blacks cannot apportion blame to something non-existent? For blacks suffer because of their own – because of being an ontological failure – existential pathology which is the state of nature. The devastating existential impact of structural violence creates a black condition, the aspect of life that shows nothing but the spectre of death, the justification that if blacks do exist, there is enough justification to render their existence unjustified. As Gordon (2000a) points out, blacks are required in the antiblack world to justify their existence. The more they justify their existence, the more they become unjustifiable. That is, the very act of justifying one's existence is the same as saying that one does not exist.

There is no way antiblack racism will recognize the existence of blacks because blacks are nothing but blacks. That is to say, they are not human beings, but blacks. They are ontologically signified as subjects outside ontology itself. Black subjects have no way of justifying their existence if they are suffering from what Wilderson (2008) refers to as the homology of absence – that is, they are just bodies which do not carry life. Building on Gordon's ontological schema of presence as absence, Wilderson (2008) introduces three layers of black absence. The first layer is absence as subjective presence, which means that the world cannot accommodate blackness at the level of subjectivity. In terms of this layer, seeing a black is seeing a black – something that precedes humanity because of the visibility of blackness is *a priori*. Wilderson (2008, 98) argues that blackness is "an ontological freeze that waits for a gaze, rather than a living ontology moving with agency to the field of vision." The second layer is the absence of a cartographic presence, which means that the life of the black is about fate, while that of the white is about freedom. According to Wilderson, the life of blacks is about *when*. In other words, when will I be arrested, when will I be stopped by police, when will I be violated, and so forth. The third and final layer is the absence of political presence, which does not allow for "the temperature of the black's grammar of suffering" (Wilderson 2008, 99). This implies that when blacks make demands, these demands are not met, since they are rendered impossible. The agency of blacks is thus negated, since blackness is something that is absent from the political world. Wilderson (2003a) argues that blackness is a scandal that does not yield any possibility of relationality for the fact of being outside structures of relations. He suggests that blackness as a subjective position presents an antagonism that cannot be satisfied. The existing structures deprive black modes of articulation; as such blacks, who are slaves, have no transactional value. Blackness does not call for taking into account and the plague of pathologies that befalls blacks in the black condition reduces them to non-entities.

The absence of ontology clearly means that there is no life at all. The recognition of blacks at the level of the body simply means that they are captive body (Spillers 1987). For blacks not to be human under the infrastructure of antiblack racism means that invisibility is at the level of being and hyper-visibility is at the level of the flesh. The captive body is not a body, but as Spillers posits, it is "a flesh." According to Spillers, the flesh is the zero conceptualization of the human, and that is a clear mark that the flesh is the site through which the exercises of dehumanization are sovereignly applied. The flesh that is racialized is regarded as a non-entity – a thing. Even though flesh is something that is part of the human, in the case of the racist logic, flesh is nothing but a thing – that is, that which is not life: flesh is something that is detached from the human being. In short, as flesh is outside the body, so blackness is outside of life. To be a thing is to be outside any form of inquiry. To be a thing is to be a slave *qua* property. It is to have no genealogy, trajectory, or horizon. Indeed, a thing is a thing because it is nothing but a thing in itself. A thing is the phenomenon with no relationality – that is, there is no existence of a thing. This has been the racist epistemology through which humanity is erased *in toto*; the humiliation of the flesh signifies

the ways in which power encounters the body in the asymmetrical
relations where racial domination is the regime of life. Bogues writes:

> [R]acial domination pressed down on black human flesh. The perfor-
> mance of power in these circumstances was a form of domination
> that one may call power *in* the flesh. It was power directing bodies
> through injury of the flesh.
>
> (Bogues 2010, 39)

The flesh of the black is a flesh, and not the human flesh. Since
it is clear that the ontology of the black is torn apart from the
human essence, this serves as enough justification for sadistic acts
of dehumanization. To render blacks a mere flesh and to turn them
into things, blackness is made to be the possession of whiteness. Of
interest is the manner in which blacks are dehumanized, and, in fact,
that the manner, shape, form, content, and acts of dehumanization
make the ontology of blackness superfluous.

To be a thing that is owned is to be that which can be crushed
absolutely at will: a thing that has no value and can be relegated to
any sadistic fantasy, and there is no moral currency or recourse to
justice. The sadistic act of denying blacks their humanity ensures
that violence that is directed at blacks is justified as violence against
things. If what is violated is a thing, then there is nothing to be
done. In point of fact, a thing cannot be violated because it is a
thing. "Affect, gesture, and a vulnerability to violence constituted
blackness" (Hartman 1997, 26). Gordon has this to add:

> The black is marked by the dehumani[s]ing bridge between individual
> and structure posed by antiblack racism; the black is, in the end,
> "anonymous," which enables "the black" to collapse into "blacks."
>
> Whereas "blacks" is not a proper name, antiblack racism makes
> it function as such, as the name of the family that closes off the need
> for further knowledge. Each black is, thus, ironically nameless by
> virtue of being "black."
>
> (Gordon 2005, 3)

The oppression of blacks is the phenomenon in excess. The
oppression of blacks, as Birt (1997) laments, is the oppression
that affects the entire aspect of the life of the black; it is total
oppression. This total oppression, Birt argues, is linked with a total
alienation. This makes the life of blacks the life without life itself. It
is for blackness to recognize its being in this racist infrastructure of

antiblackness. To deny that they are oppressed, blacks will become complicit in their own oppression. They will not be fueled by any desire to change the pathological existence to which they have been relegated. It is clear in More's work that blacks who deny the lived reality that they are in are caught in bad faith, which becomes clear through blacks being hoodwinked into the liberal cliché in terms of which they are acted upon rather than being their own agents. It is the very same liberal infrastructure of antiblackness in its guise of being compassionate to blacks, while being as racist as the very antiblackness it claims to be different from.

The Bad Faith of White Liberals

If there is a being that operates in bad faith, it is the white liberal. It is the black who is in the paternalistic, tight grip of the white liberal. In the hand of the white liberal, the black is nothing but a toy. If, as MacDonald (2012, 70) asserts, "Black Consciousness posits the primacy of a collective black self," it is clear that the white liberal is out of work in so far as the existential struggle of the black is concerned. It would seem contradictory for the black to put the white liberal to work, as the latter is concerned with being an ally with the black in the struggle against apartheid oppression. Why would the black reject the very thing that is of help in the precarious existential condition it is in, and the very thing that will help it in the struggle against oppression?

Indeed, there has not been an ontological figure that has been railed against in the struggle of oppression like the white liberal, not only in More's amplification of Biko's criticism, but even in the work of thinkers like Sartre, Fanon, and Memmi. The white liberal assumes different labels in the writings of these three thinkers, but in all cases the tendency is the same – to control the black. It is important to see the indictment of the white liberal through Sartre's figure of "the democrat," Fanon's figure of "the Left," and Memmi's figure of "the leftist colonizer." Because of the sameness in these three categories, Biko is correct in capturing them as the white liberal, the very figure that is clear in More's philosophical intervention.

It is clear from Sartre (1965) that the figure of the democrat is caught in the existential quagmire, but often clearly intentionally, because liberal hypocrisy is the very nature of the democrat. Sartre writes:

> The Jews have one friend, however, the democrat. But he is a feeble protector. No doubt he proclaims that all men have equal rights; no doubt he has founded the League for the Rights of Man; but his own declarations show the weakness of his position ... He has no eyes for the concrete syntheses with which history confronts him. He recognizes nor Jew, nor Arab, nor Negro, nor bourgeois, nor worker, but only man – man always the same in all times and places. He resolves all collective elements into individual elements.
>
> (Sartre 1965, 55)

The white liberal is out of sync with the existential reality that confronts the black and the black's continued subjection notwithstanding. As a method of the white liberal, the synthetic principle positions the white liberal as an ally, and the mode of diagnosis is nothing but a wrong synthesis. "This advice and these criticisms are to be explained by the ill-repressed desire to guide, to direct the liberation movement of the oppressed" (Fanon 1967, 80). Biko was quick to highlight the wrongfulness of the white liberal, and this is interfering in the existential affairs of blacks. The white liberal is audacious enough to dictate what the problem is for the black. Hence, it is important to understand Biko's irritation at the fact that what the white liberal wants is to speak on behalf of blacks. The white liberals are labelled by Biko (1978) as a bunch of do-gooders. The white liberal creates a regime of exceptionality and is nothing but sadistic. Sartre (1965) writes: "Actually they take pleasure in protecting these few persons through a sort of inversion of their sadism; they take pleasure in keeping under their eyes the living image of this people whom to execrate." The declaration of loving the black by the white liberal is nothing but narcissism. It is in the colonial unconscious that the white liberal still produces the inferior other – the black – even if racist intentions are hidden from sight. Thus, this declared love for blacks is nothing but a sadistic relation. This makes the white liberal, as More states, the in the closet assimilationist – that is, in *extensio* a narcissist and a sadist. The existence of the black is violated by the very fact that the white liberal speaks on behalf of the black. The black is made to disappear at the level of subjectivity and in ontology. The white liberal is nothing but the oppressor of the black.

The white liberal has everything to lose if the black is to gain liberation. The liberation of the black is the total end of oppression and this will be the end of the white liberal. It is clear that the white liberal would defend the interest to exist and will not engage in any form of suicide. That is, there is no way that the white liberal can engage in the politics of suicide, and also be the messiah of blacks by engaging in the politics of sacrifice. The white liberal who is the Other cannot sacrifice for the non-Other. The white liberal will not allow the liberation of the black. The genuine liberation that the black is fighting for is not the battle of the white liberal, since the struggle of the white liberal and the black are not the same. The existential concerns they have are not the same.

The white liberal is plagued by the "fear of the human condition" (Sartre 1965, 54). It is clear from Sartre that the white liberal fears the black coming into consciousness. Sartre writes:

> Taking this point of view, he fears the awakening of a "Jewish consciousness" in the Jew; that is, he fears that the Jew will acquire a consciousness of the Jewish collectivity – just as he fears that a "class consciousness" may awaken in the worker. His defense is to persuade individuals that they exist in an isolated state. "There are no Jews," he says, "there is no Jewish question."
>
> (Sartre 1965, 56–57)

What Sartre makes clear is that the white liberal is hostile to the liberation of the black. The fundamental point highlighted by Sartre is how the democrat seeks to isolate the Jew from existential reality, and the same applies to the white liberal and the black. The extinguishing of consciousness, its denial or ensuring its non-existence is the role of the white liberal. It is this insistence that places the existence of the white as *a priori*, and if that is the case, the black does not matter.

The problematic of the white liberal that More is dealing with is rooted in Biko's philosophical critique. It is also important to engage Fanon's figure of "the Left" and also Memmi's "left colonialist." It is in Fanon that the oppressed must take it upon themselves to struggle for liberation without any mediation from the Left. Oppression accelerates and the oppressed respond without mediation, as "the Left was paradoxically caught off guard and proved helpless" (Fanon 1967, 77). Though the Left claim to have intimate knowledge about the existential crisis of the black, for Fanon they are engaged in "active pseudo-solidarity" while being peripheral. If the Left are relegated to the peripheral positionality in the struggle of the oppressed, and the latter are asserting themselves,

Fanon writes: "The liberals abandon the struggle at this stage" (Fanon 1967, 78). They will even shout, as Fanon (1967, 79) states: "We can no longer follow you!" out of frustration as they see their paternalism wanting, and their not having control over the black. As if they were following, which is not actually the case, the Left complain of not being allowed to control the struggle of the black and dictate the terms of engagement. In laying down its conditions, Fanon shows the manner in which the Left is negligent of the existential plight of the black, and that it even goes to the extent of determining what is good for the black.

The white liberal will always dismiss the concerns of those who suffer out of hand. All the people are reduced to the figure of the universal. This will be done by highlighting the exemplar, stating how such a figure is different from the rest. The black is paraded in front of other blacks as the exemplar to be gravitated upon, and to be something to be desired. Put simply, in the hands of the white liberal, the black is nothing but a thing. It is fundamental to point out that there is no ontological relationality between the white liberal and the black, unless to point out that such relationality is nothing but the reinforcement of oppression. It is the black who is still at the ontological disadvantage in that the mechanisms of oppression that the black is enmeshed in do not have any relevance to the white liberal. By virtue of whiteness, the white liberal is the figure exempted from oppression, since the target of such oppression is the black. The white liberal practises paternalism simply because the black is still treated as the inferior being by oppression and the white liberal included, for the latter cannot be annexed from oppression that dehumanizes the black.

As soon as the white liberal becomes involved in the existential struggle of the black, then everything changes in the interests that are alien to those of the black. The struggle becomes that of the white liberal not to yield any form of liberation, but to maintain the status quo. Because the white liberal will be in charge, in no way will black subjectivity prevail. Rather, there will be black bodies with the liberal psyche – the very form of alienation in that blacks will be fighting for nothing but an illusion. In point of fact, the existence of the white liberal is sustained through the ontological and existential malaise of the black. If the liberation of the black is to come into being, this would mean the end of the white liberal. In no way can the white liberal advocate his or her own ending, unless to perpetuate his or her self-interests.

The paternalistic attitude of the white liberal leads More to state that the white liberal is the "in the closet assimilationist." It is for the white liberal to make blacks forget about their existential malaise and to live a lie of justice, equality, and freedom. If blackness fights for these ideals, which are not relevant for them but only to the white liberal, it means that blacks are operating in bad faith. This is bad faith in that Fanon (1970) referred to them as white Justice, white Liberal, and white Equality. The major concern is why the white liberal is to be obliged to be involved in the politics of blackness as opposed to fighting the very white supremacy from the existential site of whiteness. The existential ideals of blackness are diametrically opposed to that of whiteness. The former is colonized, while the latter is the colonizer. The white liberal, by virtue of being white, is the oppressor of the black. The very basis of interfering in the politics of blackness is oppression in itself. What seems to be outstanding in the subjectivity of the white liberal is the tendency to dictate the demands of blackness.

As long as there is oppression, the good intentions of the white liberal will have no significance if the sole duty is to perpetuate oppression. The political will of the white liberal is misdirected if it finds itself in blackness. For it will not understand the existential predicament of blackness, for the very fact of asymmetrical positionality and its being the subject position is nothing but complicity with oppression of blackness. The place of the white liberal is whiteness, and its existential struggle should be directly waged against the very source of its privilege.

If there is anything that appears in the consciousness of white liberals, it is what Hudson refers to as the "colonial unconscious." If the white liberal has a sole interest, it is to treat blacks as the dependable other. Being in direct control of blacks and knowing what is best for blacks is condescension. It is the very thing that the white liberal is criticized for. In the mode of the colonial unconscious, the white liberal asserts synthetic principles, as Sartre shows, deploying them as a panacea for the existential problems of the black. This means that, having been the problem, the white liberal seeks to be the solution at the same time.

If there is a question that is trivialized, if not completely denied by the white liberal, it is the question of racism. While racism is a problem to blacks, to the white liberal it should not be a problem to blacks. If the black points it out and calls it what it is, the white liberal will be quick to claim that it is not racism, but something else, or that it is something rather more complex and not as simple as racism, since to make reference to the latter is to be simplistic. To suggest that there is more to racism is to deny its validity and the lived experience of the black. The white liberal who is not affected by racism has the audacity to dictate to the black what is racism and what is not. By virtue of whiteness, the white liberal has the sovereign power to "end" racism while concealing its devastating existence.

What is to be highlighted is the fact that the white liberal has an ally – the good black – the very model of exceptionality and the exemplar of blackness. The good black is the tool of the white liberal in the sense of being hired to be the spokesperson of white supremacy. The good black is paraded around to propagate the elusive project of the politics of sameness. If there has been a problem with the existential condition of blackness it is not racism, but the specificity of antiblack racism (Gordon 1995, 2000b; More 2012, 2014). It is in this form of racism that the white liberal is bracketed off, since the white liberal has been subject to expulsion by Biko. If the problem is race, as it has always been, due to the plague of antiblack racism, the white liberal will not understand the existential predicament of blackness. Even if white liberals claim solid allegiance to the black cause, the outcome of the cause is at their own expense. That is, for there to be the elimination of black dispossession, there must be the elimination of white privilege. It is the latter which justifies the ontological standing of the white liberal. It is clear from More that there is no white liberal without white privilege. It is not a shock, then, to find the defensive mode through which the white liberal engages with the existential politics of blackness.

For Black Solidarity

If there is something that ignites the political and existential necessity of blackness, it is black solidarity. What More contends with is the misconception that black solidarity is racist. This he explicates by defending black solidarity as the politics of necessity in that racism structures black in the ontological invisibility of that being human not black *qua* black. In other words, to see the black is not to see the human, but the black (Gordon 1995, 2000b; More 2009). In response to antiblack racism, black solidarity serves as the necessary existential intervention which is informed by the struggle to end the infrastructure of antiblack racism.

If blacks are victims of antiblack racism, black solidarity gives them the structure of feeling that makes their identity with one another due to their collective experience. This is the existential pain which they have no grammar to articulate and it does not need to take the form of a "black testimony" to be an account that must be given to whiteness. Black testimony is banal in the sense that blackness narrates itself to whiteness with the aim of being heard. Blacks often explain how racism is affecting them with the aim of eliciting white empathy and sympathy. If not, then the aim will be for blacks to give testimony to whites so that whites can change their racist consciousness. Black testimony, even if given in the collective spirit, cannot reach the content and character of black solidarity. Black solidarity should not bring about a change in antiblack racism, but its absolute destruction. Black testimony will always be nothing but an empty plight, a voiceless voice, the loud deaf, and if there are any acts of compassion from whiteness, they are nothing but a façade. Why? The question of antiblack racism will always be distorted, trivialized, if not muted in the absolute, so that the existential plight of the victims of racism falls flat.

It is at this point necessary to punctuate the fact that black testimony in the face of whiteness is the nothing of nothingness. It does not carry any ontological weight, in that there is nothing that is asserted or fought for, and it is also acute to arrive at the conclusion that black testimony does not pose a threat to whiteness. The nothing of nothingness, black testimony is apolitical, and no existential demands are worthy of its foundation. What is clear is that blackness under the spell of the white liberal ceases to be any form of black solidarity, but black testimony. It is in the modes of subjectivity that the existential demands of blackness collapse completely in the face of whiteness.

It is in this structure of feeling that antiblack racism with blacks as a primary target inferiorizes, dispossesses, dominates, and dehumanizes them as a collective. Therefore, blacks in the antiblack world are ontologically erased, yet it is in black solidarity that they feel able to assert themselves against all forces that militate against their existence. That is to say, the collective lived experience of anguish and alienation will cause only blacks to act as a collective to end their existential crisis. Moreover, there would be no need for black solidarity if there were no infrastructure of antiblack racism

– whether overt or covert – that is, black solidarity is there because there is antiblack racism. In post-1994 South Africa in particular, there is often a meta-narrative that apartheid has died and there is no racism, or, that if it exists, it is a case of isolated incidents – a few bad apples, so to say. It is in this context that it is claimed that there are no victims of racism, as racism has been legislatively outlawed.

Antiblack racism creates, as More (2009) asserts, a condition of seriality. Following Sartre, More explicates seriality as "the unity of black people as a constituted group" (More 2009, 25). In a myriad of ways, they are (inter)connected and identically misplaced in the ontological realm – that is, the black is black. In the stereotypical meta-narrative that has assumed a form of common sense "they are one and all" (More 2009, 35). As members of serial groups – the condition created by antiblack racism – "blacks are constituted both as serial unities and as serial objects. By force of their position, antiblack racists hold blacks in series" (More 2009, 25). More explicates that black solidarity starts, as a form of a group in fusion, not as something to the effect of the rebellion without a cause, but as a liberation agent. If it takes this ontological form, it borders on the politics of necessity. The undesirability of the existential conditions will by any means trigger a response. Having been oppressed on the basis of a group, there is no way that the in-group fusion will not take place. More clearly argues that it is by force of circumstance that blacks in black solidarity are informed by nothing but getting rid of the existential pathologies. The aim of this is to create a new existential condition and the construction of the new being. The existential crisis that blacks are in is not their own creation, as this is the existence which has forces that militate against them.

In taking a stance in the intellectual milieu that requires self-censorship, More takes on the question of black solidarity and argues relentlessly for its defense. In post-1994 South Africa, with its myth of non-racialism, it is claimed that race is no longer relevant because apartheid came to an end, and that if there were to be any form of black solidarity, this would mark a regressive effect. Therefore, black solidarity should be always out of the question. It is clear from More's work that South Africa is antiblack in its posture owing to the plague of antiblack racism, and the victims being blacks still. If this is the case, then it is necessary for blacks to galvanize around their cause in a form of black solidarity and to rail against antiblack racism. They cannot do this as individuals, only as a collective.

Black solidarity does not emerge in a vacuum. It is the intentionality of the political – that is, the assertion of the collective spirit of humanity to bring the ultimate end to injustices that affects their existential conditions. It is even clear in Black Consciousness that black solidarity was the focal philosophical point. The ultimate aim of bringing to being the fully constitutive being of the black did not come through the individualist reference, but that of the collective. Black Conscious emphasis on blackness as their own being or being on their own is cemented on Biko's (1978) call that blacks should not be the extension of something but, as Fanon (1970) states, be their own foundation. It is therefore correct to posit that black solidarity is blackness *in-itself* and *for-itself*. The latter is the ontological constitutiveness that impels blackness to advocate for black solidarity, and it is in this struggle that blackness should act upon itself. Therefore, the white liberal should not be an ally in this struggle, in that such a figure should fight its own battles. Authentic black solidarity is the struggle of blacks, by blacks, against all latent and blatant forces of antiblack racism.

Not only is the desire and the affirmation of liberation affirmed in black solidarity, but blacks seek to rehumanize themselves in the face of dehumanization. The coming of black humanity into being is the struggle against antiblack racism. As this is the form of racism that attacks the existence of blackness *in toto*, it then means that it is not at the level of the individual that antiblack racism operates – it is at the collective level. To be black is to fall within the existential category of the collective. It is to be a thing in relation to the thinghood of blackness. It is on the basis of this logic that antiblack racism militates against the existence of blacks and thus renders the world antiblack.

The position of antiblackness has never been contradictory, since its motif has been the continued denial of the humanity of blackness. It then follows that the subjectivity of blackness and criminalization of its solidarity will assume the hegemonic form. The foremost critics of black solidarity that More confronts – Anthony Appiah, Jonathan Jensen, and Achille Mbembe – constitute the trio that accuses black solidarity of being regressive, exclusivist, and ultimately, with a degree of exaggeration, of course, racist. The trio confirm the damning account that Ture and Hamilton (1992, 84) provide, namely that: "Whenever black people have moved toward genuinely independent action, the society has distorted their intentions or damned their performance." More points out that the trio advocate "cross-racial solidarity," "a world without race," and "a broader cosmopolitanism." It is important, then, by way of extension to examine briefly the position of the trio, which entails antiblack solidarity myths. Firstly, they are correct in arguing that black solidarity is racially exclusivist. The struggle galvanizes around the black existential cause, and, if blacks find it necessary to engage in the struggle against racism, they must do so as a collective. Put simply, if blacks are confronted with antiblack racism, they must respond to it as blacks. Also, for the mere fact that they are victims of antiblack racism, they must respond to it as a collective, since antiblack racism is collectivized. They must respond out of their own subjectivity as blacks. What is punctuated is the fact that black solidarity does not need whiteness in its existential struggle, since it is not the existence of whiteness that is violated, but that of blackness. Also, whites are not affected by racism. According to More, being racially exclusivist *qua* black solidarity is not being racist, as pointed out earlier on. Rather, it is a necessary existential intervention, and blacks should be on their *own* to deal with their *own* problems. Therefore, black solidarity is nothing but a liberatory agenda.

The triad of Appiah, Jensen, and Mbembe, having adopted a stubborn attachment to antiblack solidarity, remain silent on white solidarity – that is, the racist one in the form of right-wing nationalism and liberalism. Appiah, Jensen, and Mbembe say nothing about racist white solidarity, and they are even silent on the subject of the existential plague of antiblack racism. This includes, in antiblack solidarity, the extent to which antiblack racism will invite black solidarity; the latter is not of its own making. It seems that the convenient position of the trio is symptomatic of the apportioning of blame to the victims of racism, and not the infrastructure of antiblack racism. In fact, they choose to ignore the fact that black solidarity is a response to the fallacy that the trio, as liberal humanists, try to propagate. This is the fallacy that insistently denies the black existential reality and forces itself as something that wants to be included in whiteness. The manner in which the life of blackness has been rendered meaningless by antiblack racism is something that does not matter to these three liberal humanists.

It is clear that in so far as More is concerned, the liberal humanism of cross-racial solidarity, a world without race and a broader cosmopolitanism is nothing but a myth – that is, a liberal façade which borders on what Césaire (1972) terms a decadent civilization of deception and trickery – a civilization which creates problems that it cannot solve, and yet assumes the posture of a panacea to all the existential malaise that befalls blackness. The liberal humanists are still caught in the civilization that feeds itself through antiblack racism. What Appiah, Jensen, and Mbembe also choose to ignore is the fact that the infrastructure of antiblack racism finds fertile ground under liberal humanism and, at its very worst, leaves nothing accounted for. What seems to be clear in the antiblack solidarity position of the trio is that blacks do not matter simply because the problem of antiblack racism which affects them does not matter, and they should not in any way fight to end that problem. In short, blacks must embrace liberal humanism while they are oppressed, and they should not rail against the existential reality that faults their existence. It is naive for the trio to expect black solidarity to be criminalized solely on the basis of the deception and trickery of liberal humanism with its abstract – the universal. More (2009) argues that in terms of this mode of reasoning, the liberal humanists reject claims of racial identity as such and argue for the individual in relation to the universal. However, if antiblack racism exists, in the eye of the liberal humanist it is regarded as something accidental and its mode of generation and expression is on the individual.

The liberal humanist emphasis of the individual and its embodiment as the ontological figure of the individual glosses over the existential reality that the individual is attacked by antiblack racism at the level of the collective. And, as is commonly known, the individual cannot exist in isolation. More (2009, 34) writes: "Part of the problem with liberal individualism is its intolerance of group identity, and therefore its disregard of the fact that racist consciousness always operates at the level of the collective." More goes on to amplify that the individual always exists in the realm of the collective, and the identity of the individual is the identity of the collective. Therefore, even the meta-narrative of non-racialism, color-blindness, and race transcendentalism becomes, in the face of black solidarity, the very form of existential absurdity. The liberal humanist advocates nothing but a façade. Black solidarity is a necessity in that blacks cannot fight antiblack racism as individuals, and also as liberal humanist subjects who are claimed to have the privileges of equality, freedom, and justice. It is in the collective enunciation of black solidarity that individualism is weakness and unity is strength.

There is something being avoided by Appiah, Jensen, and Mbembe's liberal humanism in that they are calling for cross-racial solidarity. However, a world without race and a broader cosmopolitanism is nothing but the apologetic stance of whiteness. In their antiblack solidarity positions, they are speaking against blacks not as blacks, but as actors of whiteness – that is, they are speaking on behalf of whites, while the latter do not raise any concern. It then seems to suggest that for there to be black solidarity, or for it to be permitted, whites must be allowed in these collective spaces. The trio seems to agree with what Ture and Hamilton (1992) label the "myth of coalition." It is in the myth that black solidarity should dissolve itself into whiteness. To be in coalition with whiteness while the struggle is for the end of the infrastructure of antiblack racism is nothing short of paradoxical in that this is the total end of black solidarity.

The myth of coalition masks the antiblack racist infrastructure and it propagates the very liberal humanist principles – a liberal façade – as if they are genuine, whereas everything is just antiblack racism. It is in the myth of coalition that the existential concerns of the black will not matter, since blacks do not matter to whites. And why should they matter, since it is the very same whiteness that creates antiblackness and the very existential crisis of the black, the latter which black solidarity seeks to bring to a total end? The myth of coalition is caught in a fundamental contradiction; that is, whites cannot be in coalition with blacks to further their interests at the expense of their own. Ture and Hamilton point out correctly that those black existential demands that inform black solidarity will evaporate, as they will be dictated to by whites in these coalitions and they will engage in the political struggle on terms that are not set by them.

There are diametrically opposed interests in the antiblack world. The interests of whiteness cannot be those of blackness. Therefore, the myth of coalition is just that whites have no affinity to black solidarity even if they are to appear genuine in that the existential demands of black solidarity are opposed to the interest of whiteness. In terms of whites understanding the interests of blackness, Ture and Hamilton (1992, 61) retort that their "perception is likely to be superficial and distorted." It means that liberal humanism has no clue about the existential pathology of blackness and the manner in which blackness seeks to liberate itself. Since black solidarity is the embodied lived reality, this is diametrically opposed to that of liberal humanism, with its emphasis on individualism and total disregard for the liberation of blacks except to sustain the antiblack world.

The myth of coalition as propagated by the liberal humanism of Appiah, Jensen, and Mbembe is responded to by Wilderson (2003a) as black solidarity being reduced to blacks becoming junior partners in a capitalist and white supremacist matrix, which is the slaughterhouse that blacks are invited into. It therefore means, as More (2009) consistently shows in his defense of black solidarity, that race does matter in that it is the very thing that affects blacks in the antiblack world. Thus, the subject position of blackness that undergirds black solidarity is turned into the politics of antagonism. But what the myth of coalition advocates is the cosmetic politics of reformism, a discourse that is outside the articulation of demands made by black solidarity and where the fundamental question of race is, as Wilderson (2003a) points out, read off from the base. It is the politics of antagonism in black solidarity that asserts that race is nothing but the embodiment of the infrastructure of the antiblack world. It is in this infrastructure that white is white *qua* white and the black is black racialization. In other words, blackness disappears into the non-racialized infrastructure, while it still remains racialized. It is only through this existential masking that blacks are made to be junior partners in the myth of coalition and their modes of inferiorization take a form of being condescended to through racist liberal humanism, which acts as if there is no race in the myth of coalition, whereas there is a huge blight of racism through covert forms.

It is in the myth of coalition that white positionality is well entrenched, and this clearly explains why there is no need to create a forum for white solidarity, as whiteness is backed up by the institutionalization, naturalization, and normalization of the existential reality as nothing but white, with blackness being existentially faulty. In short, whiteness is justification in itself. White positionality emerges in the form that is elaborated and entrenched in that all subjectivities should be under its realm (Wilderson 2003a).

> They assume that all subjects are positioned in such a way as to have their consent solicited and to be able to extend their consent "spontaneously." This is profoundly problematic, if only leaving revolution aside for a moment – at the level of analysis; for it assumes that hegemony with its three constituent elements (influence, leadership, and consent) is the modality which must be either inculcated or breached, if one is to either avoid or incur, respectively, the violence of the state.
>
> (Wilderson 2003a, 229)

Not only will black demands disappear in the myth of coalition, but blacks will cease to exist as subjects. If there are no black demands, which are the very core of black solidarity, then there is no black solidarity. It is then clear that under the spell of liberal humanism, what black solidarity will concede is nothing but dissolution in the face of the myth of coalition – the latter being white *qua* white – blacks being junior partners in the authority of whiteness *in toto*. This is clear from More's (1996, 132) philosophical intervention when he writes: "The oppressed are morally responsible for transforming the situation they find themselves in, without excuse." The insatiable demands of blackness which are the fulcrum of black solidarity should be asserted without restraint, as the aim is to see the total end of the antiblack world. These are the demands which are accentuating "a suffering that cannot be spoken because the gratuitous terror of white supremacy is as much contingent upon the irrationality of white fantasies and shared pleasures as it is upon a logic – the logic of capital" (Wilderson 2003a, 230).

If black solidarity is nothing but the politics of antagonism, there is no need for blacks to be junior partners in the myth of coalition that liberal humanism propagates. It is clear that what informs the myth of coalition is the crowding out of the demands and the politics of blacks and the hegemonic instilling of whiteness in order to leave the infrastructure of antiblack racism intact and to have no accounting for the existential misery, brutality, and horror that is directed at black bodies. The myth of coalition seems to be embedded in the underlying logic that there is no existential analogue for blackness and there should not be any form of existential cause in support of which blackness galvanizes itself.

It is clear from More (2009) that black solidarity is not only about group formation. For More, black solidarity is the basis for identity formation and existential struggle for liberation against all forms of oppression, injustice, inferiorization, and dehumanization. Black solidarity, for More (2009, 26), is the "essence of collective praxis … consciously united by a common objective or end." Biko's Black Consciousness is akin to what More explicates; it is a collective where blackness is not an individual, but the collectivized entity of black solidarity. Black solidarity is the politics of life, as the will to live is to have the end of antiblackness in totality. Also deserving of attention is the fact that it is in Black Consciousness where blacks were on their own as a collective, and what is made clear is the expulsion of the white liberal. No more will the paternalistic white liberal be the authority figure for blacks; blacks are, as a matter of black solidarity, on their own *in-themselves*, *for-themselves*, and *by-themselves*. "Every struggle for human liberation," Birt (1997, 205) notes, "is invariably a struggle for a liberated identity ... The human being must be transformed in his consciousness and self-consciousness, in his relation to self, the world and others." This clearly captures the true essence of black solidarity, which More fiercely defends as a form of political necessity in response to antiblack racism, and the creation of new pathways to liberation. These pathways are different from the creation of post-1994 South Africa, which came about through a negotiated settlement and became a liberal constitutional democracy.

Mandela's House Mystique

South Africa post-1994 seems to have undergone fundamental change, and this is a change from colonial conquest, colonialism, segregation, and apartheid to what is seen as the end of apartheid. Post-1994 South Africa is directly confronted by More (2019), who dubs it "Mandela's House," as is its post-1994 myth, which takes the form of "The Miracle." Mandela's House came into being as a gift from apartheid oppressors and it will be argued here that it still remains a colonial state. Post-1994 South Africa – Mandela's House – is neo-apartheid, as the settler–colonial arrangement is still in place, and the regime inherited by blacks as the custodians and guardians. It is not the house built by Mandela as the icon of the liberation struggle; he was acted upon, and this came from the generosity of his oppressors. The coming into being of post-1994 South Africa is the result of the liberation struggle's having defeated the apartheid legacy, and this is the propagated version. The scandal of this still stands and the testimony to this is the triad of dispossession that Mngxitama (2009) eloquently refers to as the dispossession of land, labor, and black humanity. According to More, who defies this propagation, South Africa as "Mandela's House" and "The Miracle" is nothing but a fiction of the existential reality of being black in the antiblack world where white supremacy is the defining order. This is because there has never been the realization of the ontologico-existential struggle, but what has seemed to have taken over is the tyranny of symbols, rituals, distortion of political memory, carnivalistique gestures and most of all, Mandela as a dancing native with a stereotypical colonial smile on his black face and reaching out in the populist gesture of appeasement.

It is of interest that the ontological category that More deals with is the specified phenomenon of antiblack racism. It is the form which proves The Miracle and Mandela's House a scandal. South Africa is a racist state, and in no way is the question of race and racism being dealt with. The country is plagued with intentioned ignorance, if not avoidance, and also the poverty of not wanting to account for what fundamentally racism is. Antiblack racism haunted blacks even in the euphoric days of the Mandela presidency, and continues in the present. This is not ignoring the untransformed infrastructure of white privilege which swells black dispossession to the point of its institutionalization, naturalization and normalization. If South Africa is Mandela's House, it cannot be separated from its passionate attachment – "The Miracle." According to More (2011), the last apartheid president, Frederick Willem de Klerk and his National Party acted on behalf of black subjects by telling Nelson Mandela and black people, "you are now free." Terreblanche captures this moment and period thus:

> On 2 February 1990, F.W. de Klerk – who had succeeded a faltering Botha as state president in August 1989 – stunned the world with his announcement that the liberation organi[z]ations would be unbanned, that Nelson Mandela and other political prisoners would be set free, and that the NP government is prepared to enter into negotiations with all political parties to seek a peaceful transition to a democratic political system.
>
> (Terreblanche 2002, 311)

In addition to the above, More has this to say:

> Given the disparity in land ownership, property, citizenship, voting rights, and so on that came with the oppressive apartheid regime, we need to ask the question: Was there any significant transformation after Mandela became the president on April 27, 1994? I think the initial appropriate question to be asked in order to put things into perspective is: What kind of means led to Mandela's presidency? It is well known that the transition from apartheid to Mandela came about not through a revolutionary break or complete discontinuity with the past, but through a negotiated settlement commonly dubbed the "South African Miracle."
>
> (More 2011, 181)

South Africa is the realm of the symbolic, with its carnivalesque euphoria emanating from the mythology of the rainbow nation and its discharge of non-racialism. It is the South Africa of Francis Fukuyama's "the end of history" thesis, which yielded another attachment to its name, namely the "New" South Africa. For, apartheid is rendered non-existent; it is part of the history that is no longer relevant. For More (2008, 50), the fundamental task is to unmask "the problem of racism, especially of the apartheid type." It is the very same apartheid which cemented the *longue durée* of colonial oppression and actualized it not only to be a crude and grotesque form of regime – it became the ontological bastion of dehumanization – the ontological exclusion, domination and control in excess: in short, apartheid as dehumanization par excellence. It is, therefore, important to think of the ontological positionality of blackness in relation to apartheid and also its aftermath – post-1994 South Africa as Mandela's House as More (2019) refers to it – as nothing but neo-apartheid with a black face.

This is profound and not being considered in that blackness is in the face of ontological minimization if not absolute obliteration. This is not accidental due to the fact that South Africa is interposed in the idea of the colonial state; hence blackness is in the coalface of antiblackness – the black regime notwithstanding. The postponement of the aspirations of blacks is important to engage after they have gone through the existential eclipse which was institutionalized and ideologically cemented by apartheid. The way in which the forms of lives which are created in the form of disposability and death cannot be accounted for is nothing but the pathology of the colonial state.

Mandela's House is plagued by the precariousness of the black existential condition just as it was during apartheid *qua* colonial conquest. But then the dominant narrative, which is the "house rule" in Mandela's House, is that South Africa is free from its past, racism notwithstanding. Mandela's House is claimed to be built on its own foundation that has nothing to do with the past, but everything to do with the concerted effort of being the "New" South Africa. What More (2019) brings to the fore is that Mandela's House is explicitly neo-apartheid – that is, apartheid managed by the black elite in service of white supremacy.

If this, then, is the case, there is a need to decolonize neo-apartheid, the very foundation that Mandela's House is built on. It is the infrastructure of antiblackness through economic ownership and resources, land and racism, which still reflect the colonial and its continuity of apartheid. The change that Mandela's House is lauded for is purely cosmetic. Existential precariousness still befalls blackness where their power is still symbolic in the sense that they exercise it in the ballot box, as if the liberation struggle has been about the right to vote.

The founding myth of Mandela's House is the "rainbow nation," which fails to account for the existential realities that face blacks. The myth of the rainbow nation seeks to "avoid the racism projected by the deeply racialized principles of apartheid" (More 1998, 369). After the brutal history and its solid aftermath, the insistence is on reconciliation and the bastardized notion of Ubuntu. This is avoiding reality by propagating the rhetoric of unity in diversity and the liberal cliché of equality, justice and freedom. Still, blacks are invited and crowded out in the liberal democratic consensus where they must celebrate what they do not have and become the defendants of that which does not match their aspirations for liberation. It is the liberal constitutional supremacy which claims that race is no longer a problem. "Yet there is a problem, and it cannot be ignored or simply wished away by declaring its non-existence; it needs to be confronted as part of South Africa and world reality" (More 1998, 370).

> The death of apartheid and introduction of a new liberal democratic constitution therefore meant the talk, writing, or discourse on race should stop in order to combat any semblance of racism. In point of fact, the formal elimination of apartheid laws, in a form of bad faith signified – to many people, including Mandela – the elimination of racist talk and racist practices.
>
> (More 2019, 77)

Clearly, the ethos of Mandela's House borders on bad faith, described by Gordon (1995) as fleeing from responsibility to pleasing falsehood. The pleasing falsehood is the race denialism that denies that there is racism, whereas there is racism. "The reason for the persistence of racism in South Africa can be found in the very structural foundation of Mandela's house" (More 2019, 79). To deny the existential precariousness of black existence and rhetorically propagate the liberal constitutional myth as the true foundation de-linked from the colonial and apartheid past is to be out of sync with reality that continues to haunt the present.

Indeed, what remains a scandal is the spectre that haunts; the constant reminder that blacks have only political power, and not its complement, economic power. And, what is more, they can be humiliated with impunity, as they have no ontological status like that of whiteness. In Mandela's House, there is what Hudson refers to as "colonial unconscious" where racism proliferates and expresses itself in evident yet masked forms. In an asymmetrical form, whiteness becomes the ontological formation of whiteness of white. Whiteness, as Hudson (2013, 264) laments, "is the master signifier, and it has both white and black subjects in its grip."

Moreover, as Hudson continues to show, the Constitution created black and white subjects as non-racial citizens without any reference to colonial subjecthood. These are pure subjects and liberal constitutional democracy has nothing to do with the past. It means colonial subjecthood has no place in Mandela's House. Hudson even shows that liberal constitutional democracy has three forms of denialism. The first is the fact that there is no colonial symbolic as the real. The second is that if there is colonial symbolic, it is not colonialism itself, but something else which has no colonial meaning. Lastly, the colonial aftermath should be ignored or tolerated, or its meaning understood through liberal constitutional democratic rules. The colonial symbolic puts blacks in the ontological abyss, and the very fact of its denial means that its expressions and effects should not be engaged. The bracketing off, the foreclosure and crowding out of black subjectivity in liberal democratic consensus – the ethos of Mandela's House – represents the epistemic violence of black subjectivity. To have More as a philosopher who unmasked this scandal and to render Mandela's House as bad faith is regarded as blasphemous. This is mainly because the bad faith of Mandela's House has cemented itself as *bona fide*. Its foundational myth is Mandela's sainthood and the architecture of Mandela's House will be a cathedral sanctioned by moral correctness.

If the colonial unconscious is recognized, it will be pointed out to be an individual act that is deviant, and not the existential structural reality that still shows the very ghost of apartheid and its colonial signification. More brings to the fore the aftermath of the racist infrastructure as something that still haunts black existence: the very condition which is treated at arm's length, if not made the subject of total elision, because the lived experience of blacks is not at the center. Thus, Mandela's House still allows humiliation, exclusions, denigration, and dehumanization of blacks. The mere fact that these acts do confirm these ontological violations clearly shows that white supremacy, as More (2019) notes, still reigns supreme. In other words, the existence of Mandela's House confers nothing on black existence, since precariousness continues to be a scandal.

More introduces the very important element of land, and argues that it is inseparable from life. Land restores the dignity of people, and to be dispossessed of land is to be ousted from humanity *in toto*. The recognition of blacks as humans and even their dignity is still a mirage. There is none of it to show off, let alone to claim its existence. There is no land, and there is no dignity. Landlessness is the very antithesis of dignity; More (2011) states further that dignity can be restored by the restoration of land. Since dispossession has been violent, brutal, and dehumanizing, nothing of ontological value can be said to be attached to blacks, as their very being was erased. For More, to engage in the philosophical question of land is to engage in the fundamental question of life. As More states, if there is no land there is no life; the latter is wholly dependent on land. The affirmation of life is foundational only if it has the land that it is grounded on. With no land, there is no life, but wretchedness to the point of superfluity and non-existence. The dispossession of land heralds the ontologically void subject, and there is no way Mandela's House can restore the humanity of the black without land. But then, the scandal persists, where Mandela's House claims the totality of the black as the subject that is complete, and yet there is no land that is attached to it.

In Mandela's House, the issue of land dispossession assumes the historical and silent scandal. The law that is supreme in Mandela's House is the Constitution, where the land question is tamed to docility. It is as if the ontologico-existential struggle has never been about land, but about being included in whiteness. Since South Africa is a colonial state, it is littered with the history of settler–colonial land theft, and this remains sanctioned in Mandela's House. The Constitution does not even attach the signification of settler–colonial land theft; this fundamental question has been relegated to the margins. There is no settler–colonial land theft, but instead the "land question," which needs to be solved through the land reform programme with its obscure objectives that claim to be "just" and "equitable." The manner in which the issue of land is engaged with borders on bad faith, and the date of 1913, which is marked as the historical one, seems to ignore the continued dispossession from 1652. The history of conquest and land dispossession is what South Africa is, but the narrative is different in Mandela's House, since technicism and failure to name history for what it is – settler–colonial land theft – seems to be scandalous. The willing buyer, willing seller policy, which has been a failure from the start, clearly shows that those who have had land stolen from them should buy it back. It is as if there was no history of settler–colonial land theft. It is as if there has never been a brutal continued history where land has been violently seized from blacks. In Mandela's House, Constitutional supremacy is invoked to facilitate land reform and the ministries of land since 1994 have not even dealt with the fundamental question of settler–colonial land theft. Instead, the issue has been about the land question, and this creates the impression that the struggle for liberation has not been about land but the liberal constitutional democracy. As More (2011, 181) unmasks this scandal, "the new constitution restored black people's right to land, but not the land itself."

The history of South Africa has been that of the settler–colonial state in the making, the history of violent conquest, enslavement, and dehumanization of blacks. There is no way that this history can be soothed by merely declaring South Africa a liberal constitutional state. To cement it all is the Constitution, which is progressive in the world. For there to be genuine liberation, the foundational objective as More (2011, 180) asserts, is "restoring land back to its original owners (the natives)." If no land is restored to its original owners, Mandela's House cannot have a right to fully claim to have fought and gained liberation. It is at best absurd to claim liberation while land dispossession is a continued reality. It is then important to admit that the building of Mandela's House is not the making of blacks: this is the house built for them, and yet they cannot occupy it. In other words, Mandela's House has rules that are contradictory to black aspirations. That is why it is the house founded on the myth of "The Miracle." It is the teleology in the form of a triumphant spirit and the neoliberal political imagination with its limits seems to preoccupy Mandela's House. The continued dehumanization of blacks is still the reality and More (2019) insistently argues that the triumphant myth of being free is a sham. It is so largely because black existence continues to be militated against by the black elite who are managers and guarantors of neo-apartheid with its infra-structure of white supremacy.

Sartre, Fanon, Manganyi, and Biko
Against the Manichean Axis

Sartre, Fanon, Manganyi, and Biko, as More's interlocutors, did not think and write within the limited scope of apartheid, but within the scope of the problems of the human in general, and in particular, the problem of the black in the existential condition of subjection. Their subjectivities were outside what apartheid would expect these critics to be. It is also important to assert that in their existential interventions, they were not liberals who demanded subjection to reform itself, but that it come to an end. They articulated their existential demands in such a way as to render what is happening to the black majority an existential scandal and also to bring to the fore how dehumanization institutionalizes, naturalizes, and normalizes itself.

Indeed, their criticism animates on the fundamentals of Black Consciousness philosophy – a transformative praxis – the necessity to shift the geography of reason. This is so because the infrastructure of antiblack racism remains intact. "The philosophy of Black Consciousness, therefore, expresses group pride and the determination by blacks to rise and attain the envisaged self" (Biko 1978, 82). To be in this mode of subjectivity, where More positions Sartre, Fanon, Manganyi, and Biko, is to be mindful of the fact that blacks "are beginning to rid their minds of imprisoning notions which are the legacy of the control of their attitudes by whites" (Biko 1978, 83). Black Consciousness is not racist, and nowhere does it express the desire to take over apartheid other than to bring it to an end. That said, More (2008, 54) has consistently argued that "Black Consciousness has never been espoused as a credo for subjugation and domination of whites." Its ultimate aim is the complete liberation of blacks from the clutches of subjection. To take Black Consciousness as a philosophical praxis, the affirmation of the black in the face of subjection is to shift the geography of reason in that blackness has been seen as something outside blackness. The latter claims reason to affirm itself to the world and to say it is enough to be plagued in subjection. It is to say, everything depends on blacks because it is their existence which is at stake. It is the effort of blacks to confront the white liberal myth as saviours of blacks and to affirm blacks as their own agents of liberation.

To shift the geography of reason is for blacks to think from the limits of their own being (Maldonado-Torres 2008). Sartre, Fanon, Manganyi, and Biko thought from the exterior of their being and engaged in the geography of reason to chart the terrain for ethical affirmation of subjectivity. The questions that they pose are fundamental, as they are articulated from blackness. As such, they deal with the problem of *being*. These questions turn out to be the problem of thought, that is, thinking thought not for its own sake, but thinking thought in relation to the life that is at stake through manifold processes of subjection. Fundamental questions, therefore, are ontologico-ethical in that they do confront an existential scandal of dehumanization of blacks. The actualization of these questions from their modes of articulation as pursued by Sartre, Fanon, Manganyi, and Biko demand ontologico-existentia-ethico transformation. They are informed by the desire to end the antiblack world and to give birth to another world. This is the foundation and the nature of perspective on the world, and it will differ in that it grows organically out of a radically different existential condition (Mills 1998). With regard to Fanon, More argues that he engaged in a struggle against apartheid and also had a philosophical influence on Black Consciousness. This cannot be ignored, taking into account that Fanon's influence is the very thematization of the Black Consciousness philosophical corpus, and his texts assumed a political biblical stature. More (2006) writes: "Fanon's insertion into Azania came through the two famous texts, *Black Skin, White Masks* and *The Wretched of the Earth*."

"To be constructed as either black or white in the world means one's lived-experience and perceptions of self are affected in a significant manner" (More 2006, 241). The antiblack world is structured in such a way that it makes the condition of appearance visible, while the essence of blacks as humans is rendered invisible. This is because whiteness refuses to see blackness because of its alleged ontological lack. The black body, as Mills (1998, 16) argues, "is the visible marker of black invisibility." It is the aberration from existence itself, and for it to be understood, it is important to bring in Manganyi's ontological axis, which shows the lived experiences of the black and white as being radically different. It creates two existential experiences that Manganyi (1973, 25) refers to as "being-black-in-the-world and being-white-in-the-world." The latter, of course, is a given because it is being in the world – existence – while the former is the opposite. It is in the realm of existence where there is relationality and, as Manganyi explains, in existence there is dialogue and the transaction of the individual with the environment.

The relationality of this Manichean axis is only relevant in so far as it creates the Manichean structure which Fanon aptly captures thus:

> The settler's town is a strongly built town, all made in stone and steel. It is a brightly lit town; the streets are covered with asphalt, and the garbage-cans swallow all the leavings, unseen, unknown, and hardly thought about [...] The settler's town is a well-fed town, an easy going town; its belly is always full of good things. The settler's town is a town of white people, or foreigners.
>
> The town belonging to the coloni[z]ed people, or at least the native town, the Negro village, the medina, the reservation, is a place of ill fame, peopled by men of evil repute. They are born there, it matters little where and how; they die there, it matters not where, nor how. It is a world without spaciousness; men live on top of each other, and their hurts are built one on top of the other. The native town is a hungry town, starved of bread, of meat, of shoes, of coal, of light. The native town is a crouching village, a town on its knees, a town wallowing in the mire.
>
> (Fanon [1961] 1990, 30)

The Manichean axis maintains the asymmetrical existential conditions of being-in-the-world to show that the being and the world have different meanings for those at the extreme ends of the axis. The white axis creates the hellish existential conditions for the black axis. The attended logic of the Manichean axis is that which has nothing to do with blacks as beings, but renders them powerless things worth being owned, domesticated, and dispossessed *in toto*. The Manichean axis, on top of being asymmetrical, is pathological in the sense that blacks, in all instances, act in the manner that is wholly determined by whiteness. Being-white-in-the-world produces the pathology of blackness in bad faith in Sartre's sense, where blackness reproduces white consciousness. This comes through the form of self-hate, self-negation, counter-revolutionary violence, and self–black–other elimination through what is normally paraded as "black-on-black violence." More (2008, 61) correctly notes that "oppression often makes blacks turn against their own in an attempt to flee and evade their blackness. They assert a white consciousness by adopting an antiblack standpoint on human reality." It is, of course, to become white. The manner in which they unleash their anger and the violence that comes with it has skewed directionality. Blacks in bad faith and in white consciousness violate their very own, who are not necessarily the problem, but the very same oppression that produces them. The Manichean axis of being-white-in-the-world and being-black-in-the-world creates a burden of blacks who reproduce what More considers "antiblack consciousness." Biko has this to say about blacks operating in bad faith:

> Any black man who props up the system *of apartheid and its colonial infrastructure* actively has lost his right to be considered part of the black world: he has sold his soul for thirty pieces of silver and finds that he is in fact not acceptable to the white society he sought to join.
> (Biko 1978, 92 [emphasis added])

This antiblack consciousness is profoundly deep in that it creates a false impression on the gullible blacks who think they are better than other blacks. Their yardstick of being human is nothing but to be in the midst of white approval, and being honorary whites. As it is obvious, they love the very same whiteness that reminds them in hatefulness that they are black and inferior. The Manichean axis operates through what Mills (1997) refers to as the Racial Contract, which determines who counts as white and who does not count as black. It is the ontological structuring which serves as justification for the antiblack racist infrastructure. The thing with this contract is that it is not a mutual agreement between two parties. To be specific, since it is the contract that has to do with forms of lives in the polity, it does not have ontological terms that are agreed upon. Rather, the ontological terms are imposed by whiteness onto blackness. In other words, the racial contract in this Manichean axis is set in the terms of whites *qua* whites, and these are terms that serve the interests of whites.

> Both globally and within particular nations, then, white people, Europeans and their descendants, continue to benefit from the Racial Contract, which creates a world in their cultural image, political states differentially favouring their interests, an economy structured around the racial exploitation of others, and a moral psychology (not just in whites but sometimes in nonwhites also) skewed consciously or unconsciously toward privileging them, taking the status quo of differential racial entitlement as normatively legitimate, and not to be investigated further.
> (Mills 1997, 40)

For this to happen, the Racial Contract, as Mills argues, requires compulsion through violence and ideological conditioning as whiteness has the entitlement to rule and not to be contradicted. This means that it bans all forms of black rebellion, since this will trigger standardized punishment which disciplines this rebellion never to occur again. Sartre, Fanon, Manganyi, and Biko write against the Racial Contract, as they do not recognize its terms and they have not been parties to the homology of the contractual agreement. There is no agreement, as blacks were not part of it. The Racial Contract is the contract in itself with no form of relationality whatsoever. This is not the case with being-black-in-the-world – the antiblackness which relegates blacks to what Fanon (1970) refers to as the zone of non-being. Blacks are not contractual subjects because their very being is relegated to non-existence. As Moodley (1991, 237) shows, this is on the basis that "[b]lackness symbolized evil, demise, chaos, corruption, and uncleanliness, in contrast to whiteness which equaled order, wealth, purity, goodness, cleanliness, and the epitome of beauty." The Racial Contract is the contract in-itself and for-itself – that is, its own end and very justification, since its terms are apropos exclusively for white *qua* white.

Correspondingly, the existential quad did not write in contractual ways in that the world they were in did not require any agreement. All it demanded was that blacks agree to the terms that bastardize their very existence. In Sartre (1956, 49): "[B]ad faith then has in appearance the structure of falsehood." If this is the case, then, there is no Racial Contract in the real sense of the contractual, but its falsity as white consciousness believes in it. That is, there is a contract of white per white. Everything that is contractual is, therefore, white perspectivity and the justification of subjection. More shows, through the mobilization of Sartre, Fanon, Manganyi, and Biko that the Racial Contract is bad faith, and to shift the geography of reason is to engage in the commitment of responsibility rather than fleeing to the pleasing falsehood of bad faith. To take this positionality is to take seriously Fanon's (1970) epidermal schema, to think blackness from externality of existence and insert it back to existence with its own ontological terms. This is necessary to give insight into the human condition. More places this existential quad as necessary figures to press the existential radical demands for the new world to be imagined and to be actualized. More even shows that they were fondly exposed to the South African existential reality and in their imagination and actualization they had Azania in mind – the land of the free. For, South Africa as the colonial state, and the antiblack one, for that matter, had to come to an end so that Azania can be born. It is this existential quad that took the Manichean axis of being-white-in-the-world and being-black-in-the-world not as the axis of reflection, but the ontologico-existential schema that continuously re-subjectivizes the positionality of being black in the antiblack world which must come to an end.

By foregrounding Sartre, Fanon, Manganyi, and Biko in Black Consciousness, More precisely shows that Black Consciousness is not an historical event which came and faded. It is a continued presence, a philosophical practice that is still relevant in this antiblack world. "The continued impact of Black Consciousness" as Moodley (1991, 251) concludes, "lies in its potential." Its potential is not to be realized, as it has been there from its very inception to the present. It is still informed by creating another world and bringing to an end the antiblack world. Sartre, Fanon, Manganyi, and Biko, as philosophical interlocutors, produced what Harris (1982) refers to as philosophy born of struggle. This is not a philosophy that came about out of choice or a void that will render it as some form of meditative abstractions of the universal or a pursuit of the truth that has no proximity to the lived reality of the black. Black Consciousness is a philosophy born of struggle because it arose out of the need for blacks wanting to liberate themselves from the clutches of subjection, and to live in Azania, where blacks will be fully constitutive beings and subjects who have a name to themselves and who have a name to their existence.

For More, it is clear that Sartre, Fanon, Manganyi, and Biko belong to what he refers to as the "Azanian existential tradition." It is in this tradition that centuries of the lived experience of the black in the antiblack world are meditated upon, with the resolute commitment to bringing the ethical life into being. To evoke Azania à la Sartre, Fanon, Manganyi, and Biko is to think not only about renaming a country which bears the colonial signification, but also about creating new forms of life that are outside the psychology, fantasy, histories, consciousness, and reality of whiteness and its racist infrastructure of antiblackness. The idea of Azania stems from a variety of genealogies, trajectories, and horizons. As a matter of specificity, the idea of South Africa will be engaged from Africana existential philosophy, which serves as the lens for More's philosophical practice. As the fundamental basis through which the imagination of South Africa can be fathomed, More's foregrounding in Africana existential philosophy captures the existential struggle of the will to live and the rupture that will give birth to Azania, a country with a name and outside the colonial signification of South Africa. As a philosopher of existence, More offers the imagination of Azania through the embodiment of blackness.

Ending apartheid in totality, and the colonial foundation that it rests on, also means bringing about the unmasking of neo-apartheid as the existential condition that violates blacks without white responsibility and assuaging of guilt. Blacks continue to be in the Manichean axis of the pathological as they have been systematically, systemically, and continuously dehumanized. Therefore, it is correct to point out that this Azanian existential tradition is found in the philosophical meditations of Sartre, Fanon, Manganyi, and Biko. This is because they tirelessly engaged in philosophical interventions that have to do with human reality in the antiblack world. According to More (2006, 243), the "philosophically attentive Manganyi and Biko [systematically and continuously grappled] with the everyday life of the bodily black being in an antiblack society." More shows how much influence Sartre and Fanon had on both Manganyi and Biko. He also acknowledges the fact that there are many sources of Black Consciousness, and notes that: "No doubt, Black Power has a tremendous influence on political praxis of that era in Azania" (More 2006, 253). Both Manganyi and Biko engaged in the concrete lived experience of being black in the infrastructure of apartheid with its naked and crude form of antiblackness and, by extension, their engagement still has relevance to post-1994 neo-apartheid.

Self-evidently, Black Consciousness philosophy, to Gordon (2000a), connotes "the idea that black people have perspectives on the world." To have a perspective on the world is to give a different account to the perspective of the antiblack world. The perspective of the black in the world is what Wilderson (2008) refers to as articulating the grammar of suffering – that is, blacks having a point of view about and perspective on the world. For Black Consciousness to be a philosophy born of struggle, it is then rightful for More to acutely locate the existentialist quad as critics of South Africa (the colonial state) and as imagining and actualizing Azania (the land of the free). Azania is a state that is about to come, its creation will come about through the struggle for liberation – that is, Black Consciousness as the philosophy born of struggle. The creation of

Azania is possible only if the founding and constitutive ethos is that of genuine liberation. Azania is not a Mandela's House with its flag freedoms and where white supremacy is the order of the day.

By Way of Fanon's Prayer

This meditation for More is more of an intellectual portrait than absolute detailing and a philosophical treatise. It is a meditation on the thinker thinking thought and not thought for itself – rather, thinking about the fundamental question of the human in the antiblack world and the question of liberation to end that world. It is the task of the philosopher who bears responsibility and does not abdicate that responsibility – rather, the vocation is nothing but to be responsible for responsibility itself. This is what prompts More in making a meaningful impact ontologically and existentially through what Serequeberhan (2012) refers to as the "critical negative aspect" of philosophy to undertake the responsibility of ensuring human betterment. The ontologico-existential condition of blackness is evident in More's accounts of antiblack racism and pointing out its existence, something not common in South African philosophical circles. Therefore, More is by all accounts portrayed here in this meditation as a philosopher of the human and a philosopher engaged in what Harris (1982) calls philosophy born of struggle. What would that philosophy be if not Africana existential philosophy? For it is the philosophy that is concerned with the question of the human in the antiblack world and in its shift of geography of reason; it is rethinking the question of being from its limits and modernity from its underside – that is, it is the philosophy that confronts reality by unmasking its narratives and myths to account for the human question.

By thinking from the limits of being, as Maldonado-Torres (2008) notes, the driving forces of More's philosophical interventions must be understood in relation to being black in the antiblack world and to being in combat with bad faith. Being in confrontation with bad faith is not to accept the scripted ways in which philosophy is practised as thought for thought itself, but in confrontation with the precariousness of the existential conditions that befall humanity. That is, the effort to find ways to create the ethico-political existential formations where humanity confronts the questioning of the very fact of its humanity. More's Africana existential philosophy deals with the ontologico-existential predicament of being-black-in-the-antiblack-world. It is in this instance that More also fits squarely within the canonical architecture of the ancestry of the black radical thought tradition.

What is important to highlight in this conclusion is Fanon's (1970, 165) prayer: "O my body, make of me always a man who questions!" This is not just a prayer for its own sake, but the will to live and the deepening of subjectivity. It is this prayer that affirms one's existence. It is a prayer that allows "the open door of every consciousness" (Fanon 1970, 165). More, through his philosophical interventions, is indeed invoking Fanon's prayer as he continually questions, in his embodiment, the lived experience of being-black-in-the-antiblack-world. The body of More is the body that is racialized and signified as black, and his being is that of humanity questioned. Therefore, his philosophical underpinning under the annals of Africana existential philosophy is preoccupied with the question of the black in the world, and how such a subject will rise to humanity *qua* humanity outside the infrastructure of the antiblack world, which has to end. More took the Fanon prayer to assert the right of blacks to exist and the end of the antiblack world. Moten (2013a, 766) writes: "The body that questions, because it is a body that is in question, is an experiment." But then, Fanon's prayer, as More invokes it, pushes the ontologico-existential reality to be some form of possibility. In point of fact, this possibility is the affirmation of blackness through Black Consciousness and the pursuit of another world – the decolonized world. This is the world outside the confines of the modern colonial world with its masks of antiblackness. In More, there is an authorization of the black existence and it is the articulation of the ontologico-existential structural difference.

It is clear in More's Africana existential philosophy that the re-installation of the calling for the authorization of blackness is to account for the "lived exigencies and concerns – problematic and worthy of questioning" (Serequeberhan 2012, 138). The captive black body, the body of More blackness largesse, keeps questioning through the mode of Fanon's prayer. The violence that is directed at the black body is unjustifiable, and More challenges the ways in which it is institutionalized, naturalized, and normalized. If the black body is clutched in subjection, Fanon's prayer invites a revolt for it to break from subjection; this must not be a gift from the oppressor, but the very self-authorization of blacks. As Fanon's prayer is the one that is in the mode of perpetual questioning, it means that those who have their humanity questioned are also questioning the very form of subjection that is directed at their racialized bodies. It is in this questioning that blacks are authorizing themselves through decolonial consciousness in order to affirm another existence and another world.

6

Marikana: The Conceptual Anxiety of Bare Life

The life of the black subject is always at stake for the very fact of its nearness and entanglement to wanton violence, humiliation, indignity, dehumanization, and death. The dispossessed ontology which is the negation of the other is definitional to black life. The Marikana massacre cannot be understood outside the contours of black life, which is structurally positioned in the antiblack matrix of violence. It therefore means that to account for the matrix of violence, which is a catalyst that positions the black subject at the receiving end of objectification, ontological questions should be at the center. This means going beyond hegemonic accounts that pervade the South African socio-political discourse predicated on this peripheral question: What happened in Marikana? The ontological question that is essential to pursue is of understanding the positionality of blacks in the antiblack matrix of violence, one of which Marikana is the part.

The entry point of this chapter is that the concept of bare life as articulated by Giorgio Agamben is essential for understanding the politics of life of the human in the peripheral zones. However, the concept of bare life is not sufficient to engage the politics of life in the zone of non-being, where the black subject is structurally positioned. Consequently, bare life suffers conceptual anxiety, since it cannot account for the ontology of the black subject. This conceptual anxiety is caused by the existence of the black subject located in the zone of non-being, where life has no worth and is taken at will, and Marikana presents such a reality. Bare life is concerned with the liquidation of life in the zone of being and applies to the category of the subject with ontological density – that is, the human subject in the zone of being. The contention here is that the ontological density of the black subject is that of non-existence and Marikana massacre serves as testimony to the fact that those who are in the zone of non-being can be killed with impunity and there is nothing to be accounted for.

Bare Life *Qua* Subject Erasure

The Marikana incident served as a spectacle that demonstrated the liquidation of black life. The black subject seeks to emerge, but such an attempt is made in the midst of being liquidated by objectification. What is at stake with regard to the black subject? This does not come into rupture as the black subject is denied the very fact of being alive. What is not alive cannot be a political agent, but a mere entity caught in a perpetual state of objectification where rupture is even made not to fit at the imaginary level. To be a mere entity is to be erased as a subject (and this is what Agamben regards as bare life) which is "caught in the mechanisms and calculations of power" (Agamben 1998, 71). This is objectification in its proper sense, where power is applied to the body and assuming the position that is external to the body. Being external, objectification inserts itself forcefully into the body by means of wanton violence. The life of the body is the very life of objectification. This, as Agamben notes, legitimates and necessitates total domination. It is the totality effect and operation of power to subjects who have their lives as something that they can determine but which they do not determine. "The absolute capacity of the subjects' bodies to be killed forms the new political body of the West" (Agamben 1998, 74). To amplify Agamben, Gilroy (2005, 48) argues that bare life applies to a "politically ambivalent and juridically marginal figure of the person who can be killed with impunity and of their reduction of the infra-human condition of 'bare life' that sanctions their death."

According to Agamben, the inclusion of bare life in the juridico-political order is the participation in the political life where unconditional objectification assumes the power of death. The subject in the condition of bare life means that the subject is exposed to death. For Agamben, it is the subject whose life can be killed but not sacrificed. What is of importance is that the life of the human is even exposed to death; its death is a transgression even if bare life can be institutionalized. This means that the body and the life of the human subject possesses "a natural life and a sacred life" (Agamben 1998, 61). There is no way the black subject can be closer to sacredness, since the body of the black subject is not the sacred body. This is because the body of the black subject possesses no ontological density, the density that is possessed by the body of the human. Though Agamben puts bare life as incompatible to the human world, it is the human world that hosts humans whose life is put under objectification which produces bare life. Therefore, it is clear that this poses an ethical dilemma, since human life is sacred in the politico-juridico sense. So, then, it is clear that humans are caught in the inhospitable world in which Agamben brings the condition of bare life as the ethical problem to our attention. What is seen as resolvable is the juridico-political order transforming itself to allow a move to a just and human world. But then, the predicament still remains with regard to the black subject having no recourse in the world, since the world as it is assumes the antiblack position.

The life of the human under objectification creates bare life, which is the main concern in Agamben's conceptual schema. The life of the human is that of the political agent, which should be compatible with the ethical. The ethical is, of course, evoked to condemn that which transgresses, violates, compromises, and litigates the life of the human. To be human is to be intrinsically linked to life, to be alive and to have life protected. Indeed, as Agamben notes, the condition of bare life is problematic in the ethical sense and this applies to the level of the human subject. What does it mean to exist in the absent existence? The humanity of the blackness exists as non-existence. It is the assault on humanity through the various modes of being questioned, the very questioning that displaces, disfigures, and brutalizes. The mere fact of blackness as existing is a given, which at the same time is the existence dispossessed; that is, the existence of blackness outside itself. By virtue of existing, whether perceived or real, this is the existence questioned.

Marikana is actually the very act of questioning blackness. It is the non-existence of blackness where the whole conception of humanity is suspended and what is brought to the fore is blackness. That is to say, what exists is not the human, but the black. The visibility of blackness is paradoxically the invisibility of the human.

The existence of blackness is scandalous in that non-existence precedes existence. To put the humanity of the black subject into question means blackness is the phenomenon without analogy (Wilderson 2003b). This means that blackness is incomparable in the manner in which it is objectified and there is no precise articulation of the suffering of blackness, since objectification puts blackness outside the realm of humanity. The non-existence of blackness is pathologization par excellence, which exists through objectification. By virtue of non-existence, this means that objectification serves the very role of making blackness to be that which is not supposed to exist. To exist, it seems, is the very act of contravention, which needs to be disciplined by law and order to ensure non-existence. What all this means is that the structural positionality of the black subject at the ontological level is that of perpetual erasure.

Marikana has been the existence of what actually does not exist, since erasure has taken precedence. And yet, the articulation of the Marikana massacre in the hegemonic machine of the liberal consensus does the opposite by positioning the figure of the human, which of course, aims to cause blackness to be erased. This is a scandal since blacks are not humans and what is eminent is the idea that Marikana affects all humans, while no mention is made of the black. It is only the black as the figure of the subject of objectification that featured in Marikana through being injured, shot and killed. It is, therefore, essential to pose the question: Who died? The answer which is irrefutable is that it is the black! To look at blackness *qua* Marikana is the intervention that is opposed. Opposition has to be expected to maintain the silent scandal which is the fact that only blacks were killed. Blackness is equalled to a number which is thirty-four mine workers and this number evokes the notion of tragedy and horror that affects all the things human. Blackness is added up to numbers and it is the significance of the numbers which, even if they were even more than what they are, they will not raise any form of agency. The use of numbers is to try to humanize blacks; the very fact is an impossibility. This is the very act of non-existence of blackness since it is erased from the base; the gratuitous violence that militates against blackness is unracialized, whereas it is racialized in its very logic. As Hartman (1997, 26) notes: "[A]ffect, gesture, and a vulnerability to violence constituted blackness." Objectification renders blackness to be bandaged by an antiblack matrix of violence.

The antiblack matrix of violence is omnipresent and it creates a frozen world and, according to Gilroy (2005), it perpetuates its fantasy in the form of a militarized colonial world. What is pervasive is the political ritual of condemnation, where public figures, the media, opinion makers, and the public to some extent will make the statements of condemnation; the most famous and fashionable statement is: "This is horror and gruesome as it stains our democracy." The other statement being: "We condemn these barbaric actions by the police." But the most popular is: "We are not like those barbarians." As the condemnation is made more audible, the very act of condemnation does not change anything. One black body dying is too many but, of course, since this is the body of the ontologically void subject it does not matter. So, what exists is condemnation for the sake of condemnation. What needs to be thoroughly engaged is the life of the black subject in the zone of non-being and de-linking it to the clutches of objectification which create a deathscape.

A Deathscape and the Zone of Non-Being

The life of the black subject is the life that is always interdicted. It is the life that does not belong to the very being of the subjects *qua* human, since life itself is dispossessed. The colonial encounter is the one in which Marikana needs to be traced, as this is the moment which is definitional to black life. The notion of the deathscape cannot be divorced from the colonial encounter, since it is this encounter which started to locate blackness outside the realm of life, reason, and humanity. It is from this encounter that the death of the black subject is not the act of transgression, since the very death of the subject cannot be accounted for. It is a place of objectification in that it creates natal alienation – the very basis of death (Patterson 1982). It is, according to the liberal consensus and the popular consensus that Marikana should be hailed as a national tragedy and horror. This national tragedy and horror are not seen as the lived experience of the black subject and its body being incarcerated to death.

The lived experience of the black subject cannot be reduced to a mere event, and even so, the incorrect way of regarding Marikana as an event is to displace it from the reality of black life. The deathscape is what captures the lives thrown out of the realm of life – the lives denied essence and being given to death as they are in the zone of non-being. This essentially means that the black subject is the tragedy and the horror itself, since this is what the zone of non-being (re-)produces. Maldonado-Torres (2008) declares that what creates antagonism toward ordinary social life is that the social life in the deathscape is that of the licensing of death. This means that there cannot be any social life where death is permissible, to the space which was created for death. It is known that social life should be the locus of peace, but death has superseded it. It is in the deathscape that objectification ensures that there is no life accounted for.

What is to be mentioned is that in Marikana what was killed was the black subject with no significance of a name, but the subject in totalizing terms which has the bearing of life but not as life. To have no name as a signifier means that the subject is reduced to the level of the body, and this represents an object. This act of namelessness by objectification is essentially the justification of the deathscape. The deathscape is not, as the portrayal and representation of the Marikana event an arrival, but it is the embodied lived experience of the black subject in the face of objectification. So, Marikana is the deathscape by the very fact that it renders black subjects constitutively dead, while they are alive. The space inhabited by the black subject is akin to being vulnerable to death. It is not only because the black subject is in proximity to death, but that the fabric life is death itself. In other words, the will to live simply means their will to die, unwilling to do so. The deathscape has assumed a complex character, but it is important to point out that the condition of violence in its absolute and structural form, obliterates black life. For Wilderson (2010), the deathscape exists simply because the nature of violence precedes and exceeds black life.

It is essential to understand Patterson's (1982) concept of social death when he refers to it as the natal alienation through which the black subject is positioned. To be positioned as such means that the black subject is outside the grammar of life. The black subject, according to Wilderson (2003b, 25) "assumes the positionality of subjects of social death." The grammar of life then belongs to those who are human. The realm of the human in its exclusionary sense excludes those who cannot articulate the grammar of being human. Not to have the ability to articulate this grammar is the very fact of not having the stature to engage in the politics of life. That is to say, the black subject does not have the grammar of suffering and as such, the black subject is burdened with the inability to articulate its form of life, which is tragedy and horror.

The destruction of black life is inherent in the deathscape. Marikana cannot therefore be understood outside the deathscape because it is the condition that among many other conditions is akin to the objectification of the black subject, which registers the impunity through which the black body's life can be liquidated. The deathscape entraps the black body in the state of killability which is justified by means of law and order. So, then, it is essential to attach the politics of life of those who do not carry its essence. Marikana as a deathscape is the black life itself; it is the everyday lived reality. It is in this lived reality that the impossibility of blackness yearning to have the will to life as something becomes more and more distanced. The will to live as the deathscape exists puts blackness outside the realm of life.

It goes without qualification that the modes of political engagement propagated the idea of the "mine workers" while still erasing the race question, which proves scandalous in that those who died are actually black bodies. The idea is that mine workers are ahistoricized by the fact that the idea is created that mine workers are subjects in the general sense of the term, while they are in fact blacks. The interests of white capital are clear in Marikana – that if threatened, brutality is unleashed in its full might and no black lives can be spared. For the white capital to live uninterrupted there must be a buffer zone of wanton violence, which essentially means that the deathscape should always exist. For white capital to exist, it must be nourished by black lives, even their death. To be in a deathscape means that the life of the black subject should not be spared if it is perceived as threatening. This is because it is the life that is always brought into question, the question regarding the very essence of its humanity. These are deathscapes that have assumed the level of the normal and natural through the mask of structural violence, since this is the violence that assumes the invisible form. It is, therefore, the normalization of pathologies, the very basis of deathscapes.

On Structural Violence

Structural violence, as Farmer (2004) puts it, carries with it poverty, disease, accidents, crime, and death, and these are seen as pathologies inherent in society. In no way is effort made to focus on what structural violence operates in its invisible form. Structural violence is the violence that is not visible and it is hidden in structures that signify the normality of life. Farmer insists that structural violence negates the capacity to see, name, describe, and explain the very origin and operation of structural violence. It creates the absence of the grammar of suffering and the state of noncommunicability (Wilderson 2010). In defining structural violence Farmer has this to say:

> In short, the concept of structural violence is intended to inform the study of the social machinery of oppression. Oppression is a result of many conditions, not the least of which reside[s] in consciousness. We will therefore need to examine, as well, the roles played by the erasure of historical memory and other forms of desocialization as enabling conditions of structures that are both 'sinful' and obstensibly 'nobody's fault'.
>
> (Farmer 2004, 307)

The proposition here is that structural violence is war and war is structural violence. Structural violence takes the logic of disorder and death not only to the level of the symbolic, but that of the real (Wilderson 2010). Maldonado-Torres (2004, 75) has rightly stated that "the opposition between ethics and politics is mirrored in the opposition between peace and war, and between ordinary social life of an elitist exceptionalism." The elimination of the opposites between ethics and politics can come into being if structural violence does not exist. In such a condition, there will be justice, since justice cannot be awarded to those who are not in the human fraternity. Structural violence is not symbolic but, in reality, suggests that it is absolute violence against the structural positionality of blackness. Being at the level of the real, Wilderson (2010, 75) argues, is that "the grammar of suffering of the [b]lack itself is on the level of the real." Structural violence produces the pathologized form of life which is not far from death, the death which cannot be accounted for. In support of Wilderson, Maldonado-Torres argues that what takes place at the level of the ordinary pathologies at the level of the real is the absolute expression of violence and misrecognition of the black subject. The black subject who is in the damned positionality at the level of signification is depleted. The ontological weight of such a subject disappears through erasure.

Structural violence troubles the certainty of black humanity. The attack of this violence is directed toward the black body which is caught in the state of uncertainty in terms of whether it will survive or not. Structural violence is not the innocence of power and race but the very embodiment of the two. What structural violence produces, as Hartman (1997) points out, is its pathology, which manifests itself in black suffering; a profound dimension of dispossession. Black suffering creates blackness as the dispensable other, since the violence is systematically directed against the black body, and the black condition remaining intact. As such, the institutionalization, naturalization, and normalization of black pathology, which is systematic exclusion, and dehumanization are regarded as the way of life for the black subject. It is in this logic that structural violence takes the form of invisibility and metamorphosis so that it cannot be implicated, but its victims having to be blamed by actively participating in the very acts of dehumanization. As Farmer (2004) states, structural violence is infernal machinery – it is the dominant social order which is both symbolic and material in form. As such, death is a given, since existence is survival and not life.

The Marikana massacre shows the persistence of structural violence in which the pathological form of life and the objectification that is carried with it plague the black body. The black body is always available to be violated by the mere fact of its positionality in the matrix of violence. The form of violence that explains the Marikana massacre cannot be reduced to physical violence, but it is the everyday violence which informs the forms of lives in Marikana. The operation of structural violence can hide many things, even the very form of violence itself. However, it cannot hide objectification and the pathologies that plague black subjects. As Farmer (2004, 315) states: "[S]tructural violence takes new forms in every era." Structural violence produces the life that is lived out of emptiness and these are lives that are substitutedly dead.

Black subjects are erased as the real subjects through the process of stigmatization. They are stigmatized for the mere fact of being black, and it is such a stigma that is the very basis of the justification of structural violence. Structural violence is a form of violence that takes both the signs of visibility and invisibility, articulation and disarticulation, existence and non-existence. It is a form of violence that is largely embedded in erasure, since it is not visible, while it operates by erasing the ontological essence of black subjects. The very fibre of structural violence is the erasure of humanity and is to re-appropriate objectification. Farmer raises the interesting point that says that the architects of structural violence create hegemonic accounts of reality and the primary purpose is to engage in the erasure of history. The hegemonic accounts of reality are perverse to such an extent that they are discourses beyond reproach.

Marikana is such a reality in that what is put as reality is the police killing thirty-four striking mine workers, ten police officers died in the run-up to the tragedy, making the total of forty people dead. For the fact that no structural violence is accounted for causes the very fact of its invisibility. The politics of erasure operate in the manner that assumes normality, while in fact they are the normality. The politics of erasure create a condition where it is difficult for black subjects to have the grammar through which they can articulate this violence. The state of permanence of structural violence makes it reality to such an extent that it is ingrained in the socio-political institutions that render it normal state of affairs. As Farmer (2004, 308) notes: "[T]he erasure of history is subtle and incremental and depends upon the erasure of links across time and space." It is not the first time that police have killed unarmed black subjects with impunity. So, what is different about Marikana? For example, what happened at Marikana is frozen in August 2012, where mine workers were shot and killed by the police, while this is, in fact, the daily and what Hartman (1997) refers to as "routinized violence."

The Marikana massacre is structural violence having to assume its raw form of naked violence, which is obviously targeted at the designated group of black subjects. To locate Marikana within the very nature of structural violence with its rupture of naked violence is to testify that it is the everyday existential condition of black subjects, and which unfortunately is something that is left unexplained. To regard Marikana as the very act of structural violence is something that is seen as a claim to be dismissed. Also, to regard Marikana as an event is to absolve structural violence, which is foundational and constitutive to the Marikana massacre, and to leave accountability outside the sphere of political action informed by undoing injustices inflicted upon the black body. It is the black body that is at the receiving end of violence, and that in this condition is the police violence, which cannot be detached from the state violence. As the machinery of the political, the police are the apparatus of the state and serve the interests of the state. The latter ensure that it at all times maintains the safeguarding of the white capital interests. It is this complex that constitutes the very machine that produces structural violence, which works in the ways that are complex to fathom.

The Politics of Life: The Negation of Ontology

The politics of life suggest that life is a right. To live is the right alienable to the individual and that must be protected and enhanced. The right to life is the politics of life. It means that the subject carries ontological weight by the mere fact of being. The politics of life are outside the black subject for the mere fact of this subject's being located outside the realm of being. The politics of life seem to connote the fact that they really apply to those who have life. It is reasonably so, because they are fashioned in such a way that they preserve life for those who deserve it, and they liquidate those who are not deserving it. The presence of life means to live and its absence the opposite. This is the conception of the politics of life in the world that does not offer humanity to all. But then, what emerges is that the conception of politics of life in the context of Marikana becomes questionable.

Agamben (1998) starts with the notion of bare life to account for the life suspended, which can be taken at will. It is then questionable as to how to preserve life and to live life while it is locked within the integrum of bare life. This does undercut the notion of bare life itself. Bare life points to the ways in which life in the process of its making and being lived is actually that which is rendered dead. Going back to the regime of apartheid, black killability evokes the presence of the murderous regime that puts the ontology of the black subject always at stake. So is the case with the post-1994 reality, which has the same killability instincts as its predecessor. This is the case because the black subject never mattered and never does.

The Marikana massacre shows, as with the socio-existential antiblack reality that the regime kills its own citizens, where killing en masse is something that only resonates with black bodies. It means that the very existence of black bodies is something magnetic to bullets, by the very fact that such magnetism can be justified in terms of blackness having to be in the wrong place at the wrong time, and also having engaged in the act that provokes this magnetism. This magnetism is the very fact of the justification of violence which affects the black subject, and it means that the use of the bullet was self-defense against the violence anticipated from the black subject.

Agamben evokes the concept of "ritual killing" to account for the ways in which subjects are put outside human jurisdiction and being also outside the reality of law. It is indeed the case that the violence that confronts the black body is ritualistic in the sense that police brutality, with its murderous intents, is something that has been entrenched. This takes the worst form in that the black subject is faced with the predicament that the black subject cannot account for, since the black subject has no institutions of redress. The ritualistic killing, as Agamben puts it, is the constitutive part of bare life, but then, there cannot be any bare life to that which is not human. Bare life is the life suspended, and to those who were humans. This is because the politics of bare life are for the subjects who are human.

The black subject equated with ontology assumes the state of collapsibility and the result is the nothingness of blackness. What emerges from this state of equation is bad faith for that blackness – as the condition of the state of aberration from the norm – is that which ontology has left on the wayside. The politics of agency which contend heavily to suggest that blackness is a state of mind and not a racial marker reject in absolute terms that blackness is actually the aberration from the norm. Blackness is seen as the full scale of humanity and the injustices that exist are blamed on blackness by not acting out of agency. When Marikana is applied to this set of reality, the implication is that the violence meted out to striking mine workers is justified. They are shot at, not only for the mere fact of being a threat, but for being those who are outside the realm of being.

It is important to ask: In what existential conditions does the black body matter? The claim that the black subject is the full being who is hosted by the universe with a universal connotation is that its body matters, while, to the contrary, it is made not to possess life. To place the black body in this question is to disrupt the whole universalist project of bodies having to matter and having to possess life. It is important as well to point out that black bodies do not matter, and this is because objectification squeezes out of them all the ontological essence. It is in Marikana where ontology features evaporate since the figure of non-human is taking a political stance, which is seen as that which requires discipline in that it is running against the grain of law and order. The basis of ontology in relation to the black subject represents a body not in the ontological sense, but the body of the non-human, a distinct category of the living, whose death cannot be seen as transgression but the act which can be justified. This evokes an interesting question: What does it mean to kill that which is ontologically void, the being in the zone of non-being where civility is suspended? The striking miners died and what rendered them dead is the fact that they are substitutedly dead.

Human Rights for Humans Only

The principle of human rights in the field of politico-juridico-ethics is the existential plane that applies to humans. The dominant discourses suggest that human rights apply to everybody and also emphasize how they are so important. They are enshrined in the constitution. They create an impression that they form an essential core of the conduct of the state after 1994, that it humanizes everybody in the context of a history of bare life for most and significant life for the white few. It creates the impression that resolution of conflict will be ethical in the sense that it would be to build peace rather than war in relation to idea of politics and ethics as embedded in war and peace respectively (Maldonado-Torres 2008). The constitutional framework is the language both of the neo-colonized state and white capital. It was involved in Marikana time and again. So, it means that human rights are inclusive and they are not excluding anyone as they apply to all humans. Maldonado-Torres (2017) clearly shows that human rights are, in their rooted genealogy of coloniality, still rooted in secularism, individualism, and racism. Thus, coloniality is, in the lucid terms of Maldonado-Torres (2017, 131), "part of the notion of the human in the hegemonic concept of human rights." It is important to state that human rights cannot have the full weight of application to those who are not considered humans. Therefore, the Marikana massacre, which is the black condition, is clear that human rights do not apply, since that is not the reality of the human. Since human rights are the rights that have the power to protect, this remains impotent to black subjects in Marikana.

More importantly, those who are not humans are outside the realm of human rights. As Agamben (1998, 75) notes, "inalienable rights of man show themselves to lack every protection and reality at the moment in which they can no longer take the form of rights belonging to citizens of the state." For human rights though postured as applying to all humanity, blackness is excluded by the mere fact of being given the impression of being included, and this is in fact cosmetic. It is clear that the very fact of killing those who were the striking miners by the police is the necessary order given to the police, who are supposed to execute the order as it is. It is under the suspense of human rights having to be outweighed by the order to the police.

Human rights by the act of police as the machinery of the state seem to be problematic in the sense that the police killed. The question then arises: Why it is not the system of accounting for police brutality that has been inherited from the apartheid regime? Police in their existence in South Africa have never been a service, but the militaristic terror to black bodies as the virus of violence is in the psyche of the police. The inheritance infrastructure of violence by the police is the one that is informed by criminalizing the black body and stripping of all the humanity that is left to it. The police militancy role, with its murderous instincts when it comes to black bodies, is informed by the fact that killing the black is killing the non-human and there cannot be any form of accountability.

So, the impunity that positions the black body at the state of killability is something that is institutionalized, naturalized, and normalized. Even though those actual police happen to belong in the very same communities they brutalize, and, having to share the very same objectification that affects them as they are blacks, the very role of assuming the character of the machinery makes them to think of themselves as exceptional. Police are acting in the form of bad faith as they are serving the very machinery that oppresses them. There cannot be any propagation of human rights if what exists is the regime of violence terrorizing black bodies and subjecting them to the disciplinary machine of law and order. The mere fact of blackness being a problem means that no human rights can apply.

The mere fact of being in the world as the existential loci of the political to be enshrined is made possible by the existence of human rights. The principles of human rights in the triad of the politico-juridico-ethico apply to the politics of life. Most of the evidence is about the importance of human rights. Human rights as the politics of life apply to everyone that exists. The importance of human rights cannot be overemphasized, more so as the right to exist is advocated and defended. But then, this is not accountable in minute existential terms to whom it applies to and whom it does not. The contention here is that human rights cannot apply to those who are not humans and to be exact, to those who have their humanity always questioned.

Therefore, Marikana presents a scandal and it is clear that human rights were suspended since no human beings featured there when the Marikana scandal evolved. This means that those who died there are not humans, since they are socially dead. It follows that the principles of human rights do not apply to them. In their foundational phase and with the liberal dogma as being the paragon of morality – the Declaration of Universal Human Rights when they were entrenched toward the mid twentieth century, black subjects were still under the yoke of oppression and the discourse of human rights did not have them in mind, and it is the time when Africa was still colonized. It means then, being excluded in the discourse of human rights that they were not humans. So, it is clear that the existential aspect of blackness is located outside the realm of human rights. Blackness is not humanity by virtue of its blackness.

Therefore, blackness framed within the context of Marikana is something that should be agitated rather than purporting the idea of human rights being violated. This removes ontological questions. It is then necessary to frame the context of Marikana through the force of law where the state machinery is in the form of the police where death is permissible. The permissibility of death should mean that the police are part of the structure larger than them – that is, the state as represented by the former minister of police Nathi Mthethwa. The police had to fulfil their duty of serving the state by being militant toward citizens. This is to say, the structure within which police operate, since they have been militarized since from apartheid, police act by the mere fact of order. Police are violence and violence is the police in as far as Marikana is concerned. The very same police to a lesser or larger extent are the very family members of those who were shot, injured, and killed. It essentially means that police are part of the very society they brutalize. In the claim to serve, they are part of the violent state machinery. Black bodies were in solidarity and this very solidarity presents, in the face of power, a threat to law and order. Therefore, the realm of law and order is justified in the sense that the state of killability is institutionalized to criminalize solidarity. The discipline of law and order exists as legitimated, as police must ensure they discipline black bodies in wanton terror. It is clear in South Africa how black bodies are racialized to the point of criminality and how the police are enjoying this fetish. This makes the ontology of blackness not to have any essence, any weight that make it to have that status of being. The ontological density of the blackness, in Marikana, is what is at stake.

Ontological Density

Ontology has density in so far as it applies to those who are at the realm of the human – that is, those whom the antiblack world does not antagonize and who, of course, do not have the encounter of their humanity being questioned. Only those who are dehumanized are dispossessed of their ontological density. The Marikana massacre serves as testimony to the fact that those who died do not have the ontological density. As such, they are not in their reality of the political as they are not the subjects in the fuller sense. They are the subjects of lacks and deficiencies which do not make the political agents. To be political agents, as Agamben notes, is to have the ontological position. This position still remains problematic in relation to the black subject, since such a subject cannot assume any ontological position, due to the absence of ontology itself.

Agamben's notion of the ontological position only applies to political agents. Agamben did not anticipate the problematic conceptual fidelity of the black subject's refusal to be within the realm of the human that is outside it. The ontological density of the black subject is not that which symbolizes social life in the universal code of the things human. The life of the black subject, with its lack and deficiency of ontological density, is lived in outer space (Sexton 2010). From where the black subject is structurally positioned there are no power relations, since there is no power to blackness at the level of ontology.

To be in the scheme of power relations, the black subject should be located in the social life, and not social death. The configuration of social death is indeed the world in the conception of antiblackness. The operation of power in the antiblack world is intimately linked with the lack of body and the work of power to render life (not social life, but death in life). The antiblack world is informed by violence against that which is not in the realm of the human. According to Sexton, antiblackness creates the state of invisibility at the ontological level. As such, the life of the black subject in the antiblack world is a condition of statelessness that denies every ontological possibility.

> The human need to be liberated *in* the world is not the same as the black need to be liberated *from* the world; which is why even their most radical cognitive maps draw borders between the living and the dead.
>
> (Wilderson 2011, 33)

As Moten (2008) counsels, to account for blackness is to understand it at the exterior of the ontological – a thing. What is deliberate in this structural makeup is to make sure that docility, pacifism, and pathology assume the vulgarity of blackness. The life of the black subject is one of incoherence and, as such, there cannot be any coherence to the life which is dehumanized. As Wilderson argues, the life of the black subject is captured in the structural irrationality that reduces the black body as a site through which life can be extracted. It is the extraction of life from the black subject that leaves it ontologically void, while on the other hand it gives life to the antiblack world. The antiblack world assumes the character of despotic irrationality where the life of the black subject is criminality. It is in this despotic irrationality where there are no treaties but violence, the very form that Marikana is.

The notion of bare life as articulated by Agamben is not analogous to the life of the black subject, but applies to the life of the human. When the black subject is introduced in the conceptual schema of bare life, difficulty arises by means of conceptual anxiety. That is to say, bare life cannot explain the black ontological position that is created and maintained by structural violence and the effect being that which creates a void ontology. The life of the black subject is caught in the antiblack matrix of violence which even makes the black subject have incommunicability to articulate its own suffering. The antiblack matrix of violence positions blackness not to the state of bare life, but the condition of social death. What Marikana represents is the reality of the antiblack world in which the life of the black subject is that of a thing. It is essential to account for the manner in which the black subject is unaccounted for, and having also being violated with impunity. The discourses of moral condemnation calling Marikana a horror serve the function of calling for change but not wanting change. They are just that, condemning and calling for change, while there is no change forthcoming in any direction, since the position of the black subject is fixated in the matrix of violence.

And yet, it is important to remember that Marikana is the everyday life of the black subject rather than an event. This means, Marikana as the lived experience of the black subject should be regarded as such, not as a national tragedy and horror. Of course, national tragedy and horror might at face value be regarded as essential tenants of Marikana, but it is only the black subject that is at the receiving end of systemic and perpetual violation. What is essential is the positionality of the black subject to emerge by articulating its own grammar of suffering. As the black subject is under the clutches of objectification, in no way can the black subject be at the level of the human. To be at the level of the human is the adaption of Agamben's notion of bare life, which, as it has been demonstrated, is alien to the lived experience that plagues Marikana's black life, which is social death. By contrast to bare life, which of course raises ontological questions, the scandal that confronts it is that of the black subject, which is ontologically void. Bare life is concern with the human and what is concerned with the black subject is not bare life but the formulation of ontological questions and insatiable demands that are yet to be conceded to. This is the horizon that takes the ontological position of the black subject seriously and the structures that position this subject. What happened in Marikana? This is an irrelevant question which crowds out the ontological questions relevant to black subjects' structural positionality. The ontological contrasting question is: What does it mean to live in the zone of non-being as a black subject and to be structurally positioned in the antiblack matrix of violence? This ontological question makes bare life to suffer from conceptual anxiety as far as the Marikana massacre is concerned.

Conclusion: On the Reconfiguration of the Subject

The configuration of the subject happens at a very interesting standpoint; that is, when there is no subject to reconstitute or retrieve from subjection. It means that there is no subject that can be rooted from subjection, precisely because it does not allow any form of the production of the subject. Then, what remains possible in the reconfiguration of the subject – blackness erupting from the *exteriori* of being – must be the total end of subjection. In the practices of freedom through the modes of reconfiguration of the subject, there is no fully constitutive subject when it comes to blackness, in that the figure of the subject is that which is in the making. So, the conception of reconfiguration should be understood as the Fanonian leap and the infusion of political imagination to create another world, which will be inaugurated only if the antiblack world comes to an absolute end. There is no transition, breakthrough, or democratization; there is a total end and a new beginning – *tabula rasa*. What that world will look like is not known, yet it will be deceptive to speculate and also limiting to indulge in teleological thinking.

The contact of blackness and subjection accounts for the different trajectory for the human question, where being human *qua* subject is a given for whiteness and not a given for blackness, due to the racist infrastructure of the antiblack world, which writes off the latter from the grammar of being. If blackness has been rendered to the domain of nothingness, it would mean that there is no subject. The reconfiguration of the subject, as the political project, means that the subject is that which is yet to come, in what Ndlovu-Gatsheni (2013) identifies as the murky present and the mysterious future, where the practices of freedom are not subject formation, but that of the reconfiguration of the subject precisely because blackness actualizes its ontologico-existential demands, while it is still being militated against. The reconfiguration of the subject is not teleological, it is the domain of uncertainty, since liberation is being fought for and taken from the oppressors, who have instilled in themselves the absolute subject, the one who is a given and in no need of any justification. Literally, to claim the signification of blackness as subject, is to refer to that which is not a subject in the full sense of the word. The main reason, as it has been shown, is that blackness is constituted of lacks and deficits designed to legitimate the ontologico-existential violence that shapes the antiblack world. In the antiblack world, blackness is not the category of the human and it therefore means that the conception of the subject *qua* blackness poses a number of challenges. It is framed in the form of a question: Can there be a subject without existence? This question is pertinent in the light of the fact that accounting for life that is denied to be lived demands the meta-ethical intervention in which the question of the human should be posed by those who are in the condition of blackness. There is no life, as blackness is eclipsed by being relegated to the zone of non-being.

The reconfiguration of the subject means that blackness must emerge through the politics of resurrection. This, by implication, is the significance of that which has been the positionality of the unthought, articulating the grammar of being and claiming a form of subjectivity of the political as the figure of being. The political is the figure which cannot be separated from life. Since this is a given, this raises a paradox to those who live in the black condition. It clearly shows that the question of life *qua* blackness presents a scandal, since this is the domain where life is not a given. For there to be a political, there must be a subject and this subject should be in the possession of life. The antiblack world produces itself into small fractures, which are then important to micro-politicize its functions. The manner in which the antiblack world holds its modes of subjection is seen in the nature of the racist state. It is the latter that comes into contact with its citizens and, if they are blacks, they are not citizens or subjects, they are blacks. To be black is to be rendered captive by the colonial state through its modes of interpellation and, as Althusser (1971) argues, it is to be subjected to its ideological state apparatus. What Althusser lays bare is the manner in which subjection, through the institutions that fulfils the functions of the state and sociality, finds its modes of expression in creating the possibilities of repression which might lead to dehumanization.

According to this Althusserian framework, the state is conceived as the repressive state apparatus and its existence has no meaning except as a function as the machinery of subjection. At this micro-political level, the center of the state, the latter in the service of the antiblack world, what comes out clearly is that which remains in rigidity and if there is change, it is cosmetic. In other words, the state apparatus continues to function as the executor of violence and, in this instance, the violence is directed at black bodies. This form of subjection is inscripted and legitimated by law (the instrument of the state) in order to relegate black bodies outside legality. Blackness is structured and positioned in relation to violence and, if subjection requires the repressive state apparatus (Althusser 1971), its agents of repression are not the end in themselves; they are the means that are in service of the larger structure within the antiblack world. At the macro-political level, this is where the power lies and the structure of antagonisms is located.

The articulation of insatiable demands of blackness is not limited to the anarchist ploy of ending the state. The state is at the micro-political level and not the macro-political frame, the latter is the antiblack world. The end of the state will not end subjection, since this is located in the infrastructure of the antiblack world. There will still be forces of reproduction that will maintain subjection and its proliferation. The end of the state will not end the antiblack world, and what is being argued for is the end of the antiblack world. The racist state interpellates the subject and, when it comes to blackness, which is not the subject, the racist state exercises subjection. Blackness is caught in the Manichean structure where subjection is exonerated and, yet, it is in this structure that antiblack racism expresses itself through whiteness. For whiteness to be what it is, it has to escalate its human status by dehumanizing blackness. The inscription of the subject is the sole domain of whiteness, where the latter is the chronicler and definer of what is human and non-human, superior and inferior, good and evil and so on *ad infinitum*. The asymmetrical relations that whiteness creates, to feed off itself, depend on dispossession of blackness. This ontologico-existential scandal is significant in order to understand the dehumanization that takes place through the erasure of blackness. The inscription of the subject is authorized by the whiteness *qua* the capacity of the master signifier and the subject can never be anything black, but whiteness if white. Hudson (2013, 264) writes: "The whiteness of white, where 'whiteness' = 'brimming with identity of self-possession and sovereignty' depends on blackness of black, where 'blackness' = 'without identity and self-control'." Having nothing to hold onto, blackness is the absent signifier and referent when it comes to the subject. The constitution of the subject position, to stretch Hudson's theory, is to present whiteness and the absence of blackness as the colonial relation that informs the presence of the subject through the absence of that which it reduces to de-subjectification. Thus, the question of the subject points to the intransigence of whiteness, of white as the totalization of all life forms – whiteness as the master signifier, the subject proper in the world without others, but their presence being meaningful at the non-human status, to enable whiteness to have something to compare itself with through asymmetrical relations.

The subject cannot exist without sociality (being-in-the-world) and for blackness, where there is no relationality with the world and the totality of being, the question of the subject is yet *to be*. It is the reconfiguration that attests to the fact that there is something in the making and the eventuality of its articulation means that existence, as such, has yet to come into being. The existence of blackness, as it is in the present, is the creation of whiteness, the hellish existence (Gordon 2000a). Blackness thus possesses an identity and, being twofold, this identity is, on the one hand, constructed through subjection and, on the other hand, constructed through subjectivity. The former is the one that is created by the whiteness in the capacity of the master as the oppressor who holds blackness tightly to its grip. The latter, is by blackness itself as the oppressed and who, through the insurgent politics of resistance, engages in the struggle to create its own being. What comes out clearly then is the fact that the reconfiguration of the subject is only possible through the politics of antagonism.

To be a subject in the world that is structured by violence and one that is antiblack is to be at the receiving end of violence, and only in relation to violence that comes at the level of aggression, or if it does not, it is the violence that will not be accounted for in its aftermath. The subject is fully constituted in the domain of the human and not structured ontologically like blackness. What emerges here is that there is an ontological distinction between the subject and blackness. The former is in the domain of the human, while the latter is in the domain of the non-human. The inscription of the subject, say in the politics of resistance, cannot be reduced to that which is similar to blackness. This cannot be the common struggle against subjection, more so in the world that is structured by antiblackness. The inscription of the subject, at the level of subjectivity, suggests the discursive practices outside blackness and, even if they concerned critique, such is, in fact, limited to the extent of relationality. The critique will point out, at the level of the inscription of the subject, how relationality needs to be installed to eliminate conflict. The inscription of the subject is a mere corrective to the world and not its unmaking. On the latter, what is needed is what Wilderson (2010) identified as the absence of relationality through the homology of absence that is, there is no world but the antiblack world.

The subject exists in the world and not in the antiblack world in which blackness is structured. The subject does not have anything to do with the lived experience of being black and the politics of the subject do not have anything to do with the unmaking of the world. They are based on elaborating the very same world and the focus on the gratuity of violence does not have to deal with the political ontology as such. Rather, the event, the episode, incident, temporality, etcetera, is the target. There is nothing that haunts, as everything just passes through. The inscription of the subject deals with that which can be resolved and the politics of relationality suggest that there is consensus to be reached in the quarrel between relationality (for only humans relate in the making of the world) for there to be peace and stability. If the struggle of the subject and that of blackness bears no relationality, it only attests to the fact that what exists is irreconcilability itself. It is irreconcilable to the extent that the demands of the subject are those which are structured by death, the very thing that plagues blackness. The inscription of the subject is not the demand to life; the right to life is already guaranteed and this is the right that must be protected at all times. If the right to live is a given to the subject, to blackness, it is nothing but the state of unattainability. The subject is the embodiment of rights, which means existence is a given, where belonging to the world is fundamental. The world should have the political architecture, through the erection of institutions to ensure that relationality gives the world the sense of relationality. Indeed, this civility is necessary for keeping the coherence of the world and even if there might be conflict, which might disturb this coherence, there are ways to remedy this and to reinstall civility at all times. Put another way, irrespective of the conflict among subjects, there are always political interventions to make sure that among humans, as subjects, civility should precede everything.

The making of the world, its relationality in the domain of civility, has always meant the justification of the elimination of blackness. The subject's subjectivity can continue without interruption, without citing blackness. Blackness cannot be seen as that which is necessary to interrogating the making of civility. The civil, as the necessary inscription of the subject, exists without having to be concerned about blackness. Blackness, as the "homology of absence" as Wilderson (2010) states, is that which cannot be accounted for in the sense that, for the subject to exist, in its inscription, it continually sidesteps the issue of antiblack racism, which creates the condition where there is no blackness, even if blackness cannot be avoided. The sidestepping of antiblack racism in the politics of civility cannot be seen an issue and the call for justice or the stance against injustice is made with no blacks in mind. Blackness is absent and exists in the abyss of non-existence – the zone of non-being. To be the figure of no concern essentially means that civility and the politics of non-relationality make it clear that there is a subject, and there is blackness, as distinct ontological categories. The two ontologies are opposed to the point of irreconcilability.

If there is a black subject, it is the one who is yet to be a subject proper; that is, the one who is going to live life outside the clutches of subject, the full human, who is not in the condition of lack, and the one who has the relational capacity. If, then, this is the possibility, the one in which there is a world of the human, then it is possible to talk of the subject. For Hudson (2006, 302), it is "[a] subject lacking full identity, but with enough identity to perform an act of articulation that results in its own transformation." To become the subject in relation to blackness will only be realizable if blackness sees itself and when it is in itself. Fanon (1970) is concerned about blackness being the creation of whiteness and this is the abyss from which blackness must extricate itself. For, in the antiblack condition, it is in the grip of whiteness, as Hudson says, where blackness is relegated to a collapse and a plethora of lacks and deficits.

The subjectivity of the subject (whiteness of white) is consciously defined against blackness. And, this takes the form of what Hudson refers to as the "colonial unconscious," which carries with it the racist fantasies and phobias about blackness that are often hidden, but not hidden in terms of their expressive modes. These expressions can at times appear not to be racist, while they actually are racist. These expressions are referred to by Fanon as nothing but "a paternalistic curiosity," where whiteness wants to be seen as not racist by blackness. They do not have to announce themselves as racist. In fact, in the politically correct discourse, where race is a misnomer, nobody will claim to be a racist and even people who supported racism in the past and still believe in it will not want to appear as racist. So, then, the existence of antiblack racism will be denied, even if it undercuts human relations, as there is no way there can be the antiblack world without antiblack racism. It is this colonial unconscious that renders blackness as non-existent at the ontologico-existential level and, as Hudson rightfully notes, the lived experience of blackness is not recognized by the colonial unconscious which operates under the guise of liberal democracy. Fanon writes (1970, 157): "There are laws that, little by little, are invalidated under the Constitution. There are other laws that forbid certain forms of discrimination. And we can be sure that nothing is going to be given free."

The reconfiguration of the subject will not come under liberal democracy in the case of blackness, which must become human in its own terms. Liberal democracy is maintaining the status quo and, through its accommodationist and integrationist agenda, masks the devastating impact of the antiblack world, which remains unquestioned, whether symbolically, relationally, or structurally. If there is antiblackness, it will go in the hidden realm, but that would not mean that the operating psychic economy, which has devastating ontologico-existential expression, will continue to plague blackness into dehumanization. Liberal democracy has no capacity to remedy black suffering, because it is not the ethico-political intervention of blackness. Liberal democracy is the ethical relation of whiteness of white, the exclusion of blackness par excellence. Also, liberal democracy has nothing to do with race as its register and it cannot be expected to commit to change the antiblack world. It cannot be expected to change this task, since the task is that of blackness and, as Fanon (1970) said, everything depends on it. The moral weight of liberal democracy, and it being the panacea to black suffering, is an oxymoron. The only reach of liberal democracy is whiteness as being in the world, the humanity that should be afforded rights, human rights, which do not apply to those who are not humans.

Since liberal democracy privileges the individual, the subject of whiteness of white and its prescriptions, do not have to do with the politics that are committed to the inner workings of life to produce the subject. In this terrain, the subject is a given and there is no basis to commit to an effort as such, except to safeguard the desires and the aspirations of such a subject. That is why liberty, equality, and justice are paramount to the subject – the whiteness of white, as Hudson says, which does not include the safeguarding of blackness, according to Fanon. "From time to time he has fought for Liberty and Justice, but these were always white liberty and white justice; that is, values scared by his masters" (Fanon 1970, 157). If blackness throws itself into this schema, it then dissolves in the myth of liberal democracy.

Shifting the Geography of Reason

The Black Register tries to show the precariousness of thinking in the ontological existential condition that does not permit thought. But nevertheless, as those who are affected by antiblack racism, having no duty to ask for permission to speak of the suffering, they do speak in their own name and through the politics of antagonism. This is the mode of critique and unmasking the ways in which subjection invisibilizes itself, as if its subjection is the naturalistic fate that befalls the black flesh. The very subjection that materializes itself through black suffering and its ultimate goal of dehumanization cannot be avoided when there is a resilient and impatient call that the antiblack world must come to an end, and this call is more pronounced through and through, as there is no way to tame black insurgency and its insatiable demands.

As Weheliye (2014) rightfully argues, suffering voices should not be confused with authenticity, but rather, be seen as an installation that proffers new vistas of political imagination that have everything to do with a new, different kind of politics and mode of life. Politics are the terms of engagement for blackness and this is the will to live. Blackness cannot be dictated to any more in its modes of doing politics – the politics of antagonism to be exact – since what is at stake is black life itself. What then needs to be a register is not that black lives matter, they have mattered anyway, but that the racist infrastructure of the antiblack world has led to the notion that black lives do not matter. It then means the declarative statement of "black lives matter," is not for blackness to herald its plight with the expectation that there will be a treatise as a result of this declarative statement. Black lives matter to such an extent that it is always necessary to heighten the politics of antagonism, since the antiblack world, which renders black lives impotent, still remains.

The antiblack world has not seen itself as responsible for the ontologico-existential hellish conditions of blackness, since it apportions blame to blacks themselves, for refusing to imitate their oppressors. The antiblack world exteriorizes blackness and it is on this basis that black lives do not matter. If this is the case, then blacks matter on their own and for their own, as it is their lives that are at stake and being made not to matter by the antiblack world. Black lives matter in so far as they are black on their own and not in the image that is given to them by the antiblack world, and they must assert themselves through the politics of antagonism. The limit ends there; they do not and cannot expect their lives to matter in the world that does not recognize their humanity. Blackness is structured in the ontologico-existential condition that is fundamentally and unapologetically antiblack, which in its ultimate motif renders blackness not only inferior, but non-existent. That which is non-existent does not matter. And, what more, if blackness continues to face the excess of violence and wanton death?

The redemptive register cannot be expected not to be in bad faith, precisely because it is articulated by the antiblack world, which continues to dehumanize blackness with impunity. This register is often instituted in hegemonic ways to create the impression of the world as embodying "one humanity," "peace," and "the ethics of caring." This is just a liberal façade, which has nothing to do with the ontologico-existential plight of blackness. What should be stated frankly is the fact that there is no redemption and the only alternative is the reconfiguration of the black subject in its own terms. The antiblack world cannot change itself to suit the demands of blackness, the category which does not matter, and for that which does not exist. It is necessary to shift the geography of reason and this is the task of those who have had their humanity questioned. Life worlds have shuttered to such an extent that there is no recognition of the human and yet institutionalizing, naturalizing, and normalizing dehumanization that does not have any moral responsibility to account for its deeds. For, if the necessity is to transform the world and to end its antiblackness, there is nowhere to look except to the self-generated political action of blackness. All in all, liberal democracy and its legal framework of human rights have no register to account for black suffering. "Suffering, where caused by political violence, has long functioned as the hallmark of both humane sentience and of inhuman brutality" (Weheliye 2014, 75). It is no wonder Wilderson's question, "What does it mean to suffer?" is still a fundamental one, as blackness still has no grammar to articulate its suffering, as this suffering as a phenomenon without analogue (Wilderson 2010).

The shift of the geography of reason is the fracturing of reason as it is. The political disruption is inevitable in that the shift of the geography of reason and the insistence upon another form of thought that does not allow itself to be controlled by the Euro–North-American-centric thought, shows that there is a necessity for blackness to think for itself and on its own terms. It is on this basis that the reconfiguration of the subject will allow possible avenues, to imagine other life worlds outside the infrastructure of antiblackness. This does not suggest any form of escapism, but the necessary antagonism with the hegemony of the dehumanizing practices that masquerades as thought, whereas it is subjection.

To try to describe and name the category of being is what the shift of the geography of reason is. It is to give birth to language and then to capacitate the modes of subjectivity, where the subject will be the political. To have the subject, without necessarily having the political means, means that there is no being in its absolute sense. This is the articulation of life, in that those who are written outside the modes of being are articulating the modes of being for the purpose of becoming subjects. Since blackness is not considered human, it does not allow itself to be scripted by the white gaze and its modes of dehumanization; blackness claims its being through reflective consciousness, which does not border on the triumphalist illusion of being a fully constituted subject. In its modes *to be*, blackness assumes the position of the unthought in order to facilitate the necessary condition to shift the geography of reason. The suspension of the triumphalist spirit means taking seriously the fact that the struggle is still continuing and at no stage should there be a claim that there is victory because of the cosmetic changes that are made by the antiblack world. If change is cosmetic and not fundamental, there will be no value, simply because the existential conditions that clutch blackness into subjection will remain as they are.

Amini (2010) is in opposition to the conception of the shifting of the geography of reason. For Amini, what this perpetuates is the essentialist stance that propagates ideologies and closed epistemic systems, and refers to this form of philosophy as regional philosophy. For Amini to insist that the call for the geography of reason arrests those who call for it in the borders of regionalism seems to be a claim that there are universal epistemic systems. According to Amini (2010, 32–33), "reason is subjected to regional variations." It is clear that Amini takes for granted the fact that there is no universal reason that claims to transcend regions. There are different worlds, so surely there must be different reasons – thus, the geography of reason is a necessary shift. Two questions posed by Amini (2010, 33) are of interest: "Can reason have different geographies?" and "Can the geography of reason be shifted?" To answer in the affirmative and with certainty, it would obviously be a "yes" to these questions. The possibility of this shift lies with those who are advocating for it, without any legitimation to those who see the call for the geography of reason as something to be dismissed *ad hominem*. This shift is happening at the level of what Mignolo (2007) calls "epistemic disobedience" and, where there is radical questioning of the formulated, fixed, canonical, and definitive of Euro–North-American-centric absoluteness of reason. If the geography of reason shifts, it is the black register that makes it do so. This is because the plight of blackness and that of subjects is not structurally the same, just as the ontologico-existential struggles are not the same. Amini's intervention seems to suggest that there is no geography of reason or, if there is, this is just the allegory of reason.

There should be value in the ontologico-existential struggle of blackness, and this value is linked to the elimination of dispossession, which is embedded in the triad of land, labor, and being (Mngxitama 2009). This triad of dispossession can no longer be tolerated in a situation where the political will of blackness requires that blacks themselves clearly see blackness as an attribute that holds value. It means that an effort will be made to heighten value, a recognition that life is so important that it should be fought for. In other words, blackness, as the reconfiguration of the subject, looks at the invention of nothingness. The value out of nothingness does not mean that what is nothing remains as such; in the reconfiguration of the subject, it means the radical overturning of what defines blackness as nothingness. It is then that blackness installs the political project of becoming – that is, *to be* – as the rallying call for blackness by critiquing all forms of dehumanization and bringing them to an end through revolution. The latter cannot be avoided in the circumstances that deny any form of human possibility from blackness. The ontologico-existential rupture of blackness cannot be evaded, as the world should come to an end as it is.

One of the things to be considered in the ontologico-existential struggle of blackness is that a form of defeat that continues to endure contaminates the future and also makes the spectre of the past continue to haunt the present, and yet eclipses any form of political imagination. It is the weight that continues to crush political imagination, and which in all forms tries to tame the strength that lies in the politics of resistance that are inherent in blackness. Blackness has, as the category of being that is and continues to be, dehumanized the signifier of resistance that is militated against. This does not mean that there have never been truces or victories, but it points, rather, to the importance of the struggle against the crushing weight of the antiblack world. Blackness is in confrontation with the injustice that masquerades as justice, inequality that masquerades as equality, and bondage that masquerades as freedom. This is how the antiblack world has reformulated itself in the contemporary era.

Since injustices still exist, the working of remembrance rather than forgetting is what informs resistance and the will to live. As blackness continues to resist, due to remembrance, and to assert the politics of life, in the face of dehumanization, this means assuming that the black register is the potency of subjectivity writ large. Injustices are still directed at black bodies and there has never been an epochal breaking point or a notation of its demise in history, since this happens at the exteriority of blackness. What blackness still remembers is that which is still continuing and, whatever changes that have taken place and continues to take place, cannot be expected to wipe out the history and the present of subjection with its cosmetic changes. The past is the present and the reconfiguration of the subject is not the obsession with the future; rather, it is the making of the present to be the future. If the present is still in the making, then the future is far from sight. Also, the making of the future does not mean that the future will yield better conditions. It is the mysterious, the unknown, and that which is fraught with uncertainty.

Remembrance, argues Hartman (2002), is entangled with the past. In other words, there is nothing wrong about remembering the past. That is to say, the past is the present and, not only that, subjection in the present still signifies the inner working of the past, which is to bastardize blackness and relegate it to the abyss of dehumanization. Subjection still attests to the fact that nothing ceased to happen, it is continuity as usual. What continues to happen is a repeat of what happened in the past and there is no way that there will not be any remembrance.

What then the reconfiguration of the subject is met with is denial. The antiblack world absolves itself and, in this instance of bad faith, nothing happened to blackness. Therefore, there is no past to turn to and the most important thing is to work for the future. This operates through erasure, distortion, denial, and evasion, which are all the politics of forgetting. It means, in fact, that blackness is denied its own pain and denied the opportunity to remember its own being. The continued injury to blackness has never been healed and the pain is still inflicted. The continued assault on black existence means that the past still haunts the present, the dead, the living, and those who are continuing to die "are coeval with the dead" (Hartman 2002, 759). It is this standpoint that refuses to engage in the triumphalist mode of assertion that is quick to claim the humanization of blackness, without having to think about the end of dehumanization. Hartman raises a concern about when the history of defeat assumes the hegemonic narrative of progress and the mantra of overcoming. What then would be avoided is how to put an end to black suffering at the symbolic, structural, and relational level. Hartman calls this the "rush of declarations," where no diagnostic work has actually been done concerning what keeps dehumanization of blackness intact. Like Hartman, Weheliye warns against "exalted celebrations," as if the struggle is over. What Weheliye emphasizes is how to understand subjection in its different forms of disfiguration, layers, masks, technologies, and other complexes. To claim triumph over black suffering, while the infrastructure of antiblackness still remains, is problematic in the sense that it is escapism, which might lead to fatalism, nihilism, and depoliticization, instead of to the politics of antagonism. This is what frustrates the possibility of blackness confronting dehumanization on its own terms, to ultimately end it.

What explains blackness, in relation to the question of the subject, is dehumanization. If blackness is the creation of whiteness, as Fanon says, then blackness is considered not to be human. This means that this is not creation, but destruction, which is fixed in the infrastructure of terror. This creation is, in fact, dehumanization. It is the creation of destruction. What then confronts blackness is its mode of reconfiguration as the subject and having to engage in the structure of antagonism in order to confront dehumanization. The radical installation of the human is a distinct assemblage of what it means to the human, since this is the human that is defined outside the antiblack world. This, of course, is not the construction of the liberal personhood. That is why the reconfiguration of the subject does not mean the transcendental move of overcoming or where the past will be forgotten and be put into the realm of that which happened and which is no longer relevant to the present. The past, which is marked by violations of the black body, is still happening even in the present. In no way can the reconfiguration of the subject not take seriously the fact that it is confronted with the sanitization of black suffering. What this should confront is the triumphalist narrative that claims that blackness has transcended, and it must now fashion its present for a better future. It is as if there has been no violence that happened in the past and it will, therefore, not continue into the present.

> At best, the backdrop to this defeat makes visible the diffuse violence and the everyday routines of domination, which continue to characterize black life but are obscured by the everydayness. The normative character of terror ensures its invisibility; it defies detection behind rational categories like *crime*, *poverty*, and *pathology*. In other words, the necessity to underscore the centrality of the event, defined here in terms of captivity, deportation, and social death, is a symptom of the difficulty of representing "terror as usual." The oscillation between then and now distils the past four hundred years into one definitive moment. And, at the same time, the still-unfolding narrative of captivity and dispossession exceeds the discreet parameters of the event. In itemizing the long list of violations, are we any closer to freedom, or do such litanies only confirm what is feared – history is an injury that has yet to cease happening?
>
>   (Hartman 2002, 772 [emphasis original])

What Hartman shows is the concerted effort to reconstruct the present in bad faith, in order to erase the history of violence that continues to manifest itself in the present. The reconfiguration of the subject does not mean transcendence, but it is acknowledgment of blackness coming to itself. The political is inseparable from the black self. Politics is the category of the ontological, insists Hudson (2006), the emergence of the subject – *to be*, cannot happen outside the political. "The concept of the subject is political while that of the subject-position belongs to the social – the misrecognition product of the political" (Hudson 2006, 304). The constitutiveness of blackness and politics means that the politics of life are paramount. This is the life which is being violated and, in order to assert itself, it then engages in the structure of antagonisms. Since the life of blackness is continually militated against, it then means that blackness is not allowed to emerge as the political. In short, there should not be any form of any politics in so far as blackness is concerned. Politics should exist for blackness in so far as blackness is clutched by subjection. In essence, blackness should disappear from politics as a form of human and structural relation. That is, blackness should stay outside politics and, also, outside the realm of being. The inseparability of the political and the subject attest to the fact that human life should be preserved. This is the ethical challenge that subjection cannot stand for. Sexton makes an acute observation that the antiblack world is always set violently against black bodies and, not only that, taking Fanon's cue, he argues that the actual being of blackness is violated against. In capturing the phobic nature of the antiblack world, Sexton (2015, 162) damningly declares: "The hatred of the world is upon you. It is also with you."

It happens in so far as that there should not be any insurrection from blackness – the phobic object and the stimulus of anxiety – blackness should not, according to the logic of subjection, be left to its own devices, since blackness is dangerous outside white guardianship and oppression. The reconfiguration of the subject dislodges itself from the grip of whiteness to be on its own. Blackness, on its own, does not pursue the struggle for liberation in the distorted image that is given and structurally imposed by whiteness. There is nothing Real in so far as the reconfiguration of the subject is concerned, in having to believe in what subjection presents, as such. If there is the Real, it will be overturned, as what informs the struggle *to be*, is the very becoming of blackness. The image that is given to blackness is what Gordon calls "pure exteriority" – beings seen outside the realm of the human, a thing – blackness as "perverse anonymity," "nameless," "the black of black." It is the body of the subject that is not. According to this distorted image, blacks cannot be subjects. What can be done to resolve this, at least, is for blackness to engage in imitation, to want to be white. So, to imitate permits blackness to escape the hellish life and seek refuge in whiteness, and to be accepted in whiteness, or to be white, is a fallacy. Thus, the definitive standard of blackness should be extended to blackness, again another fallacy, the impossibility that will still remain. Imitation is failure and, thus Gordon reflects:

> As imitation, what is often lacked is the original advantage of the self as standard. The imitation, in other words, is not its own standard. It is a failure, as we have seen, even of its achievement. To achieve imitation is to fail at what an imitation imitates, namely, an original.
> (Gordon 2015, 138)

The reconfiguration of the subject, if it is imitation, is not the becoming of blackness, but blackness remaining stagnantly as a distorted image of whiteness. For, blackness is not its own standard, but that of whiteness. In short, blackness is not blackness itself, but the mimicry of whiteness. Contrary to this pitfall, what the recon-figuration of the subject deploys, is the centrality of blackness as its own definer and not an imitation. In the end, what can be regarded as the supposed utopian ideal, is that there should ultimately be a subject, but not on the basis of imitation. This means, the desire is not to be white, but the desire is to be liberated and the actualization of that desire comes into being by authorizing blackness as the sole determinant of its own struggle. That is why the desire is not to have liberty, equality, or justice. Fanon (1970, 156) warned, on mimicry, that blackness will go "from one way of life to another, but not from one life to another." If this is to be understood on the basis of change, it is not change, but cosmetic change.

Blackness rises in its own name, in order *to be*, the subject emerges from the ruins of existence in its own register and grammar of suffering (Wilderson 2010). It is clear, from Gordon's emphasis, that imitation is a dead-end, a failure of failure. It is a figment of the imagination, in that the reconfiguration of the subject will never happen, it is destined to fail. If blackness insists on imitation, it will be a failure, even in the modes of articulation, because it will not speak in its own grammar, but in that of whiteness. In this instance, Gordon (2015, 138) correctly states: "To speak, the black appears as an echo of white speech." Blackness is not its own, and there is no way that there will be the reconfiguration of the subject if blackness is the figure that is exterior to the world. The shift of the geography of reason is necessary, as reason must face itself in contestation with black reason. What the latter stands against, in its quest for liberation, is to decolonize reason. The solipsism of knowledge and having the epistemic rupture of knowledges and the possibility of many worlds (Mignolo 2011) is a necessary decolonial intervention. The installation of black reason does not mean its dominance, but its co-existence with many other forms of reason.

The Black Register shows "a radical will and testament," Sexton (2015, 162) argues, it is the assertion of life and the human that is to come and is, as has been emphasized, the reconfiguration of the subject, *to be* – that which is yet to come only once the precondition that the antiblack world ceases to be in place. This rupture is necessary to create many worlds, where there is no dehumanization. The assertion of life of blackness is made in the structure of and in relation to gratuitous violence, argues Sexton, which then demands the understanding of the forms of violence which are epistemological, ontological, aesthetic, affective, and so on. It is from these sites of inquiry that violence should be unmasked. What then emerges, as well, is that the form of violence that afflicts blackness should not be understood in terms of events or episodes, but *longue durée*, in order to understand the ontologico-existential condition of blackness.

It is important to restate some positions. In the first instance, the violence that is inflicted upon the black body still continues without limit, rendering blackness to be in the state of nothingness. To theorize and to reason from this lived experience, is to make meaning through a critique and expanding the boundaries of the discourse, if not, then maybe to obliterate them. This comes into being as it is necessary for blackness to be its own register, that centers on itself, with its own modes of authorization and critique, without it being acted upon. Secondly, the re-imagining of the political, renames the consciousness that has been reanimated and it being one that is not outside the black body, but its very embodiment. This reaffirms the importance of exercising thought while in the struggle for life. Last, but not least, is the creation of the new forms of subjectivity, where blackness attempts to articulate its register. The scandal still remains that blackness articulates the suffering that is incommunicable and there is no grammar of that suffering (Wilderson 2010). Indeed, the political project of blackness in relation to the configuration of the subject wallows in the realm of uncertainty, nobody knows what will happen.

Gordon and Gordon (2009, 108) ask the following question: "What can society do when the sign continuum of the end of the world is the death of its culture?" This is a challenging question, which still depends on the need to heighten political imagination and requires tenacity to pursue the cause of liberation. This will then mean, in light of the aforementioned question, that the end of culture is the beginning of another culture. This is what Gordon (2015) calls "assembling the self," the black subject coming into its own to create the new world where many worlds co-exist. There should be, in addition to the political imagination, political will where blackness is taking a concerted effort to pursue liberation at all costs, as there is nothing to lose. The manner by which blackness asserts itself through its reflective consciousness clearly shows that there should be other forms of life. This political will is the indomitable will to live and the assertion of life in so far as this can no longer be the life that is exterior to blackness. The will to live, which is the fierce rebellion against death, is akin to Fanonian meditation of "*Yes* to life."

The World, Its End

The beginning should be anticipated and for there to be a beginning, there must be an end. Beyond the realm of the symbolic and also that of the real, there lies the horizon of possibility of other worlds. Indeed, in the pluriversal formation of pluriversity, as Mignolo (2011) argues, as opposed to the universal, which is the one that is dominantly Euro–American-centric, there should be many worlds that should exist. That which the black wants cannot be given. The existence of blackness is militated upon to rid it from any form of being a subject. It then follows that the demands of blackness cannot be met or satisfied, for they are calling the order of things to come to a halt and that includes the world too. Not only are the demands of blackness insatiable, there is no rapport and relationality in the antiblack world as the form of life that is dispatched to blackness is that of wanton structural violence, which necessitates nothing but death. The absolute cancellation of human relations is not to separate human beings from one another, but to create an ontological distinction between those who are human and those who are non-human. The reconfiguration of the subject as the political is a form of life that is not outside the ethics of relations. The relation comes into being as the category of the human – humans must relate to each other to have their place in the world – that is, the world exists in so far as it is not that of dehumanization, the current world, which is informed by subjection, the world as it is today. The kinds of politics of that are clear in this text and indicate clearly what all the thinkers attest to, the fact that it is necessary to push back and to fracture the frontiers that install all forms of dehumanization informed by antiblack racism.

If there is a continuing critique of the antiblack world and its expression – antiblack racism – there is something that blackness wants and it is only they who can satisfy that demand in their own political will. The presence of the antiblack world foils the aspirations of blackness. Blackness wants to be free and that means, to answer Fanon's question, "What does the black want?" The given answer still remains: "The black wants *to be*." This means that the demand to be free is not enough, since there are many other ontological demands of blackness. The register of human rights and that of the Trinitarian treaty of liberty, equality, and justice is the register of the demands of the subject, which are easily satisfied, but cannot be extended to black bodies. In essence, these demands have nothing to do with what the black wants and the world, as it is, is not hospitable to blackness and this extent it demands. Essentially, no value is attached to blackness by the antiblack world, let alone the fact that blackness is nothingness in the antiblack world, that is, blackness has no ontological currency and no demands can be met outside the realm of relation – the antiblack world is the world without blackness. That is to say, blackness is present in the world as something that the antiblack world can use to validate its existence and for there to be a superiority–inferiority complex it means that blackness is the state of liquidation in its existence. That, too, proves the fact that the antiblackness needs blackness for it to be relevant. If blackness renders antiblackness irrelevant, by bringing it to an end, it means that there is nothing natural about the superiority–inferiority complex.

It is the life of blackness that is at stake and the responsibility is upon blackness to articulate its demands, insatiable as they are. It is blackness that is at the receiving end of subjection and its lived experience of being black in the antiblack world means that blackness must determine what it wants and how it wants it. It is clear from the aforementioned figures in this text that they are not demanding for themselves as individuals, all of them demand for the humanity that has been put into question to be its own enunciator. What then serves as a necessity is that the ontologico-existential struggle does not require any form of paternalism, guidance, permission, or even censure, from the supposed masters, who are mainly white and outside the lived experience of blackness. This is their own struggle of blackness, since it is black life that is at stake.

What the black wants cannot be given and the articulation of the question of liberation cannot be devised from the standpoint of the oppressor. If this then becomes the case, there is no liberation. The demands of blackness, being ontologico-existential, mean that they have everything to do with life itself, every aspect of the life world to come and a total elimination of the antiblack world, the death world. The death of blackness, as the death of that which is nothing, since it is the disposable other, means that life is not a given but that which is yet to come. Since life is what is at stake, then what the black wants is not to be white, it is *to be* – that is, alive. It is precisely this that sends the infrastructure of psychic phobia to the racist infrastructure where whiteness is at the commanding heights. The consolidation of antiblackness militates against all forms of life worlds that have to do with blackness and this means that the reconfiguration of the subject is not allowed. This then leads to a necessary dimension where blackness, as a stimulus of anxiety to the antiblack world, means that there should not be any form of liberation of blackness, since this will lead to the disruption of the world. So be it, for blackness has for far too long been dehumanized. The disposable nature of blackness is what makes the antiblack world sustainable and the ontologico-existential struggle is not to make the antiblack world unsustainable, but for it to be non-existent. No gesture can be expected from the antiblack world to end itself, it has to be ended by those it dehumanizes.

Since there is no life, but survival for those who are in the black condition, the will to live is what keeps the spirit of the politics of antagonism intact. What does the black want? From Wynter, Césaire, Biko, Shakur, Jackson, and More, the answer is the existential-ontological demand to be human. To be human means not wanting to be included in the decadent frame of humanity that perpetuates ontological exclusion. Blacks are excluded in the realm of humanity and their humanity is always put into question. This questioning is the liquidation of humanity in that blacks are structured to count for nothing and the exclusionary sphere in which they are put is maintained in such a way that they are made to count for nothing. To be at the exterior of being is not the ontological position that blacks choose for themselves and it is not something that they valorize. Instead, it is to point out clearly where blacks are in the world that does not want them, and with structures that are making everyday life to be the politics of exclusions, hence the exteriorization that blackness is made to be at. So, for blacks to come to humanity, they must make the world in their own image. This making of the world is not the craft that comes for making the world a better place. It is, in point of fact, the re-making of the world. For this to come to being as the necessary condition that can only be satisfied by the end of the antiblack world, it means *to be* is the reconfiguration of the subject. All blacks want is the reconfiguration of the subject so that there will be a rupture of many worlds and life worlds outside the clutches of subjection and its dehumanizing technologies. To be human and wanting *to be* human does not mean that they want to be acted upon – they show the necessity of acting upon themselves and, also, blackness acting upon itself.

References

Abdur-Rahman, Aliyyah. 2017. Black Grotesquerie. *American Literary Thinking*, 29 (4): 682–703.

Agamben, Giorgio. 2005. *State of Exception*. (Translated by Kevin Attell.) Chicago/London: Chicago University Press.

_____. 1998. *Homo Sacer: Sovereign Power and Bare Life*. (Translated by Daniel Heller-Roazen.) Stanford: Stanford University Press.

Agathangelou, Anna M. 2011. Bodies to the Slaughter: Global Racial Reconstructions, Fanon's Combat Breath, and Wrestling for Life. *Somatechnics*, 1 (1): 209–248.

_____. 2010. Bodies of Desire, Terror and War in Eurasia, Impolite Disruptions of (Neo)Liberal Internationalism, Neoconservative and the 'New' Imperialism. *Millennium*, 38 (3): 693–722.

Ahmed, Sara. 2006. The Nonperfomativity of Antiracism. *Meridians*, 7 (1): 104–126.

Alcoff, Linda M. 1998. What Should White People Do? *Hypatia*, 13 (3): 6–26.

_____. 1991. The Problem of Speaking for Others. *Cultural Critique*, 20: 5–32.

Althusser, Louis. 1971. *Lenin and Philosophy and Other Essays*. New York/London: Monthly Review Press.

Amini, Majid. 2010. Allegories of Reason: Eurocentrism and the Native Philosophical Resistance. *Culture, Theory and Critique*, 51 (1): 29–45.

Angelou, Maya. 1975. Rehearsal for a Funeral. *The Black Scholar*, 6(99): 3–7.

Anidjar, Gil. 2004. Terror Right. *CR: The New Centennial Review*, 4 (3): 35–69.

Appiah, Kwame Anthony. 1992. *In My Father's House: Africa in the Philosophy of Culture*. New York: Oxford University Press.

Badiou, Alain. 2005. *Metapolitics*. London/New York: Verso.

Barnard, Rita. 2008. Tsotsis: On Law, the Outlaw, and the Postcolonial State. *Contemporary Literature*, 49 (4): 541–572.

Barrett, Lindon. 1995. African-American Slave Narratives: Literacy, the Body, Authority. *American Literary History*, 2 (3): 415–442.

Bascomb, Lia T. 2014. Productively Destabilized: Black Studies and Fantastic Modes of Being. *Souls*, 16 (3–4): 148–165.

Best, Steven and Saidiya V. Hartman. 2005. Fugitive Justice. *Representations*, 92 (91): 1–15.

Biko, Steve. 2004. *I Write What I Like*. Johannesburg: Picardo.

_____. 1978. *I Write What I Like*. London: Penguin Books.

Birt, Robert. 1997. Existence, Identity, and Liberation. In Lewis R. Gordon (ed.). *Existence in Black: An Anthology of Black Existential Philosophy*. New York: Routledge, pp. 205–213.

Bogues, Anthony. 2012. And What about the Human? Freedom, Human Emancipation, and the Radical Imagination. *Boundary 2*, 39 (3): 29–46.

_____. 2010. *Empire of Liberty: Power, Desire, and Freedom*. Hanover: Dartmouth College Press.

_____. 2006. The Human, Knowledge and the Word: Reflecting on Sylvia Wynter. In Anthony Bogues (ed.). *After Man, Toward the Human: Critical Essays on Sylvia Wynter*. Kingston/Miami: Ian Randle Publishers. pp. 315–338.

Buck, Marilyn. 2000. Prison, Social Control, and Political Prisoners. *Social Justice*, 27 (3): 25–28.

Bukhari, Safiya. 2003. Coming of Age: A Black Revolutionary. *Social Justice*, 30 (2): 8–17.

Butler, Judith. 2004. *Precarious Life: The Powers of Mourning and Violence*. London and New York: Verso.

Camus, Albert. 1956. *The Rebel: An Essay on Man in Revolt*. New York: Vintage.

Carter, J. Kameron and Sarah J. Cervenak. 2016. Black Ether. *CR: The New Centennial Review*, 16 (2): 203–224.

Césaire, Aimé. 1972. *Discourse on Colonialism*. (Translated by Joan Pinkhan.) New York: Monthly Review Press.

_____. 1970. *Return to My Native Land*. (Translated by John Berger and Anna Bostock.) Ringwood: Penguin Books.

_____. [1956] 2010. Letter to Maurice Thorez. *Social Text*, 28 (2): 145–152.

Chandler, Nahum D. 2014. *X: The Problem of the Negro as the Problem for Thought*. New York: Fordham University Press.

_____. 1996. The Economy of Disedimentation: W.E.B. DuBois and the Discourses of the Negro. *Callaloo*, 19 (1): 78–93.

Chipkin, Ivor. 2002. The Sublime Object of Blackness. *Cahiers d'Etudes Africaines*, 176 XLII-3: 569–583.

Coetzee, John M. 2007. *Diary of a Bad Year*. London: Harvill Secker.

Coleman, Mat. 2003. The Naming of "Terrorism" and "Evil" Outlaws: Geopolitical Place-making After 11 September. *Geopolitics*, 8 (3): 87–104.

Comaroff, Jean and John Comaroff. 2004. Criminal Obsessions, After Foucault: Postcoloniality, Policing, and the Metaphysics of Disorder. *Critical Inquiry*, 30 (4): 800–824.

Conniff, Brian. 2005. The Prison Writer as Ideologue: George Jackson and the Attica Rebellion. In Miller, D. Quentin (ed.). *Prose and Cons: Essays on Prison Literature in the United States.* Jefferson/London: McFarrend and Company, pp. 147–173.

Corrigan, Lisa M. 2009. Sacrifice, Love, and Resistance: The Hip-Hop Legacy of Assata Shakur. *Women and Language*, 32 (2): 2–13.

Dabashi, Hamid. 2015. *Can Non-Europeans Think?* London: Zed Books.

Dayan, Joan. 2002. Legal Slaves and Civil Bodies. In Russ Castronovo and Dana Nelson (eds.). *Materializing Democracy: Toward a Revitalized Cultural Politics*. London/Durham: Duke University Press, pp. 53–94.

Delantry, Gerard. 1995. *Inventing Europe: Idea, Identity, Reality*. London: Macmillan Press.

Derrida, Jacques. 1995. *The Gift of Death*. (Translated by David Wills.) Chicago/London: The University of Chicago Press.

_____. [1995] 2002. For Mumial Abu-Jamal. In Jacques Derrida *Negotiations: Interventions and Interviews, 1971–2001*. (Edited and translated by Elizabeth Rottenberg.) Stanford: Stanford University Press, pp. 125–129.

Dhondy, Farrukh. 1971. No Without Outrage. *Economic and Political Weekly*, 6 (37): 1955.

Diagne, Souleymade B. 2011. *African Art as Philosophy: Senghor, Bergson and the Idea of Negritude* (Translated by Chike Jeffers.) London and New York: Seagull Books.

Dillon, Stephen. 2013. Fugitive Life: Race, Gender, and the Rise of the Neoliberal-Carceral State. Unpublished PhD Dissertation. Minneapolis: University of Minnesota.

_____. 2012. Possessed by Death: The Neoliberal-Carceral State, Black Feminism, and the Afterlife of Slavery. *Radical History Review*, 112 (Winter): 113–125.

Du Bois, William E.B. [1903] 1997. *The Souls of Black Folk*. Boston: Bedford Books.

Esmeir, Samera. 2006. On Making Dehumanization Possible. *PMLA*, 121 (5): 1544–1551.

Eudell, Demetrius and Carolyn Allen. 2001. Sylvia Wynter: A Transculturalist Rethinking Modernity. *Journal of Western Indies Literature*, 10 (1–2): 1–7.

Fanon, Frantz. [1961] 1990. *The Wretched of the Earth*. (Translated by Constance Farrington.) London: Penguin.

_____. 1970. *Black Skin, White Masks*. (Translated by Charles L. Markmann.) London: Paladin.

_____. 1967. *Toward the African Revolution: Political Essays*. (Translated by Haakon Chevalier.) New York/London: Monthly Review Press.

_____. [1952] 2008. *Black Skin, White Masks*. (Trans. by C.L. Markmann). London: Pluto Press.

Farley, Anthony P. 1997. The Black Body as Fetish Object. *Oregon Law Review*, 76: 457–535.

Farmer, Paul. 2004. An Anthropology of Structural Violence. *Current Anthropology*, 45 (3): 305–325.

_____. 2002. On Suffering and Structural Violence: A View from Below. In Joan Vincent (ed.). *The Anthropology of Politics: A Reader in Ethnography, Theory and Critique*. Malden (Mass): Blackwell, pp. 424–237.

Ferreira da Silva, Denise. 2015. Before Man: Sylvia Wynter's Rewriting of the Modern Episteme. In Katherine McKrittrick (ed.). *Sylvia Wynter: On Being Human as Praxis*. Durham/London: Duke University Press, pp. 90–105.

_____. 2014. No-bodies: Law, Raciality, and Violence. *Meritum*, 9 (1): 119–162.

Fisher, William W. III. 2002. Ideology and Imaginary of the Law in Slavery. In Paul Finkelman (ed.). *Slavery and the Law*.

Lanham/Boulder: Rowman and Littlefield International, pp. 43–85.

Foucault, Michel. 2003. *Society Must be Defended*. (Translated by David Macey.) London: Penguin.

_____. 1989. *The Order of Things*. London: Routledge.

_____. 1977. *Discipline and Punish: The Birth of the Prison*. New York: Vintage.

Gagne, Karen M. 2007. On the Obsolescence of the Disciplines: Frantz Fanon and Sylvia Wynter Propose a New Mode of Being Human. *Human Architecture*, 5 (Double issue): 251–264.

Garraway, Doris L. 2010. 'What is Mine': Césairean Negritude Between the Particular and the Universal. *Research in African Literatures*, 41 (1): 71–86.

Gilroy, Paul. 2005. *Postcolonial Melancholia*. New York: Columbia University Press.

Giroux, Susan. 2010. *Between Race and Reason: Violence, Intellectual Responsibility, and the University to Come*. Stanford: Stanford University Press.

Goldberg, David T. 2004. The End(s) of Race. *Postcolonial Studies*, 7 (2): 211–230.

Gordon, Jane A. and Lewis R. Gordon. 2009. *Of Divine Warning: Reading Disaster in the Modern Age*. Boulder/London: Paradigm Publishers.

Gordon, Lewis R. 2015. *What Fanon Said: The Introduction to His Life and Thought*. New York: Fordham University Press.

_____. 2013. Race, Theodicy, and Normative Emancipatory Challenges of Blackness. *The South Atlantic Quarterly*, 112 (4): 725–736.

_____. 2011. Shifting the Geography of Reason in an Age of Disciplinary Decadence. *Transmodernity*, 1 (2): 95–103.

_____. 2010. Theory in Black: Teleological Suspension in Philosophy of Culture. *Qui Parle*, 18 (2): 193–214.

_____. 2008. A Phenomenology of Biko's Black Consciousness. In Andile Mngxitama, Amanda Alexander and Nigel C. Gibson (eds). *Biko Lives: Contesting the Legacies of Steve Biko*. Basingstoke/New York: Palgrave Macmillan, pp. 83–93.

_____. 2007. Through the Hellish Zone of Nonbeing: Thinking Through Fanon, Disaster, and the Damned of the Earth. *Human Architecture* (Special Double Issue), 5–12.

_____. 2006. Is the Human a Teleological Suspension of Man? Phenomenological Exploration. In Anthony Bogues (ed.).

Caribbean Reasonings: After Man Towards the Human: Critical Essays on Sylvia Wynter. Kingston/Miami: Ian Randle Publishers, pp. 237–257.

_____. 2005. Through the Zone of Non-Being: A Reading of *Black Skin, White Masks* in Celebration of Fanon's Eightieth Birthday. *CLR James Journal*, 11 (1): 1–43.

_____. 2000a. *Existentia Africana: Understanding Africana Existential Thought*. London: Routledge.

_____. 2000b. On the Borders of Anonymity and Superfluous Invisibility. *Cultural Dynamics*, 12 (3): 373–383.

_____.1995. *Bad Faith and Antiblack Racism*. New Jersey: Humanities Press.

Gready, Paul. 1993. Autobiography and the 'Power of Writing': Political Prison Writing in the Apartheid Era. *Journal of Southern African Studies*, 19 (3): 489–532.

Gross, Ariela. 2002. Pandora's Box: Slave's Character on Trial in the Antebellum South. In Paul Finkelman (ed.). *Slavery and the Law*. Lanham/Boulder: Rowman and Littlefield International, pp. 43–85.

Hardt, Michael. 2011. The Militancy of Theory. *The South Atlantic Quarterly*, 110 (1): 19–35.

Harris, Leonard. 1982. *Philosophy Born of Struggle: Anthology of Afro-American Philosophy from 1917*. Dubuque: Kendall Hunt.

Hartman, Saidiya V. 2002. The Time of Slavery. *The South Atlantic Quarterly*, 101(4): 757–777.

_____. 1997. *Scenes of Subjection: Terror, Slavery, and Self-making in Nineteenth-Century America*. New York/Oxford: Oxford University Press.

Hartman, Saidiya V. and Frank B. Wilderson, III. 2003. The Position of the Unthought. *Qui Parle*, 13 (2): 183–201.

Heller, Agnes. 1992. Europe: An Epilogue. In Brian Nelson, David Roberts and Walter Veit (eds.). *The Idea of Europe: Problems of National and Transnational Identity*. New York/Oxford: Berg. pp. 12–25.

Henry, Paget. 2000. *Caliban's Reason: Introduction to Afro-Caribbean Philosophy*. New York/London: Routledge.

Hook, Derek. 2011. Retrieving Biko: A Black Consciousness Critique of Whiteness. *African Identities*, 9 (1): 19–32.

Hudson, Peter. 2013. The State and the Colonial Unconscious. *Social Dynamics*, 39 (2): 263–277.

_____. 2012. The State and the Colonial Unconscious. Public Affairs Research Institute Public Lecture Series.

_____. 2006. *The Concept of the Subject in Laclau*. Politikon, 33 (3): 299–312.

Irele, Abiola. 2011. *The Negritude Moment: Explorations in Francophone African and Caribbean Literature and Thought*. Trenton: Africa World Press.

_____.1992. In Praise of Alienation. In V.Y. Mudimbe (ed.). *The Surreptitious Speech: Présence Africaine and the Politics of Otherness, 1947–1987*. Chicago/London: The University of Chicago Press. pp. 201–224.

Jackson, George. 1970. *Soledad Brother: The Prison Letters of George Jackson*. London: Penguin Books.

Jones, Donna V. 2010. *The Racial Discourses of Life Philosophy: Négritude, Vitalism, and Modernity*. New York: Columbia University Press.

Kazanjian, David. 2014. 'To See the Issue of these his Exorbitant Practices': A response to 'The Dispossessed Eighteenth Century.' *The Eighteenth Century*, 55 (2–3): 273–282.

Koerner, Michelle. 2011. Line of Escape: Gilles Deleuze's Encounter with George Jackson. *Genre*, 44 (2): 157–180.

Lalu, Premesh. 2004. Incomplete Histories: Steve Biko, the Politics of Self-Writing and the Apparatus of Reading. *Current Writing*, 16 (1): 107–126.

Larson, Doran. 2010. Towards a Prison Poetics. *College Literature*, 37 (3): 143–166.

Leonardo, Zeus. 2004. The Color of Supremacy: Beyond the Discourse of "White Privilege." *Educational Philosophy and Theory*, 36 (2): 137–152.

MacDonald, Spreelin T. 2012. The Emergent Self in South African Black Consciousness Literary Discourse. In Nicholas Creary (ed.). *African Intellectuals and Decolonization*. Athens: Ohio University Press, pp. 69–82.

Maldonado-Torres, Nelson. 2017. On the Coloniality of Human Rights. *Revista Crítica de Ciências Sociais*, 114 (December): 117–136.

_____. 2014. Religion, Conquest, and Race in the Foundation of the Modern/Colonial World. *Journal of American Academy of Religion*, 82 (3): 636–665.

_____. 2008. *Against War: Views from the Underside of Modernity*. Durham/London: Duke University Press.

_____. 2007. On the Coloniality of Being: Contributions to the Development of the Concept. *Cultural Studies*, 21 (2/3): 240–270.

_____. 2006a. Césaire's Gift and the Decolonial Turn. *Radical Philosophy Review*, 9 (2): 111–138.

_____. 2006b. Notes on the Current Status of Liminal Categories and the Search for a New Humanism. In Anthony Bogues (ed.). *Caribbean Reasonings: After Man Towards the Human: Critical Essays on Sylvia Wynter*. Kingston/Miami: Ian Randle Publishers, pp. 190–208.

Manganyi, Chabani. 1973. *Being-Black-in-the-World*. Johannesburg: Sprocas/Ravan.

Marriott, David. 2012. Inventions of Existence: Sylvia Wynter. Frantz Fanon, Sociogeny, and "the Damned." *CR: The New Centennial Review*, 11 (3): 45–90.

_____. 2007. *Haunted Life: Visual Culture and Black Modernity*. New Brunswick/London: Rutgers University Press.

_____. 2000. *On Black Men*. Edinburgh: Edinburgh University Press.

Martinot, Steve. 2003. The Militarization of the Police. *Social Identities*, 9 (2): 205–224.

Martinot, Steve and Jared Sexton. 2003. The Avant-garde of White Supremacy. *Social Identities*, 9 (2): 169–181.

Matthews, Sally. 2012. White Anti-Racism in Post-apartheid South Africa. *Politikon*, 39 (2): 171–188.

Mbembe, Achille. 2007. Biko's Testament of Hope. In Chris van Wyk (ed.). *We Write What We Like: Celebrating Steve Biko*. Johannesburg: Wits University Press, pp. 135–148.

_____. 2002. African Modes of Self-Writing. *Public Culture*, 14 (1): 239–273.

_____. 2001. *On the Postcolony*. California: University of California Press.

Mignolo, Walter D. 2015. Sylvia Wynter: What does it Mean to be Human. In Katherine McKrittrick (ed.). *Sylvia Wynter: On Being Human as Praxis*. Durham/London: Duke University Press, pp. 106–123.

_____. 2011. *The Darker Side of Western Modernity: Global Futures, Decolonial Options*. Durham/London: Duke University Press.

_____. 2007. Introduction: Coloniality of Power and De-colonial Thinking. *Cultural Studies*, 21 (2–3): 155–167.

_____. 1999. Philosophy and the Colonial Difference. *Philosophy Today*, 43: 36–41.

Miller, D. Quentin. 2005. On the Outside Looking. In White

Readers of Non-white Prison Narrative. In Miller, D. Quentin (ed.). *Prose and Cons: Essays on Prison Literature in the United States*. Jefferson/London: McFarrand and Company, pp. 15–32.

Mills, Charles W. 1998. *Blackness Visible: Essays on Philosophy and Race*. Ithaca/London: Cornell University Press.

_____. 1997. *The Racial Contract*. Ithaca/London: Cornell University Press.

Mngxitama, Andile. 2009. *Blacks Can't be Racist*. New Frank Talk 3. Sankara Publishing.

Mngxitama, Andile, Amanda Alexander, and Nigel C. Gibson (eds.). 2008. *Biko Lives: Contesting the Legacies of Steve Biko*. Basingstoke/New York: Palgrave Macmillan.

Mills, Charles W., Amanda Alexander, and Nigel C. Gibson. 2008. Biko Lives. In Andile Mngxitama, Amanda Alexander and Nigel C. Gibson (eds.). *Biko Lives: Contesting the Legacies of Steve Biko*. Basingstoke/New York: Palgrave Macmillan, pp. 1–20.

Moodley, Kogila. 1991. The Continued Impact of Black Consciousness. *Journal of Modern African Studies*, 29 (2): 237–251.

More, Mabogo P. 2019. The Transformative Power of Lewis R. Gordon's Africana Philosophy in Mandela's House. In danielle davis (ed.) *Black Existentialism: Essays on the Transformative Thought of Lewis R. Gordon*. Lanham/Boulder: Rowman and Littlefield International, pp. 69–95.

_____. 2018. *Looking Through Philosophy in Black: Memoirs*. Lanham/Boulder: Rowman and Littlefield International.

_____. 2017. *Biko: Philosophy, Identity and Liberation*. Pretoria: HSRC Press.

_____. 2014. Locating Fanon in Post-Apartheid South Africa. *Journal of Asian and African Studies*, 49 (6): 1–15.

_____. 2012. Black Consciousness Movement's Ontology: The Politics of Being. *Philosophia Africana*, 14 (1): 23–39.

_____. 2011. Fanon and the Land Question in (Post)Apartheid South Africa. In Nigel C. Gibson. *Living Fanon: Global Perspectives*. Basingstoke/New York: Palgrave Macmillan, pp. 173–185.

_____. 2009. Black Solidarity: A Philosophical Defence. *Theoria*, (September): 20–43.

_____. 2008. Biko: Africana Existentialist Philosopher. In Andile Mngxitama, Amanda Alexander and Nigel C. Gibson (eds.). *Biko Lives: Contesting the Legacies of Steve Biko*. Basingstoke/New York: Palgrave Macmillan, pp. 45–68.

_____. 2006. Fanon, Apartheid, and Black Consciousness. In Mariba P. Banchetti-Ronino and Clevis R. Headley (eds.). *Shifting the Geography of Reason: Gender, Science and Religion.* New Castle: Cambridge Scholars Press, pp. 241–254.

_____. 2005. *Sartre and the Problem of Racism.* Unpublished Doctoral Thesis. Pretoria: University of South Africa.

_____. 1998. Outlawing Racism in Philosophy: On Race and Philosophy. In Pieter H. Coetzee and Abraham P.J. Roux (eds.). *Philosophy from Africa: A Text with Readings.* Oxford: Oxford University Press, pp. 364–373.

_____.1996. Complicity, Neutrality or Advocacy? Philosophy in South Africa: Ronald Aronson's "Stay Out of Politics": A Review Essay. *Theoria* (June): 124–135.

Moten, Fred. 2018. *The Universal Machine.* Durham and London: Duke University Press.

_____. 2017. *Black and Blur.* Durham and London: Duke University Press.

_____. 2013a. The Suprime and the Beautiful. *African Identities,* 11 (2): 237–245.

_____. 2013b. Blackness and Nothingness (Mysticism in the Flesh). *The South Atlantic Quarterly,* 112 (4): 737–780.

_____. 2008. The Case of Blackness. *Criticism,* 50 (2): 177–218.

_____. 2003. *In the Break: The Aesthetics of the Black Radical Tradition.* Minneapolis: The University of Minnesota Press.

Moten, Fred and Stefano Harney. 2004. The University and the Undercommons: Seven Theses. *Social Text,* 22 (2): 101–115.

Mouffe, C. 1993. *The Return of the Political.* London/New York: Verso.

Ndlovu-Gatsheni, Sabelo J. 2013. *Coloniality of Power in Postcolonial Africa: Myths of Decolonization.* Dakar: CODESRIA.

_____. 2012. Beyond the Equator There Are No Sins: Coloniality and Violence in Africa. *Journal of Developing Societies,* 28 (4): 419–440.

Nolutshungu, Sam C. 1982. *Changing South Africa: Political Considerations.* Manchester: Manchester University Press.

Pagden, Anthony. 2002. Europe: Conceptualising a Continent. In Anthony Pagden (ed.). *The Idea of Europe: From Antiquity to the European Union.* Cambridge: Cambridge University Press, pp. 33–54.

Parry, Benita. 1999. Resistance Theory/Theorizing Resistance or

Two Cheers for Nativism. In Nigel C. Gibson. *The Continuing Dialogue*. New York: Humanity Books, pp. 215–250.

Patterson, Orlando. 1982. *Slavery and Social Death: A Comparative Study*. Cambridge (Mass): Harvard University Press.

Perera, Swendrini and Joseph Pugliese. 2011. Introduction: Combat Breathing: State Violence and the Body in Question. *Somatechnics*, 1 (1): 1–14.

Pillay, Suren. 2004. Anti-colonialism, Post-colonialism and the "New Man." *Politikon*, 31 (1): 91–104.

Rabaka, Reiland. 2015. *The Negritude Movement: W.E.B. du Bois, Leon Damas, Aime Cesaire, Leopold Senghor, Frantz Fanon, and the Evolution of an Insurgent Idea*. Lanham, MD: Lexington Books.

_____. 2010. *Africana Critical Theory: Reconstructing the Black Radical Tradition, from W.E.B. Du Bois and C.L.R. James to Frantz Fanon and Amilcar Cabral*. Lanham, MD: Lexington Books.

Radhakrishnan, Rajagopalan. 2008. *History and the Human, and the World Between*. Durham/London: Duke University Press.

Ramphalile, Molemo. 2011. 'Patriotic Blackness' and 'Liberal/Anti-patriotic Whiteness: Charting the Emergence and Character of an Articulation of Black/White Subjectivity Peculiar to Post-apartheid South Africa. Unpublished Master of Arts Dissertation: Johannesburg: University of the Witwatersrand.

Sandoval, Chela. 2000. *Methodology of the Oppressed*. Minneapolis/London: University of Minnesota Press.

Santos, Boaventura de Sousa. 2007. Beyond Abyssal Thinking: From Global Lines to Ecology of Knowledges. *Review*, 30 (1): 1–33.

Sartre, Jean-Paul. 1965. *Anti-Semite and Jew*. (Translated by George J. Becker.) New York: Schocken Books.

_____. 1956. *Being and Nothingness: An Essay on Phenomenological Ontology*. (Translated and with a new introduction by Hazel E. Barnes.) London: Methuen.

Scharfman, Ronnie. 2010. Aimé Césaire: Poetry is/and Knowledge. *Research in African Literatures*, 41 (1): 109–120.

Serequeberhan, Tsenay. 2012. Decolonization and the Practice of Philosophy. In Nicholas Creary (ed.). *African Intellectuals and Decolonization*. Athens: Ohio University Press, pp. 137–159.

Sexton, Jared. 2015. Unbearable Blackness. *Cultural Critique*, 90 (Spring): 159–178.

_____. 2010. People-of-Color-Blindness: Notes on the Afterlife of Slavery. *Social Text*, 28 (2): 31–56.

_____. 2006. Race, Nation, and Empire in a Blackened World. *Radical History Review*, 95 (Spring): 250–261.

Shakur, Assata. 1987. *Assata: An Autobiography*. Chicago: Lawrence Hill Press.

_____. 1978. Women in Prison: How Are We. *The Black Scholar*, 9 (7): 8–15.

_____. 1973. To my People. *The Black Scholar*, 5 (2): 16–18.

Sharma, Nandita. 2015. Strategic Anti-Essentialism: Decolonizing Decolonization. In Katherine McKrittrick (ed.). *Sylvia Wynter: On Being Human as Praxis*. Durham/London: Duke University Press, pp. 164–182.

Shelby, Tommie. 2002. Foundations of Black Solidarity: Collective Identity or Common Oppression? *Ethics*, 112 (January): 231–266.

Spillers, Hortense J. 1987. Mama's Baby, Papa's Maybe: An American Grammar Book. *Diacritics*, 17 (2): 64–81.

Stoler, Ann L. and Carole McGranahan. 2007. Introduction: Refiguring Imperial Terrains. In Anne L. Stoler, Carole McGranahan, and Peter C. Perdue. *Imperial Formations*. Santa Fe/Oxford: School of Advanced Research Press/James Currey, pp. 3–42.

Terreblanche, Sampie. 2002. *A History of Inequality in South Africa*. Scottsville/Sandton: UKZN Press and KMM Review.

Timerman, Jacobo. 1981. *Prisoner Without a Name, Prisoner Without a Number*. New York: Alfred A Knopf.

Trask, Haunari K. 2004. The Color of Violence. *Social Justice*, 31 (4): 8–16.

Truscott, Ross and Jacqueline Marx. 2011. A Response to 'Retrieving Biko.' *African Identities*, 9 (4): 481–485.

Ture, Kwame and Charles V. Hamilton. 1992. *Black Power: The Politics of Liberation*. New York: Vintage Books.

Vice, Samantha. 2010. How do I Live in this Strange Place? *Journal of Social Philosophy*, 41 (3): 323–342.

Walcott, Rinalso. 2014. The Problem of the Human: Black Ontologies and the Coloniality of our Being. In Sabine Broeck and Carsten Junker (eds.). *Postcoloniality-Decoloniality-Black Critique: Joints and Fissures*. Frankfurt/New York: Campus Verlag, pp. 93–105.

Warren, Calvin L. 2018. *Ontological Terror: Blackness, Nihilism, and Emancipation*. Durham/London: Duke University Press.

Weheliye, Alexander G. 2014. *Habeas Viscus: Racializing*

Assemblages, Biopolitics, and Black Feminist Theories of the Human. Durham/London: Duke University Press.

————. 2008. After Man. *American Literary History,* 20 (1): 321–336.

Wilder, Garry. 2015. *Freedom Time: Negritude, Decolonization, and the Future of the World.* Durham and London: Duke University Press.

Wilderson, Frank B. III. 2014. The Black Liberation Army and the Paradox of Political Engagement. In Sarbine Broeck and Carsten Junker (eds.). *Postcoloniality-Decoloniality-Black Critique: Joints and Fissures.* Frankfurt/New York: Verlag Campus, pp. 175–207.

————. 2010. *Red, White and Black: Cinema and the Structure of US Antagonisms.* Durham and London: Duke University Press.

————. 2008. Biko and the Problematic of Presence. In A. Mngxitama, A. Alexander and Nigel C. Gibson (eds.). *Biko Lives: Contesting the Legacies of Steve Biko.* Basingstoke/New York: Palgrave Macmillan. pp. 95–114.

————. 2003a. Gramsci's Black Marx: Whither the Slave in Civil Society? *Social Identities,* 9 (2): 225–240.

————. 2003b. The Prison Slave as Hegemony's (Silent) Scandal. *Social Justice,* 30 (2): 18–27.

Wilson, Lindy. 1991. Bantu Stephen Biko: A Life. In Barney N. Pityana, Mamphele Ramphele and Lindy Wilson (eds). *Bounds of Possibility: The Legacy of Steve Biko and Black Consciousness.* Cape Town: David Philip, pp. 15–77.

Wynter, Sylvia. 2006. On How We Mistook A Map for the Territory, and Imprisoned Ourselves in Our Unbearable Wrongness of Being, of *Désêtre*: Black Studies Toward the Human Project. In Gordon, Lewis R. and Jane A. (eds.). *Not Only the Master's Tools: African-American Studies in Theory and Practice.* Boulder and London: Paradigm Publishers, pp. 107–169.

————. 2003. Unsettling the Coloniality of Being/Power/Truth/ Freedom: Towards the Human, After Man, Its Overrepresentation – an Argument. *CR: The New Centennial Review,* 3 (3): 257–337.

————. 2001. Towards the Sociogenic Principle: Fanon, Identity, the Puzzle of Consciousness Experience, and What is it Like to be "Black." In Mercedes F. Durán-Cagon and Antonio Gómez-Moriana (eds.). *National Identities and Sociopolitical Changes in Latin America.* New York: Routledge, pp. 30–66.

_____. 1995. 1492: A New World View. In Vera Lawrence and Rex Nettleford (eds.). *Race, Discourse, and Origins of Americas: A New World View*. Washington/London: Smithsonia Institution Press, pp. 5–57.

_____. 1994. 'No Humans Involved:' An Open Letter to My Colleagues. *Forum N.H.I. Knowledge for the 21st Century*, 1 (1): 42–73.

_____. 1991. Columbus and the Poetics of the *Propter Nos*. *Annals of Scholarship*, 8 (2): 251–286.

_____. 1989. Beyond the Word of Man: Glissant and the New Discourse of the Antilles. *World Literature Today*, 63 (4): 637–648.

_____. 1984. The Ceremony Must be Found: After Humanism. *Boundary 2*, 12 (3): 19–70.

X, Malcolm. 1970. *By Any Means Necessary: Speeches, Interviews, and a Letter by Malcolm X*. New York: Pathfinder.

Index

rhetoric of 66, 67, 68–69
class perspective 9
Coetzee, John M. 114, 115
Coleman, Mat 113
colonial subjecthood 209
colonial unconscious 195, 209,
     246
colonial world
     Césaire's critique of 63–93
     exclusionary sacredness of 15
     genealogy of 234
     hierarchization 54
     militarized 226
     paternalism 88
     patriarchal infrastructure 38
     settler-colonialism 94, 184
     unmaking 31
     Wynter's critique of 30–62
     see also apartheid; Imperial
         Man
colonized subject 64, 65, 67, 69,
     70
     assimilation 75, 79–80
     dehumanization of 55, 73, 77,
         82, 89, 91, 92–93
     dispossession 79
     erasure of 75
     human rights, outside 71
     non-human status 70, 71, 79
     ontologico-existential
         conception of 71, 77, 82,
         86, 89
     positionality of 83, 87–88
     return to itself 83–93
     subjectivity of 64, 83, 91, 93
     thingification 71, 89
Color Line 42, 43
colour-blindness 201
Comaroff, Jean and John 118,
     119, 120
combative breathing 49, 50, 51,
     52
community of masters
     foundational logic 41

Imperial Man 38, 39, 41, 42,
     50, 54, 60
     police as 121
Conniff, Brian 153, 156–157
consciousness 184
     antiblack 215
     decolonial 86, 91, 221
     history of 70–71
     race 183
     see also Black Consciousness
Corrigan, Lisa M. 172
cosmetic politics of reformism
     28, 108, 203, 208, 242,
     249–250, 251
criminalization
     of black bodies 20, 29, 112,
         163, 235
     of solidarity 140, 141, 142,
         199, 201
     see also outlaw figure; prison
         slave narrative
critique, limits of 10, 19
culture
     end of 257
     philosophy of 16

Dabashi, Hamid 21
damné 48, 49, 51, 52, 53, 55,
     57, 59, 62
     existential condition of 48, 50,
         52, 54, 58
     imperial guardianship 59, 60
     political unconscious 61
     socio-historical formation 54
     solidarity 49
     subjection of 59, 60
     subjectivity 54, 61
     "undeservingness" of freedom
         59–60
Dayan, Joan 163, 164, 165, 166
de Klerk, Frederick Willem 206
death 7, 8, 12, 17, 39, 40, 43,
     46, 57, 63, 67, 69, 107,
     124–125, 185, 186, 187

disciplinary power 156
monologue of power 166
phallic 31, 119, 177
sacred nature of 157
see also community of masters;
    white supremacy
prison gulag 177
prison slave narrative 29,
    146–177, 220
carceral apparatus 150, 152,
    154, 155, 156, 157, 159,
    160, 163, 164, 166, 167
collectivist struggle 147
dehumanization 149, 152, 165
fugitive figure 146, 147, 148,
    160–161, 163, 164, 165,
    166, 169, 170
legislative defeat 161, 168–169
logic of domination 159
loving subjectivity of blackness
    170–177
monologue of power 166
non-being of blackness 171
political communiqué 161, 162
prison slaves' demands 147,
    148, 161, 170
prisoner–warder relationship
    153, 154, 157–158, 165,
    166, 167
resistance 147, 150, 159, 162,
    169
ritualization of the incarcerated
    body 149
rooted in desire 174
tyranny of justice 162–170
writing the prison slave
    148–149, 150–151, 152,
    155, 156, 157, 159, 160
Pugliese, Joseph 50

Rabaka, Reiland 80, 81, 82,
    83–84, 85
race 9–10
as burden of blackness 10

consciousness 183
denialism 9, 19, 28, 101, 103,
    208, 246
as floating signifier 9, 10
as social construct 9
transcendentalism 101, 103,
    201
Racial Contract 215, 216
racial essentialism 82
racialized bodies 39, 40, 42, 43,
    138, 143, 189, 220, 221,
    237
see also niggerization
racism 7, 10, 12, 98, 100, 101,
    109, 129, 138, 139, 143,
    178, 181, 182, 183–191,
    196, 198, 199, 200, 201,
    206, 219, 245, 246, 247,
    258
apartheid see apartheid
born-again racism 101–102
hierarchized power relations
    185
infrastructure of 30, 46, 122,
    183–191, 197–198, 201,
    202, 212, 215, 240
institutionalized 102
legitimation of 103
logic of 30, 96, 102, 116, 145,
    178
in the private realm 101
reverse racism 102, 196
white liberal anti-racist project
    100, 126–136, 191–196
see also colonized subject;
    dehumanization; prison slave
    narrative; subjection
racist gaze 9, 97
racist state 20, 21, 111–1117,
    242
assumption of high moral
    ground 112
Ideological State Apparatus
    112